Literary Disability Studies

Series Editors
David Bolt
Liverpool Hope University
Liverpool, UK

Elizabeth J. Donaldson
New York Institute of Technology
Old Westbury, NY, USA

Julia Miele Rodas
Bronx Community College
City University of New York
Bronx, NY, USA

Literary Disability Studies is the first book series dedicated to the exploration of literature and literary topics from a disability studies perspective. Focused on literary content and informed by disability theory, disability research, disability activism, and disability experience, the Palgrave Macmillan series provides a home for a growing body of advanced scholarship exploring the ways in which the literary imagination intersects with historical and contemporary attitudes toward disability. This cutting edge interdisciplinary work includes both monographs and edited collections (as well as focused research that does not fall within traditional monograph length). The series is supported by an editorial board of internationally-recognised literary scholars specialising in disability studies: Michael Bérubé, Edwin Erle Sparks Professor of Literature, Pennsylvania State University, USA; G. Thomas Couser, Professor of English Emeritus, Hofstra University in Hempstead, New York, USA; Michael Davidson, University of California Distinguished Professor, University of California, San Diego, USA; Rosemarie Garland-Thomson, Professor of Women's Studies and English, Emory University, Atlanta, USA; Cynthia Lewiecki-Wilson, Professor of English Emerita, Miami University, Ohio, USA. For information about submitting a Literary Disability Studies book proposal, please contact the series editors: David Bolt (boltd@hope.ac.uk), Elizabeth J. Donaldson (edonalds@nyit.edu), and/or Julia Miele Rodas (Julia.Rodas@bcc.cuny.edu).

More information about this series at
http://www.palgrave.com/gp/series/14821

Elizabeth J. Donaldson
Editor

Literatures of Madness

Disability Studies and Mental Health

Editor
Elizabeth J. Donaldson
New York Institute of Technology
Old Westbury, NY, USA

Literary Disability Studies
ISBN 978-3-030-06485-3   ISBN 978-3-319-92666-7 (eBook)
https://doi.org/10.1007/978-3-319-92666-7

© The Editor(s) (if applicable) and The Author(s) 2018
Softcover re-print of the Hardcover 1st edition 2018
This work is subject to copyright. All rights are solely and exclusively licensed by the Publisher, whether the whole or part of the material is concerned, specifically the rights of translation, reprinting, reuse of illustrations, recitation, broadcasting, reproduction on microfilms or in any other physical way, and transmission or information storage and retrieval, electronic adaptation, computer software, or by similar or dissimilar methodology now known or hereafter developed.
The use of general descriptive names, registered names, trademarks, service marks, etc. in this publication does not imply, even in the absence of a specific statement, that such names are exempt from the relevant protective laws and regulations and therefore free for general use.
The publisher, the authors and the editors are safe to assume that the advice and information in this book are believed to be true and accurate at the date of publication. Neither the publisher nor the authors or the editors give a warranty, express or implied, with respect to the material contained herein or for any errors or omissions that may have been made. The publisher remains neutral with regard to jurisdictional claims in published maps and institutional affiliations.

Cover credit: Brain light/Alamy Stock Photo

Printed on acid-free paper

This Palgrave Macmillan imprint is published by the registered company Springer Nature Switzerland AG
The registered company address is: Gewerbestrasse 11, 6330 Cham, Switzerland

MORE PRAISE FOR LITERATURES OF MADNESS

"Elizabeth Donaldson's collection, *Literatures of Madness*, represents a landmark contribution to madness and disability studies. With attention to historical constructions of madness based upon gender, ethnicity, class, and nationality, this collection considers these legacies through an impressive diversity of literary traditions and theoretical perspectives. From canonical feminist and lesbian fiction, to indigenous texts, to Caribbean and Indian novels, contributors develop innovative readings, grounded in knowledge of madness as a complex lived experience—as a source of community, a crucible of survival, and form of resistance. This is a path breaking anthology, a must-read for anyone interested in the complicated meanings of madness in contemporary thought."
—Michelle Jarman, *Associate Professor of Disability Studies at the Wyoming Institute for Disabilities, USA*

Acknowledgements

Thank you first and foremost to all the contributors whose hard work made this collection possible. And special thanks to those authors who made it through some difficult and challenging obstacles to bring their work to fruition. I deeply appreciate your commitment to this project and I feel fortunate for having such a great group of people as collaborators. My heartfelt appreciation to our external reviewers for their time, close attention to, and enthusiasm for the manuscript. Thank you also to my colleagues in the English department at NYIT, especially Amanda Golden, who kindly read parts of this manuscript and whose expertise in Sylvia Plath was a great resource to us. And thank you to the wonderfully helpful JoAnn Politis in NYIT's Interlibrary Loan Office.

My research into Mary Jane Ward was conducted at the Howard Gotlieb Archival Research Center at Boston University, and I owe a debt of gratitude to Miriam Pepoon Cronin, Kevin Cronin, and Paula Haines for their hospitality while I worked at the Mary Jane Ward Collection there. Thank you, Peter Naccarato, for inviting me to share my Ward research at the Conversations on Diversity and Social Justice speaker series at Marymount Manhattan College. I also greatly appreciate Wilbur Farley's help in reviewing the Ward chapter, and for support throughout the process of putting this collection together.

To all my family and friends, thank you for your patience with me and for understanding the time commitments that this project involved. An especial gracias to Kate Buck in Playa del Carmen for her amazing friendship and hospitality over the years. Thank you to Kit Kincade,

Keith Byerman, and the English department at Indiana State University for inviting me to share my related work on S. Weir Mitchell. My work in disability studies wouldn't be possible without the network of disability scholars who have given me an intellectual home and support, especially my sister from another mother, Catherine Prendergast. My warmest thank you to my Dante's family and my Facebook disability studies friends for the extended community that you give me. And a special thanks to the Columbia University Seminar in Disability, Culture, and Society, founded by Rachel Adams, and presently chaired by Julia Miele Rodas and Lotti Silber, with Liz Bowen as rapporteur.

Finally, thank you to my fellow Literary Disability Studies series editors, David Bolt and Julia Miele Rodas, whose friendship and early support helped make this book possible, and thank you to the great folks at Palgrave Macmillan—especially Ben Doyle, Allie (Bochicchio) Troyanos, and Rachel Jacobe—who have been a fantastic editorial team.

Contents

1 Introduction: Breathing in Airless Spaces   1
   Elizabeth J. Donaldson

Part I Mad Community

2 Coming Out Mad, Coming Out Disabled   11
   Elizabeth Brewer

3 Going Barefoot: Mad Affiliation, Identity Politics,
   and Eros   31
   PhebeAnn M. Wolframe

4 "Hundreds of People Like Me": A Search for a Mad
   Community in *The Bell Jar*   51
   Rose Miyatsu

5 Writing Madness in Indigenous Literature: A Hesitation   71
   Erin Soros

Part II Mad History

6 "Is the Young Lady Mad?": Psychiatric Disability in Louisa May Alcott's Fiction 91
   Karyn Valerius

7 *The Snake Pit*: Mary Jane Ward's Asylum Fiction and Mental Health Advocacy 109
   Elizabeth J. Donaldson

8 Alcoholic, Mad, Disabled: Constructing Lesbian Identity in Ann Bannon's "The Beebo Brinker Chronicles" 127
   Tatiana Prorokova

9 Seeing Words, Hearing Voices: Hannah Weiner, Dora García, and the Poetic Performance of Radical Dis/Humanism 145
   Andrew McEwan

Part III Mad Survival

10 "My Difference Is Not My [Mental] Sickness": Ethnicity and Erasure in Joanne Greenberg's Jewish American Life Writing 165
    Gail Berkeley Sherman

11 Resistance, Suffering, and Psychiatric Disability in Jerry Pinto's *Em and the Big Hoom* and Amandeep Sandhu's *Sepia Leaves* 183
    Srikanth Mallavarapu

12 Mental Disability and Social Value in Michelle Cliff's *Abeng* 199
    Drew Holladay

13 It Doesn't Add Up: Mental Illness in Paul Hornschemeier's *Mother, Come Home* 215
    Jessica Gross

Index 235

Notes on Contributors

Elizabeth Brewer is an Assistant Professor of English at Central Connecticut State University. Her research focuses on rhetorics of mental disability, and she teaches classes in disability studies (and disability studies and literature), rhetoric, and composition. She has co-authored the "Arts and Humanities" volume of *The SAGE Reference Series on Disability* and has published in *Composition Studies*, *Disability Studies Quarterly*, *Kairos*, and the *Writing Program Administration* journal. She is currently co-editing a collection titled *Cripping the Computer: A Critical Moment in Composition Studies*.

Elizabeth J. Donaldson is Associate Professor of English at New York Institute of Technology, where she teaches courses in bioethics and American literature and directs the Medical Humanities program. She has published essays on LSD-inspired disability-immersion experiences of schizophrenia, mental illness in film, antipsychiatry in Lauren Slater's memoirs, and physiognomy and madness in *Jane Eyre*. She is a member of the editorial board of the *Journal of Literary & Cultural Disabilities Studies* and is co-editor (with Catherine J. Prendergast) of the special issue, "Emotion and Disability" (2011). She co-edited *The Madwoman and the Blindman: Jane Eyre, Discourse, Disability* (2012) and co-edits the book series *Literary Disability Studies* with David Bolt and Julia Miele Rodas. Her current research project focuses on psychiatry and American literature.

Jessica Gross has a Ph.D. in Comparative Literature from the University of Wisconsin and is Assistant Professor of English at St. Louis College of Pharmacy. She works in English, French, Spanish, and Tagalog, focusing on the modern novel and comics and on questions of identity, mental illness, and war and violence. At St. Louis College of Pharmacy she is currently teaching two courses she developed: "Comics and Conflict" and "Invisible Made Visible: Comics and Mental Illness." Current projects include the way comics about mental illness use landscapes to portray mental states, and analyses of Southeast Asian comics.

Drew Holladay is Assistant Professor of English at the University of Maryland, Baltimore County and received a Ph.D. in Rhetoric and Composition from the University of Louisville. His research combines rhetorical theory, sociolinguistics, and critical disability studies to examine writing about medicine and mental health. Outside of academic research, he has worked with non-profits to promote community engagement and awareness of disability issues, including co-editing the short film *Voices Together: The Art as Memory Project* and producing promotional videos for the Council on Developmental Disabilities in Louisville, KY.

Srikanth Mallavarapu has a Ph.D. in English from SUNY Stony Brook. He has been a Brittain Postdoctoral Fellow at Georgia Tech and a SAGES Fellow at Case Western Reserve University. He is currently an Associate Professor in the English department at Roanoke College and one of the coordinators of the Peace and Justice Studies Concentration. His research and teaching interests include the negotiation of modernity in the postcolonial context, contemporary South Asian literature and film, critical theories of literature, and of science, technology, and culture.

Andrew McEwan researches self-representations of mental disability, mental illness, and madness in postmodern and contemporary avant-garde poetics. His academic writing has appeared in or is forthcoming in *Open Letter* and *The Routledge Encyclopedia of Modernism*. He is the author of the books *Repeater* (Book*hug 2012), a finalist for the Gerald Lampert Award; *If Pressed* (Book*hug 2017); and *Tours, Variously* (forthcoming from Talonbooks in 2019). He is also the author of the chapbooks *Input/Output* (Cactus 2008), *Conditional* (Jackpine 2013), *I can't tell if this book is depressing or if I'm just sad* (No. Press 2015), *Theory of Rooms* (Above/Ground 2015), and numerous other periodical and anthology publications in Canada and the USA. He lives in Ontario, Canada.

Rose Miyatsu completed her undergraduate degree at UCLA, where she wrote her honors thesis on mental disability in the work of William Faulkner. She is currently a doctoral candidate in English Literature at Washington University in St. Louis, where she focuses on 20th and 21st century American literature and disability studies. Her current dissertation project is on asylum novels of the post-WWII period, and examines how a nuanced perspective on mental difference can foster more inclusive forms of community.

Tatiana Prorokova is currently working on her second book project that examines representations of the environment and climate change in fiction since the Industrial Revolution (financed through the Equal Opportunity Scholarship for Outstanding Female Junior Scholars, MARA, the University of Marburg, Germany). She holds a Ph.D. in American Studies from the University of Marburg, Germany, a European Joint Master's Degree in English and American Studies from the University of Bamberg, Germany, and a Teaching Degree in English and German from Ryazan State University, Russia. In 2016, she was a Visiting Scholar at the University of South Alabama (English Department and Center for the Study of War and Memory). Her research interests include war studies, ecocriticism, gender studies, and race studies. She is a co-editor of *Cultures of War in Graphic Novels: Violence, Trauma, and Memory* (Rutgers University Press 2018).

Gail Berkeley Sherman (B.A., Barnard; Ph.D., Princeton) is Professor of English and Humanities at Reed College. While teaching a wide variety of courses, she seeks to make academia a family- and female-positive space, for instance by successfully working to bring on-site child care to Reed. A rhetorical and ethical focus characterizes her scholarship, from the first USA dissertation on the fourteenth-century female English mystic, Julian of Norwich, to her work on fiction by twentieth-century American Jewish authors. Her current writing project inscribes Joanne Greenberg's literary oeuvre in an account of the intersection of Jewish, feminist, and disability concerns in American post-Shoah fiction. Encountering her own and family members' depression spurred her interest in disability studies. She lives in Portland, Oregon, with her husband, with whom she has launched four children into a world she trusts they will help to repair.

Erin Soros is a Mellon Postdoctoral Fellow at the Jackman Humanities Institute at the University of Toronto. She has published fiction and nonfiction internationally and her stories have been produced for the CBC and BBC as winners of the CBC Literary Award and the Commonwealth Award for the Short Story. Her academic articles have appeared in such peer-reviewed journals as *differences: A Journal of Feminist Cultural Studies*, *The Journal of Intercultural Studies*, *The Journal of Curriculum Theorizing*, and *The Canadian Journal of Women and the Law*. She has been a visiting writer at four universities, most recently University of Cambridge which funded travel to research Inuvialuit oral history in Canada's Western Arctic. Soros has performed a one-woman show at University of Oxford, University of Glasgow, McGill University, Lion's Gate Hospital Hope Centre, and psychoanalytic conferences that explores trauma-induced madness. The script is forthcoming in *Women and Psychosis: Multidisciplinary Perspectives*.

Karyn Valerius is Associate Professor of English at Hofstra University and Director of the Women's Studies and Disability Studies programs. Her teaching and research interests include disability and literature, medicine and literature, American women writers, and reproductive politics past and present. Her publications include "A Not-so-silent Scream: Gothic and the U.S. Abortion Debate," *Frontiers: A Journal of Women's Studies* 34.3 (September 2013) and "'So Manifest a Signe From Heaven': Monstrosity and Heresy in the Antinomian Controversy" in *The New England Quarterly* 83.2 (June 2010). She is working on a book manuscript, "Misconceptions: Maternal Impressions in U.S. Literature, Medicine and Popular Culture."

PhebeAnn M. Wolframe is a queer and mad-identified psychiatric survivor, sometimes mad activist, and independent scholar. She completed her Ph.D. dissertation "Reading Through Madness: Counter-Psychiatric Epistemologies and the Biopolitics of (In)sanity in Post World War II Anglo-Atlantic Women's Narratives" at McMaster University in 2013. Other published work in Mad Studies includes the article "The Madwoman in the Academy, or, Revealing the Invisible Straightjacket: Theorizing and Teaching Sanism and Sane Privilege" in *Disability Studies Quarterly* (33.1) which has also been translated into French by Marina Rodrigues at zinzinzine.net.

List of Figures

Fig. 6.1	"Sisterhood," from Louisa May Alcott's *Work*	104
Fig. 9.1	Hannah Weiner's *Public Access Poetry* reading of *Clairvoyant Journal*	155
Fig. 13.1	"To drift merrily," from Paul Hornschemeier's *Mother, Come Home*. Image copyright © 2017 Paul Hornschemeier, courtesy Fantagraphics Books	218
Fig. 13.2	David faces his doctor at the psychiatric hospital, from Paul Hornschemeier's *Mother, Come Home*. Image copyright © 2017 Paul Hornschemeier, courtesy Fantagraphics Books	225
Fig. 13.3	Thomas, wearing his lion mask, faces his father, from Paul Hornschemeier's *Mother, Come Home*. Image copyright © 2017 Paul Hornschemeier, courtesy Fantagraphics Books	228

CHAPTER 1

Introduction: Breathing in Airless Spaces

Elizabeth J. Donaldson

In 1998, Shulamith Firestone published *Airless Spaces*, a slender collection of vignettes about her life in and out of psychiatric hospitals. The book begins with a nightmare: "I dreamed I was on a sinking ship" (5). Firestone's narrator flees from a manic, drunken party on an upper deck and seeks shelter deep in the watery bowels of the ocean liner. Searching for a protected air pocket, she stows away in a refrigerator, "hoping to live on even after the boat was fully submerged until it should be found" (5). Unfortunately, the ship sinks in the Bermuda Triangle, where no one is willing to search. Unlike the buoyant, repurposed coffin that saves Ishmael in *Moby Dick*, Firestone's basement refrigerator sinks like a rock, lost to obscurity in the Bermuda Triangle of mental illness. These are "deadpan, deadend stories," the back cover warns.

Airless Spaces, with its psych ward sketches and tales of "losers" and suicides, nevertheless contains and beautifully preserves these last gasps of breath. These are tales that are devastating in their brevity, for the monumentally small acts of courage and resistance and for the neglected moments of grief and loss that they encapsulate and record. The fact that the book even exists is itself an unlikely wonder. Beginning her activist work in the late 1960s, Shulamith Firestone was a force to be

E. J. Donaldson (✉)
New York Institute of Technology, Old Westbury, NY, USA

© The Author(s) 2018
E. J. Donaldson (ed.), *Literatures of Madness*, Literary Disability Studies,
https://doi.org/10.1007/978-3-319-92666-7_1

reckoned with. A radical feminist leader and organizer, Firestone published a groundbreaking manifesto of second wave feminism, *The Dialectic of Sex: The Case for Feminist Revolution*, in 1970 when she was only 25. But as Susan Faludi describes in her memorial essay, "Death of a Revolutionary," bitter divisions in the feminist movement led Firestone to "self-exile" (58). And Firestone's emerging, concurrent mental health problems made her almost disappear. Diagnosed with paranoid schizophrenia, she spent time in and out of psychiatric hospitals on involuntary committals (Faludi 60). But in the early 1990s, a makeshift support system of women organically emerged to help Firestone survive, meeting with her weekly to "help her with practical needs, from taking her anti-psychotic medications to buying groceries" (Faludi 61). Lourdes Cintron was at the core of this support group, which included friends who admired Firestone's work and friends who were healthcare professionals. As a caseworker for The Visiting Nurse Services of New York, and an ardent admirer of *The Dialectic of Sex*, Cintron successfully advocated for Firestone to receive nursing support services, even though she had no insurance (Faludi 61). Bolstered by the care of this community of women, Firestone's health and standard of living improved, and her hospital stays were less frequent. *Airless Spaces*, which is dedicated to Cintron, is a product of this special period in Firestone's life. Yet in the late 1990s her support group began to fall apart just as organically as it had formed: Cintron became ill, and other women, including Firestone's psychiatrist, moved away. Firestone relapsed more often, spent more time in hospital, and increasingly withdrew from family and friends. She died in August 2012: her body was discovered in her apartment, only after her landlord noticed that her rent bill sat untouched on her doorstep for several days (Faludi 61).

Airless Spaces exists because a feminist community of carers worked both within and beyond the traditional mental health care system to support Firestone when she wanted and needed it. The book is a product of feminist ethics of care in action, of a web-like interdependency among women. But its origin story is secondary to the remarkable content of the book. *Airless Spaces* is the muckraking, realist, disability studies antidote to the misogynist fantasy psych world of Ken Kesey's *Cuckoo's Nest*. Firestone's work is sparse and direct, mired in the mundane details of case workers and day programs, involuntary commitments and missed rent payments, homelessness, taking meds, not taking meds, and the hard and rarely glamorous work of surviving with a chronic psychiatric disability.

Airless Spaces should be a classic in a canon of literature about mental illness; it should be a text that disability scholars routinely turn to when they discuss disability and mental illness. But chances are you haven't read it. Yet.

Literatures of Madness is an initial step in creating a tradition of literary disability studies of mental illness, mental disability, madness. The collection itself embodies a search for primary texts like Firestone's and a search for the language and methodologies of analyzing these texts within a disability studies framework. The collection is meant to function as a provisional hub or way station: a point at which to meet together collectively, to commune, build on synergies, and honor differences, before continuing on the longer journeys forward.

The book is organized into three sections: Mad Community, Mad History, and Mad Survival. These themes directly correspond to aspects of Firestone's life and work. The Mad Community section is about the importance of connection among people with disabilities, and the often invisible networks that link them together, which is reflected in both the content of Firestone's vignettes and the creation of *Airless Spaces*. This section begins with Elizabeth Brewer's "Coming Out Mad, Coming Out Disabled." Brewer examines the historically uneasy fit between mad studies and disability studies and explains some of the fundamental ideological differences between the two. Brewer notes, for example, that many psychiatric survivors do not identify as being disabled, and likewise many disabled people do not identify as psychiatric survivors. In an effort to bridge the divide between mad studies and disability studies, Brewer analyzes scholarship by three authors who strategically come out as both disabled and mad: Margaret Price, Katie Aubrecht, and A.J. Withers. The form of Brewer's chapter also reflects and reinforces her larger argument about coming out and coalition building: she weaves her critical readings together with her own personal stories to reveal her positionality, perspectives, and motivations for analyzing the tricky contacts between madness and disability.

In a similar vein, PhebeAnn Wolframe's "Going Barefoot: Mad Affiliation, Identity Politics, and Eros" bridges mad and queer communities. Wolframe examines the ways in which consumer, survivor, ex-patient, and mad (c/s/x/m) communities, like LGBTQIA communities, are bound together across messy identity categories and shared experiences of otherness. Beginning with a reading of Persimmon Blackbridge's novel *Prozac Highway* (2000), Wolframe explores how c/s/x/m people forge a sense of kinship through online listservs. Wolframe further theorizes mad reading practices as a form of community building by analyzing excerpts from *MadArtReview*, a private blog she created. Reading *MadArtReview* alongside *Prozac Highway*, Wolframe considers the way mad people undermine the fixing of madness as identity, instead carefully negotiating their identifications and affiliations, and consciously blurring boundaries. This blurring, Wolframe argues, offers the possibility of messy affiliations across difference, and the re-emergence of a kinship between queerness and madness.

The next two essays in the Mad Communities section examine different types of structural, institutional barriers that complicate the creation of mad communities. In her essay, "'Hundreds of People Like Me': A Search for a Mad Community in *The Bell Jar*," Rose Miyatsu provides a new, alternate reading of madness in Sylvia Plath's canonical asylum novel. As Miyatsu points out, previous readings ignore the fact that while Esther is searching for and rejecting female role models, she is also searching for identity and community as a person with an enduring mental illness. It is rare, Miyatsu argues, for any critic to even mention characters like Valarie, the lobotomized patient Esther meets, or Miss Norris, her mute neighbor in the asylum. When critics dismiss these friendships as symptoms of illness rather than a legitimate attempt at community building, they deny the personhood of those who cannot "recover," people who end up getting left behind as Esther moves toward normalization. Although the hierarchical structure of the asylum, an institution based on progress and "cure," ultimately dampens Esther's attempts at forming bonds, her experiences there encourage her to imagine what a community that can incorporate pain might look like, even if it is currently unrealizable.

Erin Soros explores very different types of institutionalized barriers to mad community building in her chapter "Writing Madness in Indigenous Literature: A Hesitation." Soros grapples with how her embeddedness in a history of colonial violence against Indigenous communities in Canada troubles her desire to write, as a non-Indigenous, mad-identified scholar, about madness in Indigenous texts. Soros attempts to reconcile or balance her wish to share with a general audience her deep appreciation for the insights into madness that she has gained from texts like Alicia Elliott's "A Mind Spread Out on the Ground" and Lee Maracle's *Celia's Song* with her gut feeling that her "act of literary witnessing…can only quite helplessly fail." Out of this project, Soros envisions creating a collaborative hypertext designed to further develop the historical and cultural context of the Indigenous texts she describes here, with the hope that it will lead "to a potentially unending series of conversations." And so her essay will ultimately extend beyond the page—creating a new mad community online to bear witness, however conflicted and complicated that act may be, to madness in Indigenous literature.

The essays in the Mad History section recover women writers and texts—like Firestone and *Airless Spaces*—that are part of an often unacknowledged or hidden mad legacy. In "'Is the young lady mad?': Psychiatric Disability in Louisa May Alcott's Fiction," Karyn Valerius offers a fresh reading of the author most popular for her nineteenth-century *Little Women* novel series. As a careful reading of Alcott's journals and letters reveal, Alcott herself was "moody" and experienced periods of depression, which included a disturbing suicidal episode. In this chapter, Valerius examines how madness and mental maladies inform three of Alcott's lesser well-known texts: the sensationalist short story, "A Whisper in the Dark"; her first novel, *Moods*; and the autobiographical fiction *Work*. "Whisper in the Dark," Valerius argues, reconfigures Gothic tropes in order to illustrate the gendered double bind of madness; in *Moods*, Alcott's tragic, manic-depressive heroine destabilizes a conventional marriage plot; and Valerius reads *Work*, certainly the most optimistic of the three, as a feminist narrative of depression and recovery.

Elizabeth J. Donaldson's chapter "*The Snake Pit*: Mary Jane Ward's Asylum Fiction and Mental Health Advocacy" reconstructs the publication and reception of Mary Jane Ward's autobiographically-based novel about her experiences as a psychiatric patient in a state mental hospital. This book and the successful feature film that followed helped to garner public support for reforms in psychiatric institutions and made Ward famous. This chapter examines the close and productive relationship between Ward's fiction writing and her later work as a mental health advocate in the 1950s. While Ward's *The Snake Pit* had great success in its day, its popularity has not been lasting. And Ward's later novels have been ignored by critics. Using archival evidence from Ward's papers, Donaldson argues that Ward's life and her books are an untapped, important resource for disability scholars of mental health.

Similarly, Tatiana Prorokova claims the work of Ann Bannon in the "Golden Age" of lesbian pulp fiction as territory ripe for literary disability studies of mental illness. In her chapter "Alcoholic, Mad, Disabled:

Constructing Lesbian Identity in Ann Bannon's 'Beebo Brinker Chronicles," Prorokova argues that Bannon's novels reveal the connection between lesbianism and madness in ways that both resist and complicate medical models of homosexuality as pathology. For Bannon's characters, madness is engendered in part by the patriarchal, heterosexual norms of 1950s–1960s America. Beebo Brinker's alcohol-fueled jealousy transforms her into a madwoman and almost ruins the life of her partner. Another mad heroine, Vega, is obsessed, suicidal, and disfigured from surgeries related to her tuberculosis. Bannon's portrayals of lesbians as addicted, alcoholic, physically and psychologically mutilated women are historical reflections of a culture that uses the power of psychiatric diagnosis to pathologize lesbians, yet they are also pioneering characters in the history of lesbian literature.

Andrew McEwan closes the Mad History section with his analysis of a unique lineage of mad poetry in "Seeing Words, Hearing Voices: Hannah Weiner, Dora García, and the Poetic Performance of Radical Dis/Humanism." McEwan begins with Hannah Weiner's 1977 televised reading of her *Clairvoyant Journal* poems. Weiner saw words, and she incorporated these linguistic visions—big words that sent commands and also little words that criticized—into her autobiographical poetry. Thirty-seven years after Hannah Weiner's performance, the Spanish artist Dora García staged a similar recorded reading of *Clairvoyant Journal* as part of her *Mad Marginal* project. García's project moves Weiner's poetics into an interconnected linguistic investigation of radical marginality and antipsychiatric movements, and further blurs distinctions between literature, experience, and performance. McEwan places these performances in conversation with critical disability studies critiques of subjectivity and with emergent posthumanisms. This mad history of seeing words and hearing voices prompts McEwan to forge a new theoretical space, a non-binary radical dis/humanism, that demands a redefinition of relations from a mentally disabled, outsider, and avant-garde perspective.

The final section, Mad Survival, is about strategies of resistance and resiliency, searching for and finding that pocket of air on a sinking ship where you can still manage to breath, at least for a while (Firestone 5). An empathic relationship between doctor and patient, one that acknowledges mutual dependence and vulnerability, can provide that method of survival, as Gail Berkeley Sherman explains in her chapter "'My Difference Is Not My [Mental] Sickness': Ethnicity and Erasure in Joanne Greenberg's Jewish American Life Writing." Sherman analyzes

Greenberg's autobiographical novel, *I Never Promised You a Rose Garden*, through the lens of Emmanuel Levinas and post-Holocaust Jewish ethics. *Rose Garden*, Sherman argues, challenges stereotypes of psychiatric disability and purposefully works to undermine the hierarchical binary of sane/insane and even doctor/patient. Although the 1977 movie version of *Rose Garden* erases all discursive performance of Jewishness, the original 1964 novel explicitly counters the historical anti-Semitic association of Jews and mental illness. As Sherman's fine-tuned close reading reveals, the respectful therapeutic conversations in the novel demonstrate Greenberg's moral insistence that all human beings are both dependent on, and obligated to, the varied others whom we encounter through speech.

Srikanth Mallavarapu's chapter, "Resistance, Suffering, and Psychiatric Disability in Jerry Pinto's *Em and the Big Hoom* and Amandeep Sandhu's *Sepia Leaves*," shares a similar faith in the possibility of human connection and survival in response to chronic mental illness. Using Arthur Kleinman's model of resistance and suffering in the context of the lived, embodied experiences of patients, families, and caregivers, Mallavarapu analyzes two recently published Indian novels that deal with schizophrenia. *Em and The Big Hoom* highlights the social and intersubjective experiences of illness and suffering, which include not just the patient but also the extended network of family and caregivers. And in *Sepia Leaves*, the young narrator tries to simultaneously make sense of a dysfunctional family and a dysfunctional nation. Together *Em and the Big Hoom* and *Sepia Leaves* offer a nuanced representation of disability and mental illness in India, as well as the struggle to construct meaning out of these experiences for individual families.

The final essays in this section map out Mad Survival on two very different conceptual landscapes, which are both marked by trauma. Drew Holladay's chapter, "Mental Disability and Social Value in Michelle Cliff's *Abeng*," explores the value of difference in postcolonial culture. Cliff's 1984 novel *Abeng*, Holladay argues, creates spaces for individuals that colonial culture would otherwise reject as mad, unintelligent, bizarre, or inefficient. *Abeng* critiques the deleterious effects of disability in Jamaican society while also recognizing and valuing people with mental disabilities. Holladay examines four central characters in *Abeng* who have a mental disability and bear its stigma—but whose circumstances and relationships lead to varied personal consequences. Cliff's portrayal of these disabled characters reveals a new picture of difference and *créolité* in Caribbean literature. *Abeng* shows us that mental disability, and disability more generally, should be recognized as an essential part of the global project of social justice.

Holladay's comprehensive and global perspective is a productive juxtaposition to Jessica Gross's focus on an inner landscape. In "It Doesn't Add Up: Mental Illness in Paul Hornschemeier's *Mother, Come Home*," disability studies meets comics studies and graphic medicine. Gross offers a detailed reading of trauma in *Mother, Come Home*, a graphic narrative of a child's experience with his father's depression and suicide, which he witnesses after encouraging his father to abscond from a psychiatric hospital. In the comic, the father floats through what Gross describes as a "traumascape"—a bizarre, surrealistic illustration of how the world seems to the survivor of trauma. Graphic novels and comics, Gross argues, are important modes of communicating trauma: they can present experiences of disability in images when words fail. This is especially important when dealing with mental illnesses, which have symptoms that may be impossible to express in words and are also often not visible to others. *Mother, Come Home*'s visual format powerfully and insightfully represents the dissociation and embodiment of trauma and depression, making these experiences legible in new ways.

We hope that *Literatures of Madness* makes literary disability studies of mental health legible in new ways for our readers. And for Shulamith Firestone, who survived as best as she could for as long as she could in airless spaces, and for others like her, we hope this work finds them and gives them new space and more breath.

Works Cited

Faludi, Susan. "Death of a Revolutionary." *The New Yorker*, 15 April 2013, pp. 52–61.

Firestone, Shulamith. *Airless Spaces*. Semiotext(e), 1998.

———. *The Dialectic of Sex: The Case for Feminist Revolution*. William Morrow and Co., 1970.

PART I

Mad Community

CHAPTER 2

Coming Out Mad, Coming Out Disabled

Elizabeth Brewer

2008. "Can I do disability studies?" Near the end of my first disability studies class and introduction to the field when I was a graduate student, I visited my professor in her office hours. I asked her this very question, essentially searching to understand if a scholarly place in the field of disability studies might exist for me. My interest was in mental difference and distress, and the ways in which psychiatric survivors seek to establish credibility in opposition to psychiatry. I wondered, in what contexts and using what strategies were those with psychiatric disabilities deemed rhetorically credible? Since psychiatric disability creates stigma around individuals, I wanted to know how one speaks from the position of a spoiled identity, to borrow a phrase from Erving Goffman. It would be a couple years before I'd learn about the consumer/survivor/ex-patient movement or about mad studies, and even at that point I wondered if my inquiry was an uneasy fit within disability studies.

At least in part, my concern about my place within disability studies came from the field's important commitment to disabled people speaking for themselves, claiming their identities, and demanding "nothing about us without us"; this is because my position was complicated. One year before the conversation with my disability studies professor, my brother had been

E. Brewer (✉)
Central Connecticut State University, New Britain, CT, USA

diagnosed with schizophrenia and shortly thereafter took his own life. I was still grieving and trying to reconcile my own memory of my brother with tidy narratives that others used to understand him. Most of these narratives were based on psychiatric knowledge. The year my brother died, a study was published in the Annals of General Psychiatry *that explained my brother's circumstance as statistically unsurprising. Suicide rates are high for people with schizophrenia, especially for those who are young, male, white and never married. These facts summed up my brother's death clearly enough for most people. But for me, I never saw my brother again after he told me his diagnosis, and the task of retroactively reading his life through a diagnostic lens felt incomplete and inauthentic—not necessarily wrong, but not representative of my understanding of him.*

I had many personal and professional issues with which to grapple when I spoke to my professor in her office hours that day. I candidly asked her questions that are at the heart of my inquiry in this essay: Is disability studies a hospitable theoretical framework for humanistic inquiry into mental difference? What is my position: am I still a sibling if my sibling is gone? If I am, how tolerant is disability studies of sibling narratives? What if my position as a nondisabled person changes? Must I account professionally for new diagnostic labels of my body and mind as they may arise? How do I—but, more so, how does anyone—delve into mental difference and distress from a disability studies perspective, given the field's overwhelming focus on physical and sensory disabilities?

In recent years, disability studies publications have increasingly included perspectives on psychiatric disability. Any disability studies journal routinely publishes articles on madness along with work on physical and sensory disabilities; this was not the case even fifteen years ago. In 2013, *Disability Studies Quarterly* published a special issue on "Disability and Madness," and the guest editors, Noam Ostrander and Bruce Henderson, identified recent scholarly work on madness as "draw[ing] heavily on Disability Studies to trouble the borders of normal/abnormal and sane/insane." At the same time, mad studies emerged in 2008 as its own location of humanistic inquiry into psychiatric disability, and scholars writing in that field repeatedly make their connections to disability studies clear. Richard Ingram claims in defining mad studies that it owes a great debt to disability studies. Similarly, Jennifer M. Poole and Jennifer Ward express feelings of indebtedness to disability scholars like Eli Clare who have told stories before them, encouraging them and others to "break open the bone" by narrating their mad experiences (100).

Despite this cross-pollination, critical discussion of the points of overlap and the tensions between madness and disability are scarce. The notable exception is Peter Beresford's thread of scholarship, stemming from his 2000 publication in *Disability & Society* of "What Have Madness and Psychiatric System Survivors Got to Do with Disability and Disability Studies?" to his present work that questions disciplinary relationships. However, even in the limited intersectional work on disability and madness, very few writers claim a position of madness *and* disability or include coming out narratives. This absence is surprising given the value placed on identity politics in both disability studies and mad studies.

This chapter analyzes scholarship by three authors who strategically come out as both disabled and mad: Margaret Price, Katie Aubrecht, and A.J. Withers. I use the description of "coming out" purposely, as Brenda Brueggemann and Debra Moddelmog have, recognizing that "coming-out conversations in gay and lesbian studies and [mad] and disability studies have obvious differences, [but] they share a number of points, not the least of which is their interest in exploring the connection of traditionally discredited identities to a larger historical and political picture of the fit citizen and thus the fit teacher" (311). While their identity claims might be especially stigmatized from a medical model perspective, I argue that claiming both identities increases the authors' credibility and allows the writers to powerfully critique scholarship and activism related to mad and disabled people's rights. The texts I analyze also model coalitional scholarship, in part because they share their own identities as examples that cut across divisions between who "counts" as mentally or physically different. I have woven my own stories throughout this chapter to provide readers with information on my postionality, perspectives, and motivations for analyzing the tricky contacts between madness and disability.

MAD STUDIES IN RELATION TO DISABILITY STUDIES

Before delving into my analysis of coming out claims within peer-reviewed publications, I want to contextualize the overlaps and rifts between mad studies and disability studies and to clarify terminology. Doing so will provide greater exigence for analyzing these particular coming out narratives. The tensions between the two disciplines show that claiming disability identity on the basis of madness is contested ground.

Mad studies is an emerging academic field of study comprised of activists and scholars who share similar critiques of psychiatry. As described by the authors of *Mad Matters*, the field "incorporates all that is critical of psychiatry from a radical socially progressive foundation in which the medical model is dispensed with as biologically reductionist whilst alternative forms of helping people experiencing mental anguish are based on humanitarian, holistic perspectives" (LeFrancois, Menzies, and Reaume 2). Mad studies refers to a constellation of approaches in higher education that have roots in psychiatric survivor activism. Bradley Lewis explains that psychiatric survivors are activists for whom psychiatry has been a damaging force (*Moving Beyond Prozac* 63). Some use the abbreviation of c/s/x, or consumer/survivor/ex-patient, to refer to the range of identities and interactions an individual might have with psychiatry. The disparate approaches within mad studies are in part due to its status as a "broad church" of psychiatric survivors who fear endorsing one rigid understanding of mental difference that would "divid[e] rather than unit[e] survivors" (Beresford and Wallcraft). At its core, mad studies scholars oppose the illness model of mental difference and the hegemony of psychiatry. Beresford and Peter Campbell explain that for many people, "A mental illness diagnosis..., although sometimes helpful in easing confusion and distress, effectively marks out the individual as a citizen of lesser value ... isolated, distrusted, largely unemployed and dependent on the welfare system" (327). As a result of the stigmatized place in society that mental patients occupy, survivors "talk back," as Linda Morrison terms it, to psychiatry.

Disability studies takes a broader mission, though it, of course, shares mad studies' critique of pathologizing human difference. The Society for Disability Studies states on its website that disability studies "explore[s] models and theories that examine social, political, cultural, and economic factors that define disability and help determine personal and collective responses to difference." Simi Linton provides the foundational idea that disability studies inquires into disability as "a marker of identity" and a "social/political category" (12). Linton's definition creates space for people with a range of impairments and diagnoses to claim disability and disability studies as their home. As she explains it, "people with significant impairments, people with behavioral or anatomical characteristics marked as deviant, and people who have or are suspected of having conditions, such as AIDS or emotional illness, that make them targets of discrimination" are all part of a coalition of people who might claim disability.

The key is identifying with some sort of difference and studying lived experiences from the assumption that difference is neither deviance nor the ultimate negative signifier.

While disability studies and mad studies are distinct from any medical approach, such strong lines of separation cannot be drawn between the two theoretically similar lines of inquiry. Despite Linton's inclusive vision of disability studies, a perusal of the scholarship discourages a conclusive stance on whether or not madness can or should be considered a disability. Some scholars and activists like Henderson and Ostrander strategically ally mad studies and disability studies because both disciplines contend that mental and physical differences are a defining feature of humanity. Disability studies scholars writing about madness sometimes refer to it as a subset of the disability experience, terming it "mental disability" (Lewiecki-Wilson; Price). One argument for considering madness as a disability is that the motto of the disability rights movement, "nothing about us without us," is useful for psychiatric survivors and disabled people alike. It applies to both groups' desire to be seen as authorities on their own experience and to be included in individual and large-scale policy decisions.

Despite the overlaps between mad studies and disability studies, the two disciplines are an uneasy fit in some ways. A deep rift between the approaches exists because many psychiatric survivors do not identify as being disabled, and likewise, many disabled people do not identify as psychiatric survivors. More than a problem of recognition, members of both communities sometimes actively resist the other identity. Psychiatric survivors who view themselves as mentally different and celebrate their uniqueness might reject the label of disability or impairment and its implied pathology to explain their experience. On the other hand, a common trope in disability autobiography or personal narrative is to assert that physical disabilities or illnesses do not interfere with one's mental functioning. Such assertions along the lines of, "I may use a wheelchair, but my mental functioning is all there!" imply that impaired mental functioning is an undesirable state, which runs counter to the views of most psychiatric survivors.[1]

Whether or not an individual identifies as mad or disabled, madness can be covered under the Americans with Disabilities Act (ADA). Thus, from a legal perspective, a connection exists. Beresford, in particular, has noted that regardless of how "we as disabled people or psychiatric system survivors may think of ourselves, we are still lumped together within the same externally imposed definitions, administrative categories and statistics," and "we are both subject to discrimination and oppression" (169). The choice to accept any identity is an individual one, but regardless of whether an individual identifies with the psychiatric survivor movement, the disability community, or neither, legal and bureaucratic systems frequently devise policies and procedures that consider mental difference to be a disability.

Claiming Madness and Disability

Beresford's point remains that often institutions label individuals, rather than individuals choosing their own labels. But as mad and disabled people talk back to institutional discourses and claim their own preferred terminology, they position themselves in relation to certain models of disability. *How* one claims an identity reveals one's views on embodiment and on epistemology. Coming out as mad, rather than mentally ill, makes a statement about how one views their experience and the nature of mental difference. But no single alternatives to terms like "mental illness" or "handicapped" exist, and word choice is hotly contested. A discussion thread from the Disability Studies and Humanities listserv in March 2011 supports this point, as many list members joined a conversation about the range of language used to name psychiatric disability. The discussion prompted members of the list to identify their preferred terminology for psychiatric disability, which are listed in the box below:

> Consumer/survivor/ex-patient
> Disabled people
> Disability of the mind or bodymind
> Mental and physical disabilities
> Mental disability
> Mental illness
> Neuroatypical
> Neuro-cognitive and affective disabilities
> Neurodiversity
> Personality disorder
> Psychiatric disability
> PsychoCrips
> Psychosocial disability

The range of responses is striking—thirteen different terms were mentioned by far more than thirteen respondents to the discussion thread. But even more interesting to me is that the conversation about terminology is not confined to this one listserv thread from 2011.

In July 2012, a similar thread on the DS-HUM listserv resurfaced when a member of the list, Genevra Jones, posted the following:

> Since I've been a member of DS-HUM the term "mental illness" has repeatedly been used on this listserv. Although at various times posters have tried to call attention to the obviously (or not??) problematic politics of the term, the conversation never really seems to have gone anywhere. I simply hope that DS [disability studies] scholars might endeavor to be a little bit more careful or self-conscious when invoking biomedical constructs (i.e. "illness") that not only clash with socioecological theories of disability, but have been actively opposed by many, many members of the user/survivor activist movement.

The result of Jones' post was that many members of the list wrote in defense of their own preferred terms for psychiatric disability, some of which relied on biomedical constructs that others vehemently opposed. But the motivation that each person had for one term over another was rooted in the term's power to construct mental difference in a particular way.

Choosing to disclose one's relationship to disability has been framed in disability studies as an ethical and even epistemological decision. The logic follows that if lived experience provides insight into inaccessibility or ableism, then it is to an author's benefit to name that experience, position, and identity. Of course, disclosure is never without risk. Corbett O'Toole is perhaps the strongest proponent of disclosing one's relationship to disability in one's own scholarship. She argues in her 2013 *Disability Studies Quarterly* essay that disability studies takes up disclosure as a topic, but paradoxically, most scholars do not publicly or professionally claim disability status. This silence regarding identity is certainly true in publications on madness and disability, making the analysis of coming out claims in the next section a needed contribution to this topic. O'Toole's point is that disclosure is necessary for readers to frame and interpret the information they read. When scholars do not disclose that they, for example, have disabled family members, other disability studies scholars with similar experiences lose an opportunity to identify with and benefit from this shared perspective. In short, coming out creates role models for others. And role models are particularly important for those who claim stigmatized identities. As Eli Clare puts it, "I am in particular need of role models. I think many of us are" (227).

2011. *"Should madness be considered a disability?" I asked my undergraduate students in an Introduction to Disability Studies course this question near the end of the semester. We had just finished reading excerpts from Margaret Price's* Mad at School *and Bradley Lewis' "A Mad Fight: Psychiatry and Disability Activism." We had spent all semester learning about the models of disability, disability pride and culture, and the history of discrimination and ableism within the United States. It is possible to go an entire semester on the foundations of disability studies without discussing psychiatric disability in depth, but I wanted it to be a meaningful part of the course. I also wanted to know where my students marked the boundaries of the field. I still have our class notes that I copied onto paper from the board, where we drew textual evidence from Price and Lewis to ask a question Simi Linton posed in 1998: what is/is not disability studies? In our case, we limited our inquiry to mad pride and c/s/x activism, along with mad studies* (Table 2.1).

I asked my students what they thought should *be—not what is—the relationship between madness and disability, admittedly expecting either apathy or consensus that any person should be able claim a disabled or mad identity, or both. I assumed that the young adults in my classroom would take the approach that they were in no position to mete out judgment on identities or disciplinary boundaries. I enjoy the fire-in-the-belly idea exchanges, but I would have understood a neutral stance from novices in the field. To my surprise, the class was split on this deliberative question, and in the next class, we held a debate. Ultimately, I couldn't decide on a winner or answer to whether or not disability studies should include mad studies, but the thorniness of the issue got driven home yet again for me. My students volleyed reasons for over an hour, expressing strong positions for the benefits of coalition building that resists diagnostic boundaries, and on the other hand, the positive impact of claiming a distinct mad identity untethered to the mainstream baggage of that prefix dis-. In the end, I think we all felt like we couldn't possibly choose. We wanted space for both.*

Table 2.1 Transcribed notes that I recorded in an Introduction to Disability Studies class that I taught in 2011. The column on the left includes threads within disability studies, and the column on the right includes threads within mad studies. The middle column indicates shared inquiry between the two fields

Disability studies	Both	Mad pride
	Challenge representations of medicalized/individualized notions of disability (Lewis 340)	
Ableism (Lewis 340)		"Mentalism" or "Sanism" (Lewis 340)
Don't want the "mad" label (Lewis 340)		Don't want the "disability" label (Lewis 340); view mental difference positively (Price 14)
Concerned with confinement and accessibility (Lewis 340)		Concerned with state coercion and involuntary commitment (Lewis 340)
	Concerned with impairment (Lewis 341)	
	Rights-based model (Lewis 341)	
	Political activism in response to the Bush triple-play (Lewis 348)	
	Question what a "normal" mind is (Price 4)	
	Passing (Price 7)	
	Challenges how spaces and places encourage particular minds and bodies (Price 13)	
	Community/coalition is created (Price 18–20)	
	Interested in reassigning the meaning of terms (Price 20)	

COMING OUT MAD AND DISABLED

Naming one's relationship to madness, disability, or both is always a negotiation of risk and benefit. One risks discrimination, but stands to gain understanding, disseminate uniquely situated knowledge, and connect with others. The scholarship on tensions between mad studies and disability studies notably lacks voices that speak from *both* positions. This perspective is necessary, particularly because publications within disability studies increasingly include madness, yet few writers candidly navigate the historically uneasy mad/disability relationship. When writers disclose, they model how one contributes to both mad studies and disability studies by identifying with both. They also move the discussions forward about tensions between the fields by troubling neat boundaries and explaining the personal consequences (good and bad) stemming from the intersection of madness and disability.

I analyze texts by Margaret Price, Katie Aubrecht, and A.J. Withers that take up the fraught intersection of madness and disability within academia. I chose peer-reviewed texts written for disability studies and mad studies audiences that were published after 2008, the year mad studies coalesced into a separate field. I selected texts after 2008 knowing that by that time writers had the option to claim mad studies as a singular disciplinary home, so their identification with both disability and madness is strategic. Disability studies cannot be argued as the only disciplinary home for humanistic studies of madness, if it ever could be. I also chose texts on the basis that they explicitly and thoroughly engaged the lines between madness and disability, and crafted their interventions using personal narrative and statements of disclosure. These three scholarly texts serve as examples of how the position of mad and disabled can create a credible ethos and can allow incisive critique of both mad studies and disability studies.

PRICE AND DISABILITY COMMUNITY

In the introduction to her 2011 monograph, *Mad at School: Rhetorics of Mental Disability and Academic Life*, Margaret Price comes out as both mad and disabled. She bluntly writes: "I am crazy (although I don't usually use that word to refer to myself)" (1). And shortly after, she states that "although I use *mental disability* as my own term of choice, I continue to use others as needed, and my overall argument is for deployment of language in a way that operates as inclusively as possible, inviting coalition, while also attending to the specific texture of individual experiences" (9). Price follows Cynthia Lewiecki-Wilson in her preference for the term *mental disability*, which unites disabled people while retaining helpful information about her focus (18). Price's call for coalition responds to the history of isolation and separation that disabled people have faced. Precisely because of its impact on individuals' lives, the language of psychiatric disability is a significant portion of the introduction. Price weighs the merits and limitations of terms ranging from mental illness to psychiatric survivor to neurodiversity. And she adds commentary on her personal response to the terms, from her position of claiming both madness and disability. For example, Price shares that the label *mental illness* in her experience encourages a well/unwell binary that discourages holistic care and has been an uneasy fit for her need of long-term therapy. She remembers a point at which her insurance company deemed her "well enough" to no longer need talk therapy (12). In this case, an illness paradigm clearly worked against Price's needs.

The introduction's reflection on terminology is unique and important for both mad studies and disability studies particularly because it is driven by Price's own coming out. Without her overt identity claims, her analysis of language would make a scholarly intervention, but would fail to provide a human weightiness, if you will—a reason why debates about whether one is mad, disabled, or both affect one's life. Price writes, "I have chosen to use a term that includes *disability* explicitly" because it provides community (19). This community is one that includes reaching across differences and does not depend on shared diagnoses or experiences. Price illustrates this vision of disability community through a story she shares about hugging Neil Marcus, a disability activist and writer who uses a wheelchair, at a conference. Regardless of their different embodiments, both strategically choose to identify with one another and claim disability. Price's coming out narrative is one of personal gain, in terms of the benefits of identity and community that positioning her mental difference as disability have brought her. In the face of medical model narratives that define disability by the loss of function, and madness by the loss of rationality, Price talks back with a story of her personal gain.

In addition to Price's personal benefit in the form of a disability community, her ethos as both mad and disabled enhances her authority to speak on language and disciplinary positioning. That claiming madness and disability might enhance one's position is no small point; in most cases, these labels increase stigma (O'Toole). But in fields like mad studies and disability studies that are built on the lived experiences of individuals, writing from marginalized positions creates valuable knowledge. Tobin Siebers contends that "identity politics remains in my view the most practical course of action by which to address social injustices against minority peoples and to apply the new ideas, narratives, and experiences discovered by them to the future of progressive, democratic society" (321). In other words, Price's identification with both madness and disability names a position from which knowledge about social inclusion resonates. In her introduction, this knowledge takes the specific form of broadening disability studies beyond its focus on physical and sensory disabilities (5); interrogating threads within disability studies that marginalize chronically ill, "unhealthy disabled" (Wendell) people, regardless of the mental or physical nature of that illness (14); and demanding space for "*both* local specificity *and* broad coalitions for maximum advantage" (18). This last call for a both/and approach echoes Ingram's urging for mad studies scholar-activists to "carv[e] out spaces of relative autonomy while simultaneously taking up the many 'communalities' and points of intersection between parallel fields of inquiry and action" (qtd. in LeFrancois et al. 12). Price declines the opportunity to present a "view from nowhere" (Nagel 3) on the intersection of madness and disability, instead embracing her personal experience—of navigating word choice and finding community with other disabled people—as having scholarly importance.

Aubrecht and the Language of Mental Illness

The next two examples of writers who come out as mad and disabled in their scholarship, Katie Aubrecht and A.J. Withers, use their complex identifications to critique exclusionary practices in either disability studies or mad studies. By positioning themselves as both mad and disabled, their disclosures challenge any attempts to destigmatize or legitimize one experience at the expense of the other.

Aubrecht's 2012 article, "Disability Studies and the Language of Mental Illness," published in the *Review of Disability Studies*, weaves disclosure and identification throughout its argument for disability studies to stop relying on the language of psychiatry. Aubrecht positions herself almost immediately as "someone whose body, mind, and senses bare the mark of the mental health system," and she notes (it seems strategically in the passive voice) that she *has been* "named mentally ill." At no point does Aubrecht claim the label of mental illness, but she reflects that the label's application to her led her to disability studies. While Aubrecht initially orients readers to her identity as a mad person, she also claims the term disability, invoking phrases like "we in the disability community." And she spends considerable time questioning person-first language as she expresses preference for *disabled person* over *person with a disability*. She writes, "In identifying as a *disabled person* and not a *person with a disability*, I seek to 'transgress' (Titchkosky 137) the normative demand to remove and distance myself from disability through the use of the word 'with.'" Similar to Price, she claims disability in this article apparently because of madness, and understands these subject positions as intertwined.

Whereas Price uses narrative (her story of hugging Neil Marcus at a conference) to describe the community that she gains from identifying as disabled, Aubrecht employs narrative to relay the pain of being denied that same community. She moves out of a third-person engagement with scholarship to a first-person claim that she has experienced discrimination on the basis of not appearing to be disabled. She recalls that despite asserting her disability identity, as Linton claims is sufficient for inclusion within the disability community, she has not always been recognized as disabled. Aubrecht is savvy in her reflection on this incident; she realizes that regardless of the stigma associated with disability status in mainstream culture, "in disability studies, just saying you are disabled has 'credibility,'" because it signals valuable experience and perspective from which knowledge can be shared. It stands to reason, then, that such a position of credibility might be contested or guarded. She goes on to consider what markers of disability culture one might bear, beyond claiming it, to benefit from this ethos. I read her considerations as essentially concluding that claiming disability is a privilege dependent upon holding certain priorities, such as fighting ableism. Disability identity and community are founded on those shared values, rather than on diagnoses or identifications with madness. Aubrecht reaches this conclusion through reflections on her own identity and the pain at not being granted in-group status by other disabled people. As I elaborate in the next section, Withers reaches a similar conclusion about the need for coalition based on shared values rather than similar bodies or minds.

Because Aubrecht has been personally "marked by the language of the mental health system," she is particularly apt to notice language within disability studies that dehumanizes psychiatrically disabled people. She warns of "serious consequences" that will come from "ignoring questions that point to conflicts in the relationship between psychiatric survivors, madness, distress and disability" because people experiencing either madness or disability face an inaccessible, ableist world. Aubrecht's position as both mad and disabled allows her to speak with authority on oppression facing both populations. She critiques narratives that separate the two groups and contribute to crip-casting, or categorizing certain disabilities as less desirable than others. One case in point is Lynn Manning who can accept that he is blind apparently based on the relief that he has not been hallucinating. Manning's narrative uncritically contributes to conversations about madness and disability by expressing a clear preference for blindness over madness. Aubrecht criticizes the logic in disability narratives that goes, "Do not worry. You are disabled, not crazy." Such logic effectively buys status for the disabled person by demonstrating that madness is not only fundamentally different, but fundamentally worse. Through this analysis of disability narratives that deprecate madness and rely on psychiatry's authority and conception of mental illness, Aubrecht demonstrates that challenging psychiatry should, in fact, be a shared mission that aligns with disability studies and mad studies. Her personal experience of being denied acceptance within disability communities illuminates the personal cost and pain to drawing boundaries between madness and disability communities. Just as many narratives in disability studies chronicle the cost of passing as able-bodied (see Stephen Kuusisto's *Planet of the Blind* for an apt example), we better understand identity and coalition building when we know how these affect individuals.

WITHERS AND DISABLISM

A.J. Withers' 2014 chapter "Disability, Divisions, Definitions, and Disablism: When Resisting Psychiatry is Oppressive," published in the edited collection, *Psychiatry Disrupted: Theorizing Resistance and Crafting the (R)evolution*, admonishes the consumer/survivor/ex-patient movement for separating itself from disabled people. Withers comes out as a physically disabled person who is also psychiatrized on the basis of being a trans person (114). And it is because of this complex identification that Withers experiences boundaries between madness and disability that clash with their[2] own embodiment. Withers' coming out begs the question of how madness and disability could possibly be disentangled when they are not mutually exclusive. Whereas Aubrecht spoke from her dual position to indict disability studies for defining itself against madness, Withers critiques mad activists for defining themselves as *not* disabled. However, Withers' specific relationship to disability and madness emphasizes the author's identification with disability and queerness more so than with madness. A footnote to Withers' claim of being psychiatrized clarifies, "I am not claiming an 'insider' position here, however.

Like most trans people I know, the psychiatrizaion of my trans identity is a relatively insignificant part of that identity" (127). Withers' footnote is a crucial signal to readers that the position of madness has been applied *to* trans people, but that they do not necessarily identify with this. In fact, Withers' first person perspective at times claims only physical disability and not madness, particularly in the author's description of their preferred model of disability:

> While the primary developers of this radical model that I am promoting are *physically disabled* (myself and Loree Erickson), our work was done *in close consultation with psychiatrized people*, and draws on many of the important contributions that the psychiatric survivor movement has made. (my emphasis 126)

Withers' unique position as someone who claims a disabled identity but has been labeled as mad on the basis of being trans creates the foundation for their critique in this chapter: that activist movements of mad people have been inhospitable to the larger disability community.

Withers establishes credibility on the basis of having multiple, interlocking marginal identities, a position that allows critique of groups that "purchase privilege" at the expense of another (125). In Withers' chapter, this indictment describes the ways the c/s/x movement makes a case for respect on the basis that it is *not* populated by disabled people and it does not desire disability. Withers, speaking primarily from the position of a disabled person, expresses resentment at having disability identity framed as something "in need of being prevented and the result of [psychiatric] harm" (117). From this position, then, the author builds the case that the c/s/x movement uses disablist[3] language and resists the label of disability. Ultimately, the call to action in this chapter is for activists to redirect their energy away from defining themselves against other marginalized groups, to instead end categorizations of people that deem some groups deviant—on any basis. Withers speaks from a position of a trans, disabled, psychiatrized person, and in locating similar oppressions across groups, reframes the debate about madness-disability relations to one of coalition building across all oppressed people.

2017. "How do we place Kay Redfield Jamison within disability studies? Does she identify with the field? Do you think she belongs on our reading list?" I asked my upper-level undergraduate English majors in a Disability and Literature class these questions. We had read Jamison's An Unquiet

Mind *and discussed Jamison's word choice regarding her identity and diagnosis, specifically her preference for "manic-depressive illness" over "bipolar disorder." We also analyzed the models of disability that Jamison seemed to employ in her memoir, namely her reliance on the medical model and the distancing moves she makes between herself and those with sensory and mobility impairments. I argued that these aspects of the text make it clear that Jamison does not position herself within the field of disability studies or mad studies. She certainly never explicitly identifies with either. As a psychiatrist herself, she vehemently supports biomedical interventions and finds alternative models unethical. While we might find value in Jamison's perspective and even view it as empowering using G. T. Couser's work on disability autobiography—in other words, we might apply disability theory to Jamison's text—we cannot uncritically claim that Jamison is furthering the mission of disability studies. This seemed to me, a point beyond debate. But some of my students seemed puzzled and wanted to further understand my point. They asked in class discussion why Jamison wouldn't claim disability studies as a disciplinary home. After all, they asserted, she has a disability and is writing about it. Shouldn't disability studies be the larger umbrella for all models, perspectives, and mental and physical differences? I turned the question back to them: Is this disability studies' role though? Should it be? From Jamison's perspective, what does she lose if she rejects disability studies (and mad studies, for that matter)? My students agreed: community.*

Conclusion

While disability studies and mad studies scholarship frequently reference both experiences seamlessly and without comment, both fields also include word choice and comparative claims that actively separate the communities. And for scholar-activists who value "nothing about us without us," it makes sense that a crucial source of knowledge on the madness/disability identification should be individuals who publicly claim both positions. Though few examples exist as yet in our publications, the analysis of the three examples above demonstrate that claiming both madness and disability can be a position of credibility and coalition building. And they tell us what often matters most to us as readers, scholars, and people: why claims to certain communities matter to individuals. One of the lessons of these three coming out narratives from Price, Aubrecht, and Withers is that gatekeeping moves limit opportunities for community building. More than this though, we see that drawing boundaries between what counts as madness and disability causes personal pain. Regardless of how one identifies, purchasing privilege at the expense of another identity causes damage.

This analysis of coming out claims also reinforces the value of authors disclosing their positions, especially when these disclosures directly inform the argument and even when they are difficult. In light of my analysis, I want to revisit the question I began with almost ten years ago: can I do disability studies? The tensions that Price, Aubrecht, and Withers expose between disability studies and mad studies demonstrate, yet again, that despite Linton's broad definition of disability studies, the field has not agreed on who can comfortably occupy it. I believe that in part we lack consensus because we do not regularly disclose our relations to disability in our scholarship. The three essays I analyze in this chapter are the exception. However, I do not pretend that disclosure is an easy solution or that everyone is in a position to publicly identify without significant consequences. My point is that we do not know how many of us have complex identifications like I do and like the authors I analyze. If we did, the line between madness and disability might be a less contentious boundary because we would be aware of how many in the field relate to disability in complex ways.

If my students today asked me my original question of whether or not they could do disability studies, I would reframe it to *how* can you do disability studies, or *what* do you need to value to work in the field? If we have more scholarship that self-consciously grapples with disciplinary fit and complex identifications, our questions might shift to these. We would also have more role models undertaking ethical scholarship from different positions. When we choose not to name our relationships to disability in our scholarship, we limit opportunities to serve as role models and to build community because others simply do not know why we have come to the field or how we imagine it. Corbett O'Toole posits that when we do not disclose an identity, we reinforce the idea that disability is undesirable and shameful. I would add that when we do not publicly claim more complex relations to disability, like mine and like the authors I analyze in this essay, we let readers come to their own conclusions about who populates our scholarship. I worry that we perpetuate fear about being discovered to have a messy or uncommon relationship to disability, when in fact these complex identifications can create role models and can catalyze interventions into debates, such as the border between madness and disability.

Notes

1. In my analysis of Katie Aubrecht's article later on this chapter, I return to this discriminatory move and explain how it creates a caste system of sorts by distinguishing physical disability as more desirable than psychiatric disability.
2. I follow other writers, including Jaime R. Brenes Reyes, who use and note that Withers' preferred pronoun is *they*.
3. Fiona Kumari Campbell defines *disablism* as the counterpoint to *ableism*, which describes "a set of assumptions (conscious or unconscious) and practices that promote the differential or unequal treatment of people because of actual or presumed disabilities."

Works Cited

Aubrecht, Katie. "Disability Studies and the Language of Mental Illness." *Review of Disability Studies*, vol. 8, no. 2, 2012, n.p.

Beresford, Peter. "What Have Madness and Psychiatric System Survivors Got to Do with Disability and Disability Studies." *Disability & Society*, vol. 15, no. 2, 2000, pp. 167–72.

———, and Peter Campbell. "Participation and Protest: Mental Health Service Users/Survivors." *Democracy and Participation: Popular Protest and New Social Movements*, edited by Malcolm J. Todd and Gary Taylor. Merlin Press, 2004, pp. 326–42.

———, and Jan Wallcraft. "Psychiatric System Survivors and Emancipatory Research: Issues, Overlaps and Differences." *Doing Disability Research*, edited by Colin Barnes and Geof Mercer. The Disability Press, 1997, pp. 66–87.

Brueggemann, Brenda Jo, and Debra A. Moddelmog. "Coming Out Pedagogy: Risking Identity in Language and Literature Classrooms." *Pedagogy*, vol. 2, no. 3, 2002.

Campbell, Fiona Kumari. "Refusing Able(ness): A Preliminary Conversation about Ableism." *M/C Journal: A Journal of Media and Culture*, vol. 11, no. 3, 2008.

Clare, Eli. "Gawking, Gaping, Staring." *Disability and the Teaching of Writing: A Critical Sourcebook*, edited by Cynthia Lewiecki-Wilson and Brenda Jo Brueggemann. Bedford/St. Martin's, 2008, pp. 224–28.

Couser, G. Thomas. "Disability, Life Narrative, and Representation." *Disability Studies Reader*, 3rd ed., edited by Lennard J. Davis. Routledge, 2006, pp. 399–402.

Goffman, Erving. *Stigma: Notes on the Management of Spoiled Identity*. Touchstone, 1986.

Ingram, Richard. "Mapping 'Mad Studies': The Birth of an In/Discipline." Disability Studies Student Conference, 3 May 2008, Syracuse University, Syracuse, NY.
Jamison, Kay Redfield. *An Unquiet Mind: A Memoir of Moods and Madness.* Vintage, 1996.
Jones, Genevra. "Re: 'Mental illness' and Let's Pretend This Never Happened." *Disability Studies in the Humanities Listserv*, 2 July 2012. Accessed 2 July 2012.
Kuusisto, Stephen. *Planet of the Blind: A Memoir.* Delta, 1998.
LeFrancois, Brenda A., Robert J. Menzies, and Geoffrey Reaume, editors. *Mad Matters: A Critical Reader in Canadian Mad Studies.* Canadian Scholars Press, 2013.
Lewiecki-Wilson, Cynthia. "Rethinking Rhetoric through Mental Disabilities." *Rhetoric Review*, vol. 22, no. 2, 2003, pp. 156–67.
Lewis, Bradley. "A Mad Fight: Psychiatry and Disability Activism." *Disability Studies Reader*, 3rd ed., edited by Lennard J. Davis. Routledge, 2006, pp. 339–52.
———. *Moving Beyond Prozac, DSM, and the New Psychiatry.* University of Michigan Press, 2006.
Linton, Simi. *Claiming Disability: Knowledge and Identity.* New York University Press, 1998.
Manning, L. *Weights.* 2003. http://www.kennedy-center.org/programs/millennium/artist_detail.cfm?artist_id=LYNNMANING.
Morrison, Linda J. *Talking Back to Psychiatry: The Psychiatric Consumer/Survivor/Ex Patient Movement.* Routledge, 2005.
Nagel, Thomas. *The View from Nowhere.* Oxford University Press, 1986.
"On mental disability." *Disability Studies in the Humanities Listserv*, 9 Feb 2011. Accessed 11 Feb 2011.
Ostrander, Noam, and Bruce Henderson. "Editors' Introduction." *Disability Studies Quarterly*, special issue of *Disability and Madness*, vol. 32, no. 4, 2012.
O'Toole, Corbett Joan. "Disclosing Our Relationships to Disabilities: An Invitation for Disability Studies Scholars." *Disability Studies Quarterly*, vol. 33, no. 2, 2013.
Pompili, Maurizio, et al. "Suicide Risk in Schizophrenia: Learning from the Past to Change the Future." *Annals of General Psychiatry*, vol. 6, no. 1, 2007.
Poole, Jennifer M., and Jennifer Ward. "'Breaking Open the Bone': Storying, Sanism, and Mad Grief." *Mad Matters: A Critical Reader in Canadian Mad Studies*, edited by Brenda A. LeFrancois, Robert J. Menzies, and Geoffrey Reaume. Canadian Scholars Press, 2013, pp. 94–104.
Price, Margaret. *Mad at School: Rhetorics of Mental Disabilty and Academic Life.* University of Michigan Press, 2011.

Reyes, Jaime R. Brenes. "Review of *Disability Politics and Theory*, by A.J. Withers." *Canadian Journal of Disability Studies*, vol. 2, no. 3, 2013, pp. 135–38.

Siebers, Tobin. *Disability Theory*. University of Michigan Press, 2008.

Titchkosky, Tanya. "Disability: A Rose by any Other Name? 'People-First' Language in Canadian Society." *The Canadian Review of Sociology and Anthropology*, vol. 38, no. 2, pp. 125–40.

Wendell, Susan. "Unhealthy Disabled: Treating Chronic Illnesses as Disabilities." *Hypatia*, vol. 16, no. 4, 2001, pp. 17–33.

"What Are Disability Studies?" *The Society for Disability Studies*, 14 June 2017. https://disstudies.org/index.php/about-sds/what-is-disability-studies/.

Withers, A. J. "Disability, Divisions, Definitions, and Disablism: When Resisting Psychiatry Is Oppressive." *Psychiatry Disrupted: Theorizing Resistance and Crafting the (R)evolution*, edited by Bonnie Burstow, Brenda A. LeFrancois, and Shaindl Diamond. McGill-Queens University Press, 2014, pp. 114–28.

CHAPTER 3

Going Barefoot: Mad Affiliation, Identity Politics, and Eros

PhebeAnn M. Wolframe

As a psychiatric survivor[1] and mad studies scholar, I am interested not only in *why* mad people come together in community, but also *how* mad communities come together, fracture, and reconfigure, changing and developing over time. What are the ties that bind mad communities? Are the tensions within mad communities merely sources of strife, or are they also a wellspring of resilience? Is eros, the unreasoned expression of love, which Foucault posits as the lost link between eroticism and madness, one of the ties that binds mad and queer communities together across difference?

To answer these questions, I examine a mad community I created for research purposes. The community took the form of a blog, called *MadArtReview*. In *MadArtReview*, which operated from 2011 to 2012, participants were asked to post reviews of texts of their choice—including novels, films, music, advertising, video games, television shows, news media—which depicted madness/mental illness and/or psychiatric treatment. In addition to posting reviews where they reflected on how they related to this media as "mad readers," participants could comment on one another's posts and generate discussion. They were recruited from

P. M. Wolframe (✉)
Thunder Bay, ON, Canada

© The Author(s) 2018
E. J. Donaldson (ed.), *Literatures of Madness*, Literary Disability Studies, https://doi.org/10.1007/978-3-319-92666-7_3

existing psychiatric consumer/survivor and mad[2] listservs, message boards, and Facebook groups, and live all over the world, but primarily in Canada and the United Kingdom. Participants did not have to identify themselves or their politics in any particular way; they only had to self-identify as having had experience of the mental health system.[3]

In addition to the blog, I also turn to a literary representation of madness and mad community: Persimmon Blackbridge's semi-autobiographical novel *Prozac Highway*. The novel is unique in that it brings together queer and mad politics, and central to its narrative is a consideration of the way consumer, survivor, ex-patient and mad communities have been shaped and fuelled by global Internet culture. As such, it is an apt literary text to pair with the online *MadArtReview*. *Prozac Highway* takes place in the 1990s in Vancouver and revolves around Jam, a middle-aged lesbian performance artist and housecleaner who has experience of madness. Jam is struggling with an episode of depression and writer's block, as well as her ex-lover, best friend and artistic collaborator Roz's possible breast cancer relapse.

Much of the novel's narrative happens through Jam's interactions on a peer-support listserv called ThisIsCrazy, which is populated by mad people from all over the world. In an email welcoming Fruitbat, a new member, to ThisIsCrazy, Jam responds to questions about the terminology the community uses. She writes:

> Hey Fruitbat, welcome to the Crazy family… C/S/X is a mad movement abbreviation for Consumer (someone who's on the receiving end of psychiatric services)/Survivor (an uppity consumer: someone who's been there and thinks it sucks)/eX-inmate (someone who really really thinks it sucks). Very awkward, I know, but it's fairly inclusive, which is the point. Used to be if you were a C and I was an X, we wouldn't speak to each other except to yell, but there's been a lot of blood under the bridge since those days. (13)

Here Jam reveals to Fruitbat, and Blackbridge reveals to her readership, three of the most common of many labels people use in the c/s/x/m community—excluding mad, which is more commonly used today—as well as the tensions that exist between those who choose to use them. These tensions run throughout the listserv portions of *Prozac Highway*, particularly when various members of ThisIsCrazy debate psychiatric drug use, an issue on which most have strong opinions (37, 63, 121).

Jam's initial message to Fruitbat reveals that despite the tensions among members the community has embraced, for the most part, its multiplicities (Blackbridge 13).

As on the fictional ThisIsCrazy, one of the things I found most interesting as I survey *MadArtReview* is the nuance in the way blog participants identify themselves and their attention to the complexities of mad experience. Since participants were drawn from existing online mad communities, however, the prevailing sentiment on the blog is one critical of the medical/psychiatric model of madness, which frames mental difference and/or distress as biologically-based illnesses, rather than social, cultural and/or spiritual phenomena. This said, many *MadArtReview* participants shared an ambivalent relationship with psychiatric labelling. For example, participant Anne O'Donnell, explains:

> For those not in the UK, for the past few years, this government (Conservative-Liberal Democrat coalition) and the previous one (Labour) have been working to cut back on welfare benefits... To justify this, politicians and the media have been portraying benefit claimants in various derogatory ways...
> How does this affect me?
> I am on benefits because of mental health problems/distress/madness. (I don't really have a preference at the moment for what term to use.) I've been aware of this growing campaign against disabled people for a long time, and it has fed into my own paranoia at many times. Because my impairments (I am diagnosed as bipolar, and I also have a liver condition and have to battle fatigue and pain and side-effects) are invisible, I am often part of conversations which turn to the subject of benefits....

Here, the language issues that are a source of conflict to varying degrees within mad communities become irrelevant in the face of the material consequences of media representation and government policies for mad and disabled people in neoliberal Britain. Anne remarks that she doesn't have a terminology preference. It is less important to self-label according to a particular model of madness and more important—as her arresting question "how does this affect me?" suggests—to have others understand the lived reality of being identified as mentally ill/disabled in a climate of austerity measures and stereotyping. Anne also states that she is "diagnosed as bipolar." This choice of phrasing is interesting because it neither accepts bipolar as an identity (as in "I am bipolar") nor rejects it. In a post discussing Dissociative Identity Disorder, participant wheelchairdemon writes:

> I don't like diagnoses but the alternative can be so simplistic. 'X is over-diagnosed' can so easily become 'there's nothing wrong with the majority of people who get that label.' Either way, it is a way of invalidating people's experiences of trauma, distress, madness, and denying us what we need to heal and recover or just simply live well.

As wheelchairdemon points out, dismissing diagnostic labels altogether can make invisible the experiences that get attached to them, experiences which are legible only when psychiatrizable; it is perhaps to gain recognition that Anne chooses to use her diagnostic label in a cautious phrasing. Naming "bipolar" as a label and placing it alongside other possible labels ("mental health problems/madness/distress") can be read as a refusal to pin down her experiences within one framework.

In *Prozac Highway*, Jam's tongue-in-cheek definition of the terms consumer, survivor and ex-patient, as well as her embracing of the more encompassing acronym c/s/x indicates her likewise fraught relationship with identity politics. The mad community—like the queer/LGBTT2QQIA+[4] community, of which Jam is also a part—has an ambivalent relationship with identity politics, with some groups and individuals disavowing categorization at times, and embracing it at others. This ambivalence plays out in *Prozac Highway* through Jam's relationship to psychiatric and sexual categorization, and in *MadArtReview* through participants' use of both description and labelling. I posit that these textual negotiations of one's own and others' identities through and against the lens of established categories functions as a theorization of the mad community's necessarily fraught relationship with identity politics. I furthermore argue that in *Prozac Highway*, Jam's embracing, rejecting and pondering of labels establishes a little-explored connection between mad and queer communities.

In her welcome message to Fruitbat, Jam describes ThisIsCrazy as an online "family," thus setting up an expectation of the closeness, caring and conflict she should expect from the listserv (13). This metaphor of family becomes particularly salient when one Toronto-based listserv member, Junior, ends up hospitalized. The members of the listserv—even those who do not get on well with Junior—phone the hospital from all over the world, claiming to be concerned family members. They do this in part because they know that patients who have involved families tend to be better treated (113). Junior receives 28 messages from various members of his surprisingly far-flung family, including his "cousin" Jam in Vancouver, his "father-in-law" Howard in Kansas City and his "sister" D'isMay in Tokyo. The idea of Junior's having such a motley family is apt; Junior, a young gay man whose parents disapprove of both his madness and his queerness, feels more kinship with his chosen family (214). *Prozac Highway* thus establishes a link between mad and queer communities through the tradition of creating chosen families. As Kath Weston argues in her classic study of friends-as-kin in queer communities, queer chosen families challenge the split between acts and identities because the very mention of one's queer family invokes sex, serving as a reminder that kinship and sexuality are not so easily split into public and private as those who admonish queer folks to "keep [sexuality] in the bedroom" might like to think (xii).

As Lynn Huffer argues in *Mad for Foucault*, to frame acts and identities in terms of either/or is essentially to recreate the Cartesian split between mind and body which she argues is inextricably linked to the rise of bourgeois morality, the splitting of reason and unreason, and the "great confinement" of the mad in asylums. Huffer, following Foucault, critiques the American concept of identity, which disregards the affective dimensions of sexual experience, and risks pinning down the queer into "rigid categorical positions" (82). While queerness may have emerged as a force of resistance, an "other" place to consciously inhabit, it has become an affiliative rallying point which reifies our "our perversions and our genders" (82).

While Huffer links the homosexual to the lunatic as figures of a largely undifferentiated cast of others who were excluded in the great confinement, Robert McRuer, in a similar intervention in *Crip Theory*, links compulsory heterosexuality to compulsory able-bodiedness (1). He posits that marginalized social groups, while rejecting a reification of their experiences, may find that this very method of resistance is appropriated and contained for political purposes other than those for which they were originally mobilized (2).

Drawing on McRuer's concept of "cripping," transforming "the substantive, material uses to which queer/disabled existence has been put by a system of compulsory able-bodiedness," I propose the related term maddening for the way in which mad communities highlight and redefine the ways in which bodies deemed mad are used discursively and materially (32). One of the ways in which mad people engage in critical maddening is by pointing out—like Foucault in *History of Madness*—the material and discursive conditions out of which particular tropes of "mental illness" emerge and behind which madness retreats.

Both *MadArtReview* and *Prozac Highway* describe the conditions surrounding the emergence of madness, which include the invocation of the labels and discourses used to pin it down. While *MadArtReview* and *Prozac Highway* describe experience a great deal, this description is not included as a way of trying to pin madness down; rather, these descriptions are queries, landscapes, emotions and textures. They are the bumping of bodies against discourses. They are the lyricism Huffer finds in Foucault's *History of Madness*. I argue that this descriptive mode is a way of maddening the dominant discourses of madness, allowing madness-the-experience to, as Foucault puts it, "speak of itself" in moments of linguistic slippage (Huffer 65).

In *MadArtReview*, participants madden texts by directly commenting on each one's social, historical, cultural and political background, and by reflecting upon their own experiences. For example, in their comparison of two films featuring mad protagonists, *Take Shelter* and *Shutter Island*, retropotamus argues:

> When compared to Scorsese's *Shutter Island* the film *Take Shelter* provides what I thought was a much more complex and interesting portrayal of mental illness and the psychiatric industry. Both films link paranoid social critique to psychosis, but the plot twist at the end of Scorsese's film re-privatizes and neutralizes these critiques, depicting the protagonist's discovery of repressive and exploitative biomedical experimentation as the delusions of a mental patient....
>
> The ending of [*Take Shelter*] leaves us wondering if there might not be a collective, social crisis behind the intuitions and anxieties the main character suffers... Curtis's [the protagonist's] mental illness is symptomatic of a larger social context which though not as explicitly located as the paranoid critique of *Shutter Island* (the crisis seems to have something to do with environmental degradation and systemic economic issues) is validated as real....
>
> *Take Shelter* draws on the trope of the mad individual as social prophet...There is a scene in *Take Shelter* when Curtis addresses his community from the perspective of an ostracized, mad individual. This scene...

argue[s] that mad individuals… have insights into our collective, social ailments that people 'need to hear' but are unwilling to confront.

Retropotamus's critique of *Shutter Island* is based on the film's unwillingness to show the conditions of madness's emergence. Rather than highlighting the social and political aspects of the protagonist's madness, the film's conclusion reifies "mental illness" and personal trauma as the explanation for its protagonist's unpopular, and not even fully intelligible—"the crisis *seems to have* something to do with environmental degradation…"—political commentary. Retropotamus praises *Take Shelter*, on the other hand, for using the premodern trope of the mad prophet as a way of making visible the complex factors that result in somebody being defined as mad. This maddening happens in *Take Shelter* through a moment of "letting madness speak of itself": when the mad individual addresses the community, calling them to account for their silencing and exclusions. Although the mad prophet becomes worthy because his words are useful to all the "sane" people around him, retropotamus reads Curtis's speechifying as talking back to community structures that exclude mad people.

A further maddening occurs in the comments posted on retropotamus' review of the two films. Directing their remarks at *Shutter Island*'s trailer which retropotamus posted, wheelchairdemon observes:

> I've been in the forensic ward of a psych hospital and this depiction comes nowhere near close to the truth. I was the only non-criminal there (i.e. sent there by the courts). Most patients had murdered someone and to be honest with you, when you met them in real life, they could be forgiven.
>
> Their families were never there emotionally or, oftentimes, physically. The patients often expressed a deep sense of longing for love, companionship, and MOST IMPORTANTLY OF ALL, direction….
>
> As for the 2nd movie, it was closer to reality in that the impact of mental illness and hallucinations can be scary. That being said, I've not experienced them without being inadvertently given too much psychiatric medications that triggered the bad reaction. When the reaction came, it was scary, but the hallucinations matched nothing real (like swarms of bugs). When I tried to describe them, the staff didn't get it, so I often changed my description to something that came closer to what they would understand….

People are individuals so, perhaps for someone else, this video comes closer to the truth…. I'm saying this based on personal experience. (emphasis original)

Both retropotamus and wheelchairdemon are interested in the discursive and social conditions of madness; they get at these issues, however, through different approaches. Rather than reading the discourses of madness which frame each text's protagonist, wheelchairdemon uses their experience to call into question the assumed links between madness, dangerousness and biology. Even though wheelchairdemon establishes some distance from their fellow inmates, who were convicted of previous violence—"I was the only non-criminal there"—wheelchairdemon also sympathizes with them, explaining that there are reasons why the inmates did what they did, including family neglect and trauma. Wheelchairdemon furthermore explains that their experience of hallucinating, unlike Curtis's in *Take Shelter*, was not particularly frightening, but also that it could not be defined in words that were understandable to the "sane" people around them. In their words, "the hallucinations matched nothing real," and so they had to resort to describing them as being "like swarms of bugs" so that others could understand. This comment serves as a reminder of Foucault's assertion that madness and reason do not share a language, and that experiences of being mad are typically not intelligible in a culture structured by reason (549). The closest we can get to capturing madness is to—as wheelchairdemon does here—describe the moment at which it retreats into unintelligibility. Wheelchairdemon is also careful, however, to note that their experiences are not universal. This insistence upon multiplicity—"people are individuals so, perhaps for someone else, this video comes closer to the truth"—refuses a fixing of either mad experience, or the specific experience of hallucinating, as experiences that can be known, described and categorized.

This sense of multiplicity permeates *MadArtReview*. Participant Anne writes: "I don't think madness is necessarily an evil, I don't really look for cure—but many people do. I don't like stories which talk about tragedy and overcoming it and how the right drug and/or therapist cured it. But if that is someone's experience, or interpretation of their experience, then it is as valid as any interpretation of mine." Elsewhere in *MadArtReview*, Anne ties this desire to claim her viewpoint as personal to the creation of community. At the end of one of her posts, she includes a clarifying note on her language use: "me/us and I/we [are used] to distinguish between and to include my individuality and our collectivity." Here, Anne shows the way in which she is manipulating language to try to capture both a sense of common experience among mad people but also a sense of being an individual who cannot speak for all psychiatrized people. I picked up this sense of a coexisting individuality and collectivity again in ingridjoanne's post about the impact of science fiction author David Gerrold's work on their life. Like Anne, ingridjoanne explains their use of terminology: "this series [Gerrold's 'War Against the Chtorr' novels] works as self-help literature for people with societal damage (my way of saying 'dysfunction' or 'personality disorder')." By connecting the commonly understood language of psychiatry (dysfunction, disorder) to their own way of understanding their experiences, ingridjoanne borrows the legitimacy of psychiatric discourse in order to make their own perceptions intelligible. This juxtaposition positions ingridjoanne's terminology as equal to but different from psychiatric language, maddening psychiatric discourse and questioning its primacy. Ingridjoanne's use of the first person ("my way of saying") makes clear that their perspective is their own, and exists alongside others, including, but not limited to, the medical model. Their perspective—that madness is a sign of having been damaged by society—while proclaimed as an individual standpoint, opens a space for thinking about madness a collective rather than a personal issue.

Despite moments where participants frame madness as a source of collective identity, *MadArtReview* never, as I had hoped, functioned like the mad listservs and blogs I have been a part of outside of research, or like the fictional ThisisCrazy. One of the reasons that participants identified for this lack of community were the restrictions imposed by research ethics protocol. When I was planning this project, I received extensive advice and help from a Research Ethics Board advisor who enjoined me to make it mandatory that the participants in my research use pseudonyms, and be identified only by these in any of my written work, and indeed, this advice was reinforced in my research on online research methodologies (Simsek and Veiga 225–226; Eysenbach and Till 1004). I was also advised to caution participants against sharing personal information, including stories that may make them identifiable to others. The ethics advisor explained that people who have experience of the mental health system are a "vulnerable population" and that, as a researcher, I am ethically obligated to protect "their" identities.

This framing of people who have mental health system experience as a group that needs to be regulated (via consent forms, discouragements about "outing" oneself and management on the part of the assumed-to-be reasoned researcher) reveals the university's institutional and epistemological investment in the biopolitical management that underpins the mental health system.

My concerns about the ways in which these confidentiality measures would restrict participation in *MadArtReview* were affirmed when participants addressed this issue directly in the blog. For example, participant Don Roberts wrote:

> Just want to express my thoughts on Confidentiality. My opinion:
> Confidentiality works against us, or is actually used against us. It keeps us apart and alienated.
> I want to just tell you who I am and what my life is like, and has been like. Makes it easier to have conversations.
> Truth is I was tempted to post my personal information but I think it might muck up the study.

He goes on to say later, in the comments:

> Confidentiality is a mechanism of control because it isolates us from the community and that isolation breeds fear. We become afraid of the community and the community becomes afraid of us. Within a sphere of confidentiality I am nothing more than a disease to be 'treated' – outside the protection of that bubble I am [a] human who has stories of struggles with adversity, poverty, and hardship.

The importance of being open about experiences of madness and psychiatrization, and of attaching those experiences to whole, complex, embodied lives was echoed throughout *MadArtReview*. Some participants joined the project precisely because they wanted a space to talk about their experience of madness and psychiatrization, a place where they did not have to hide these experiences as though they are shameful, as Don reflects here.

Mad people are often prohibited from getting in contact or staying in contact with one another outside of clinical or research settings because of restrictions involving confidentiality, or because it is assumed that this interaction will compromise the research or therapy in some way.

In fact, this resistance to confidentiality is at the foundation of the mad movement. The Vancouver Mental Patients' Association, formed in 1971, for example, was initially made up of a group of ex-patients who met in a day hospital. The hospital had rules against patients contacting one another outside of hospital hours; following the suicide of a fellow patient, however, the patients secretly circulated a phone list so that they could provide each other with support during the hospital's off hours (Chamberlin 78).

While the set-up of *MadArtReview* did not allow any way for participants to get in touch with one another outside of the blog environment, participants did madden *MadArtReview*'s ethics protocol. They resisted their anonymity by posting identifying information about themselves in their blog entries: they stated where they live, described their personal appearance and experiences, referred to their membership in other mad groups, linked to their personal blogs, posted pictures of their faces as their user icons, chose pseudonyms which closely resembled their real names, or which they used in other locations online, and wrote about the problems of confidentiality itself. When I explained, in the comments to Don's post, that my Research Ethics Board advisor had required that the study have a mandatory confidentiality protocol, participant Anne O'Donnell even suggested the direct action of the blog participants writing a letter to the research ethics board asking them to change their policies about "vulnerable people." Eventually, I revised my ethics protocol so that participants could be identified by name if they chose to do so. Unfortunately, by the time I did this, the participants had essentially vanished from *MadArtReview*. I only received two revised consent forms, one from Anne O'Donnell and one from Don Roberts, whose real names you see here.

Despite a deficit in participation, *MadArtReview* provided me with more rich commentary and exchanges that I could discuss here. Participant responses to the problems in the blog project's design, moreover, showed me that the greatest impediment to developing and sustaining mad communities is not divisiveness along political or identity-based lines; rather, it is the subjectifying of mad people as "vulnerable" (incapable of speaking in our own best interests; risky, at risk, and liable to be "triggered") that prevents and fractures mad community.

Both *MadArtReview* and ThisIsCrazy give a sense of the diversity of experiences, identities and perspectives among mad folks, however, there is both more conflict and a closer sense of community on

Blackbridge's fictional listserv. ThisIsCrazy members continually assert their experiences of queerness, racialization and psychiatrization as valid counter-narratives to perspectives which differ from their own. I argue, however, that the marrying of tension and connection on ThisIsCrazy allows for a sense of eros, or mad love, to emerge in *Prozac Highway*. We encounter eros in the passionate debates between listserv members: when D'isMay, a black woman living in Tokyo, and Cloudten, a white man living in Denver, debate whether gender, race, sexuality and nationality have meaning in "a global electronic reality" or not; when D'isMay (a psychology grad student) and Junior debate whether it is possible to work for change from inside the mental health system; or when George and Parnell fight constantly about the efficacy and safety of psychiatric drugs (11, 16, 36). These conflicts are part of ThisIsCrazy being a chosen family, a place where differences can be discussed safely because members will still care for one another despite them. Notwithstanding their feud, Parnell calls George "old friend" in an email showing support of George's advocacy work, and D'isMay mobilizes the listserv when the police show up at Junior's home (67). These are signs of love between ThisIsCrazy family members. The place where eros—an uninhibited love, felt in the body and soul—emerges most markedly in the narrative, however, is when eroticism, madness and conflict mix together in Jam and Fruitbat's online affair. While Roz is Jam's queer family, she does not understand Jam's madness or need for mad community. When Jam went into a full-time therapy program for her depression, Roz accused her of "pissing off in the middle of a project" and being "a pain in the butt" (135). Roz furthermore sees the Internet as "another way to be passive and isolated consumers" and chastises Jam for wasting time online (82). When Roz finally encounters Jam's online mad family herself near the novel's end she comments, "are these people all hets or what?" (260). Since Roz primarily affiliates around her lesbian identity, she assumes that Jam, who was, until recently, active in the lesbian community, likewise affiliates primarily through her lesbianness. Roz does not consider the possibility of madness as identity or a basis for community.

While Jam affiliates with others through her lesbianism, she has never fit in with its norms, coming out in the 1980s as a femme bisexual woman (22, 52). Much as Jam is critical of mainstream understandings of madness, so too does she call into question the immutability of lesbian signifiers and belonging. The fact that these signifiers and boundaries shift over time is made clear when Jam tries to search for information

3   GOING BAREFOOT: MAD AFFILIATION, IDENTITY POLITICS, AND EROS   43

on lesbian cybersex and realizes that "kewl queers don't use the word lesbian anymore. It's old and stodgy, like Womyn-loving-Womyn. Get modern. But I always liked the word lesbian, the tang of danger and desire" (52). Exploring online sex sites, Jam finds that, as in the 80s, her queerness does not jive with community norms. When she encounters someone ambiguously named Peter on the CyberDyke personals site, Jam wonders, "if you're having virtual sex, does it matter what your virtual girlfriend wears between her legs in the meatworld?" (53). She realizes that in online space, away from physical signifiers, it is difficult to maintain categories of identity and desire. While she is unsure about Peter, Jam is even more wary of "Suzi" who is "24, tanned, fit, waiting to hear from You!!!" (52). Jam's imagined description of herself as "42, basement-white, mentally unfit, and not really Interested!!!" comically points out her difference within the lesbian community, even given the relative fluidity of identity online (52). Jam is queer even within the queer community, and as her descriptor "mentally unfit" reveals, her difference is her madness. Roz's inability to recognize Jam's madness and the lack of mad visibility even within the online lesbian community is an affirmation of McRuer's claim that "able-bodiedness, even more than heterosexuality, still largely masquerades as a nonidentity, as the natural order of things" (1). Even on the sexual margins, mental and physical "fitness" are the norm, and there is little consideration of "unfitness" as a way of being.

While Jam is ambivalent about both lesbian and mad affiliation, these overlap in her understanding of herself, illuminating each other's limitations and possibilities. Fruitbat points out some of the problems of mental illness as identity when she advises Jam:

> Go barefoot. Believing in your diagnosis is big time trouble.... Shrinks rewrite the story of your life to fit your DSM category. Then your friends watch for symptoms: 'Oh no, too many mixed metaphors, she's schizing out!' I guess some folks find it a useful road map to their inner landscape or something, but I just get lost. It turns a situation (I hear voices) into an identity (I'm a schizophrenic). (33)

While Jam is aware of the pitfalls of identity politics, she finds it difficult to think outside of madness norms. For one thing, she, like ingridjoanne—who, on *MadArtReview*, describes her difference using both psychiatric terminology and her own term "[person] with societal damage"—grapples with the lack of non-psychiatric language available to describe her experiences. Jam in part negotiates madness-as-experience and madness-as-identity by maddening terms, and making them her own. Jam tells Fruitbat: "I use the word depression in its slippery sense, a description of how I feel, subliminally shaped by drug ads and my new shrink" (153). For Jam, "depression" cannot be pinned down as either something shaped by public and psychiatric discourses, or as a descriptor for "feeling shitty" (153). Instead, the term captures an experience that is inseparable from its discursive context.

Given the difficulty of separating madness-as-experience from the discourse of "mental illness," Jam struggles to decide whether it is possible for madness and erotic desire to coexist. She muses:

> How do you write about the erotic bonding possibilities of unpleasant psych-drug experiences? You don't. It's been a long time since Allen Ginsberg howled for Carl Solomon and madfolks were almost respectable, in some circles at least. Nowadays there's something seriously strange about being turned off by Suzi 'tanned and fit' and turned on by Fruitbat 'do you really want the whole pitiful story of my incarceration?' dirty girl talking to herself in the park, picked up by the cops and spat out into a psych home—how can she be the sex interest in a story unless you're going for that creepshow thrill? Watching weirdos doing it. (168)

While Jam and Roz made lesbian fucking visible through their art, Jam struggles to break through the discursive walls which separate desire from madness. Just as Jam finds herself using psychiatric language, because it is the language that has shaped her experiences, and the only language available, she finds it difficult to describe desire outside the established tropes of erotica. These tropes—captured in the figure of "Suzi tanned and fit," and in the description Jam's friend Cynthia, a phone sex worker, gives of the "intellectual type… wearing a pearl-grey suit" and "black lingerie"—are all based on classist and sanist ideals which Jam and Fruitbat do not fit (52, 138, 154, 183).

Finding established tropes unsuitable, Jam must create a new kind of fantasy. In the midst of a conversation about what counts as desirable, Jam and Fruitbat begin to have cyber sex. While they are having sex in an email thread titled "whoever you are," they also continue a conversation about their medicalization in a thread titled "morning." It proves difficult to keep these conversations separate and linear, however. In one thread, Fruitbat has asked her to pull up her t-shirt and play with her breasts. In the other, she is asking Jam about the antidepressant Elavil. Jam becomes frustrated with the two simultaneous conversations and writes, "how long did I take it? Take what? Sitting here with my shirt up, you staring, fingers flicking my nipples, the other hand, my hand, trying to type some conversation about psych drugs? It's no longer morning, whoever you are. I can't take it" (161). As it turns out, Fruitbat, too, "can't take it anymore," and is "so turned on [she] can hardly sit still" (161). Jam and Fruitbat's subsequent fantasies involve Jam picking up Fruitbat, who is panhandling in the park, and Jam being a fellow resident in Fruitbat's psychiatric boarding home and sneaking into bed with her (200, 217). Rather than hindering the sexual charge of their encounters, invoking their experience of madness and psychiatrization adds an element of danger and improbability—two key ingredients in fantasy—and is "*très* hot" (168).

In Jam and Fruitbat's cybersex encounters, eros seeps into *Prozac Highway*. Their fantasies repeatedly turn away from established discourses of sexiness, and fall outside of linear time and material place. These fluid fantasies rediscover an affinity between madness and queerness, an affinity Jam sees in Allen Ginsberg and Carl Solomon's relationship, and which Foucault represents in the Ship of Fools, where madfolk and queerfolk live in kinship, negotiating the watery threshold between madness and reason (Huffer 61, 103). Jam and Fruitbat's erotic exchanges suggest the possibility that even in the modern age, mad desire is capable of blurring the boundary between sanity and madness.

While eros disrupts boundaries in *Prozac Highway*, it is, before long, forced to retreat back into the dominant discourses of psychiatry and sexuality. Fruitbat, who has been slowly withdrawing from Thorazine without the knowledge of her psychiatric team, is found out, and is given a high dose weekly injection of Haldol instead of pills. Fruitbat ends her relationship with Jam after this change (235). That the eroticism of madwomen will be violently foreclosed is reinforced when Jam tries to write a "normal" erotic story for Roz. Jam envisions her protagonist Judy running along the beach and then picking up a jogger reminiscent of "Suzi tanned and fit" (52, 200), but in the story Jam actually writes, Judy comes across a naked woman masturbating. Judy thinks that she should report the "crazy person" on the beach, but instead, she becomes aroused watching the woman, and then punishes the woman for this desire by throwing rocks at her (222). Jam's story only indirectly suggests the possibility of a reciprocal mad love. Her story of mad desire, like her relationship with Fruitbat, is taboo, so Jam hides both from her "meatworld" friends.

The possibility of a community that crosses queer/mad and meatworld/online boundaries emerges when Jam becomes suicidal. While dusting at housecleaning client Stephen's house, Jam accidentally breaks an urn filled with ashes belonging to Stephen's late lover Bruce. Jam vacuums up Bruce's ashes, and, unable to throw them out, brings the vacuum cleaner bag home (230). Jam puts the vacuum cleaner bag on top of her computer beside her lithium, which she is trying to decide whether to take therapeutically, throw out, or to use to kill herself. The vacuum cleaner bag, speaking in Bruce's imagined voice, becomes a counterpoint to Jam's lithium (230). Every time the lithium says "kill yourself" Bruce says "no" (246).

Bruce's counsel, along with care from Roz at the height of Jam's depression, suggests the possibility of Jam's mad and queer communities coming together as a messy chosen family (257). When Jam, who has begun to take Prozac, accidentally cuts her arms too deep while self-injuring, Roz takes her to the hospital. Roz cares enough that, despite her aversion to computers, she goes on ThisIsCrazy to try to find out what has been happening in Jam's life (255). Jam is unsettled by Roz interacting with ThisIsCrazy, and particularly Bones, a former medical student who is as opinionated as Roz; nevertheless, Jam prefers Roz asking Bones for advice rather than calling the emergency doctor, and Roz complies with Jam's wishes (257). With prompting from Bones— who realizes that Jam is suicidal from a coded message that she dictates through Roz—Roz asks Jam whether she wants her lithium disposed of. Jam's assent nixes the suicide plan that she has been contemplating. This willingness to let Jam decide what she needs opens the possibility of Roz learning to madden her perspective, and even to link her experiences of queer marginality—especially in the course of her cancer treatment—to Jam's experiences of madness and psychiatrization. While Jam is uneasy about the overlapping of her mad and queer affiliations, the fact that Roz and the ThisIsCrazy family interact with each other on Jam's behalf is hopeful. As Bruce's imagined voice reminds Jam, while he counsels her through the coming together of her disparate chosen families, "life is supposed to be complicated" (257). His statement serves as a reminder that, like the participants of *MadArtReview*, Jam does not have to pin down her identity, deciding to be only and indefinitely lesbian or queer, mentally ill or mad. In Huffer and Foucault's terms, Blackbridge posits a kinship between madfolks and queerfolks characterized by a continual "turning into something other" (83). Jam's identity, and her story, can remain unfinished, always being (re)created.

At the novel's end, Jam plans to spread Bruce's ashes beside the lupins she planted with her queer friend Cynthia. This decision symbolically suggests a recognition of the interdependence of Jam's madness (represented by the talking ashes) and her queerness (represented by both the lupins and the ashes). Laying these aspects of her experience together underneath the lupins, which, as a prolific perennial, are a symbol of growth and renewal springing up from the ashes, represents mad and queer perspectives and communities coming back into kinship. This kinship, through the metaphor of the lupins, is imagined as ever-spreading, seasonally ebbing and forever re-emerging out of the divisive ruins of liberal humanist identity politics. Invoking the differences within and between communities may be messy—like the dust and ashes in the vacuum cleaner and the dirt around the flowers—but it is also promising. In *MadArtReview*, what prevented community from forming was not the differences of the participants, but the restrictions that prevented them from coming to share, as do Jam and Roz, the shared experiences of individuals who may identify differently, and from finding ways both online and in person to gather as community. *Prozac Highway*'s conclusion opens the possibility of what Heather Love calls "sticky" associations across experiences and labels (185). The coming together of mad and queer people in *Prozac Highway* offers generative—if always contested—ways to queer and madden dominant discourses and identity politics. Paired together, *Prozac Highway* and *MadArtReview* question neoliberal identity politics as they are taken up in grassroots activism, psychiatry, research ethics, and state policy, and offer instead messier models of understanding and describing identity and community.

Acknowledgements I would like to extend thanks first and foremost to all who participated in *MadArtReview* and made this research possible. Thank you also to Drs. Dilia Narduzzi, Sarah Brophy, Geoffrey Reaume, Lorraine York and Brenda LeFrançois for their encouragement and helpful feedback on this piece.

Notes

1. For background on the history of the Canadian consumer/survivor/ex-patient/mad movement, see LeFrançois et al., *Mad Matters: A Critical Reader in Canadian Mad Studies* (2013); Morrison, *Talking Back to Psychiatry* (2005); Shimrat, *Call Me Crazy* (1997); Burstow and Weitz, *Shrink Resistant* (1988); and Chamberlin, *On Our Own* (1978).
2. For more information on the terms people use in the consumer/survivor/ex-inmate/mad movement and the naming of the movement itself, see Reaume "Lunatic to Patient to Person" and Burstow "A Rose by Any Other Name." I use "mad community" here as an umbrella term to describe c/s/x/m+ communities.
3. I did not seek out or track any characteristics besides country of residence from this group of 18 participants so I do not know whether this group represents the diversity of the mad community in terms of class, race, gender, sexuality, religion, age, etc. Ensuring diverse representation would be an important consideration in any future attempt at a mad reading community.
4. Acronym for the Lesbian, Gay, Bisexual, Transgender, Transsexual, 2-Spirit, Queer, Questioning, Intersex, Asexual community. The + indicates other identities that may not be represented by the acronym but are also part of the community.

Works Cited

Blackbridge, Persimmon. *Prozac Highway*. Press Gang Publishers, 1997.

Burstow, Bonnie. "A Rose by Any Other Name." *Mad Matters: A Critical Reader in Canadian Mad Studies*, edited by Brenda LeFrancois et al. Canadian Scholar's Press, 2013, pp. 19–91.

Burstow, Bonnie, and Don Weitz. *Shrink Resistant: The Struggle against Psychiatry in Canada*. New Star Books, 1988.

Chamberlin, Judi. *On Our Own: Patient Controlled Alternatives to the Mental Health System*. Hawthorn Books, 1978.

Eysenbach, Gunther, and James E. Hill. "Information in Practice: Ethical Issues in Qualitative Research on Internet Communities." *British Journal of Medicine*, vol. 234, 2001, pp. 1103–5.

Foucault, Michel. *The History of Madness*. Routledge, 2009.

Huffer, Lynn. *Mad for Foucault: Rethinking the Foundations of Queer Theory*. Columbia University Press, 2009.

LeFrançois, Brenda A., et al., eds. *Mad Matters: A Critical Reader in Canadian Mad Studies*. Canadian Scholar's Press, 2013, pp. 19–91.

Love, Heather. "Queers ___ This." *After Sex? On Writing Since Queer Theory*, edited by Janet Halley and Andrew Parker. Duke University Press, 2001, pp. 181–91.

McRuer, Robert. *Crip Theory: Cultural Signs of Queerness and Disability*. New York University Press, 2006.

Morrison, Lydia. *Talking Back to Psychiatry: The Psychiatric Consumer/Survivor/ Ex-patient Movement*. Routledge, 2005.

Nichols, Jeff. *Take Shelter*. Perf. Michael Shannon, Jessica Chastain, and Tova Stewart. Sony Pictures Home Entertainment, 2012.

Reaume, Geoffrey. "Lunatic to Patient to Person: Nomenclature in Psychiatric History and the Influence of Patients' Activism in North America." *International Journal of Law and Psychiatry*, vol. 25, 2002, pp. 405–26.

Scorsese, Martin. *Shutter Island*. Perf. Laeta Kalogridis, Mike Medavoy, and Arnold W. Messer. Paramount Home Entertainment, 2010.

Shimrat, Irit. *Call Me Crazy: Stories from the Mad Movement*. Press Gang Publishers, 1997.

Simsek, Zeki, and John F. Veiga. "A Primer on Internet Organizational Surveys." *Organizational Research Methods*, vol. 4, no. 3, 2001, pp. 218–35.

Weston, Kath. *Families We Choose: Lesbians, Gays, Kinship*. Columbia University Press, 1991.

Wolframe, PhebeAnn, and Participants. *MadArtReview: Research Blog for Psychiatric Consumers and Survivors to Review and Discuss Media*, private blog on wordpress.com. 25 Oct 2012.

CHAPTER 4

"Hundreds of People Like Me": A Search for a Mad Community in *The Bell Jar*

Rose Miyatsu

It is no secret that contemporary American culture places a high value on happiness. As Barbara Ehrenreich puts it in her book *Bright-Sided*, "being positive—in affect, in mood, in outlook—seems to be engrained in our national culture" (1). Having positive affect is almost mandatory, and the compulsion toward happiness has become a strong guiding force in community formation, especially with the growth of identity politics in the post-WWII era. Marginalized groups, such as racial and sexual minorities and most recently the disabled, have seen the march from shame into pride, from negative to positive affect, as a large and necessary stepping stone toward creating a communal identity. But what about those who cannot be happy, who refuse to orient themselves toward positive affect? What community is available to them? This is a question that a number of prominent queer and feminist theorists, including Heather Love, Ann Cvetkovich, Sara Ahmed, and others, have been grappling with over the past several decades. In *The Promise of Happiness*, for instance, Sara Ahmed describes the compulsion toward happiness as a kind of "world-making" that can justify oppression and

R. Miyatsu (✉)
Washington University in St. Louis, St. Louis, MO, USA

value certain ways of living over others by labeling them as paths that lead to happiness. Such world-making, she argues, forecloses other possible ways of being together and leaves behind those (like "feminist killjoys" and "unhappy queers") who cannot be enfolded into this happiness, leading her to conclude that "Ethics cannot be about moving beyond pain toward happiness or joy without imposing new forms of suffering on those who do not or cannot move in this way" (Ahmed 216). If relationships centered on happiness can cause such suffering, then how *do* we create a community that can incorporate painful histories, and that, most importantly, leaves no one behind?

One of the most productive places that I propose we begin to look for an answer to these questions is in a subgenre of literature that I will call "asylum novels," which became especially popular after WWII when a number of exposés on mental hospitals, and later a growing antipsychiatry movement, drew national attention to the treatment of mental illness. In asylum novels, ostracized characters are thrown into community with other isolated and stigmatized figures, often against their will. While this involuntary treatment of the mentally ill is of course hugely problematic from an ethical standpoint, the distress and isolation that the mentally ill characters experience as a result of their community's inability to incorporate their mental difference or suffering leads them to critically examine the (often hierarchical and patriarchal) "normal" ways of relating with friends, family, colleagues, and others who they feel have failed them. Visions of new forms of community that would refuse to leave even the most unresponsive, the most difficult, and the loneliest people behind comprise a large, if sometimes ignored, theme in a broad range of asylum-based texts from classics like Mary Jane Ward's *The Snake Pit*, Sylvia Plath's *The Bell Jar*, Joanne Greenberg's *I Never Promised You a Rose Garden*, and Ken Kesey's *One Flew Over the Cuckoo's Nest*, to recent works of young adult fiction like Suzanne Young's *The Program* and Ned Vizzini's *It's Kind of a Funny Story*. In this essay, I will look at how one of the most canonical of these asylum texts, Sylvia Plath's *The Bell Jar*, imagines what a community of people who identify as mentally ill might look like, and who gets left behind when "getting better" and being well is privileged over methods of being together that can incorporate psychic and emotional pain.

Criticism on *The Bell Jar*: Making Space for Communities of the Ill

To say that *The Bell Jar* is a book about identity and finding (or not finding) community is merely to state the obvious. Several critics have referred to the book as a female *bildungsroman*, and almost every piece of criticism on the novel makes some mention of the main character Esther Greenwood's continuous attempts to discover her identity and find her place in a community that, as critic Susan Coyle puts it, "seems hostile to everything she wants" (161). Almost all of this criticism, however, focuses on Esther's search for identity as either a woman or a writer, and chronicles her attempts to compare herself to various female models. Diane Bonds, for example, argues that the novel is about Esther negotiating her identity as a woman through systematically examining almost every female model she comes in contact with. In a more recent essay, Nicholas Donofrio writes about how Esther looks to her internship experience for models of her options as a woman. Other critics, such as Linda Wagner-Martin, Lynda Bundtzen, Luke Ferretter, Paula Bennett, Gayle Whittier, Miller Budick, Marjorie Perloff, Marilyn Boyer, and Maria Farland, just to name a few, have made similar statements about Esther's search for a female community, identity, sexuality, and language throughout the novel, and rightly so. It would be very difficult to argue that Esther's search for identity and community is not influenced by her gender in an era when, as Marjorie Perloff puts it, "female roles are no longer clearly defined" (515). What I believe these texts miss, however, is that while Esther is searching for and rejecting female role models, she is also, or perhaps even primarily, searching for identity and community as a person with an enduring mental illness.

Throughout the novel, Esther makes multiple attempts to imagine herself as a part of a community of people with mental or even physical ailments, yet critics have failed to acknowledge the efforts Esther makes to connect with others who share her mental distress as legitimate attempts at community building. It is rare for any critic to even mention characters like Valerie, the lobotomized patient Esther meets, or Miss Norris, her mute neighbor in the asylum, let alone the suicides Esther follows in the papers. Although no critic that I know of goes so far as to say so, it is clear from these omissions that most of them view these attachments to the mentally ill as mere symptoms of Esther's madness to be replaced with more "legitimate" identifications once she is "healed" or reintegrated back into the larger society. Even scholars who see the novel as a critique on the patriarchal institution of psychiatry, as Luke Ferretter and Maria Farland do, tend to ignore the relationships that Plath forms in the asylum, perhaps because they see madness as a temporary stop before a feminist awakening rather than a piece of her identity that she might build an identity or community around. Seeing the bonds Esther forms as a mere symptom of mental illness and not a legitimate attempt at community building denies the personhood of those who cannot "recover," people who end up getting left behind as Esther moves toward normalization and a place in the canon of feminist heroes. I want to explore the importance of a mad community to Esther, and how the novel might be looking toward a vision of community in which no one gets left behind.

"A Classical Neurotic": *The Bell Jar's* Definition of Mental Illness

In order to understand how Esther Greenwood is searching for an identity and community not just as a woman, but also as someone with an enduring mental illness,[1] it would be helpful to have a clear definition of what mental illness is. Unfortunately, this definition is not always clear even to Esther. Every character in the novel seems to have his or her own definition of mental illness, and for a majority of these characters, medical definitions of mental illness are suffused with popular stereotypes that have little medical or scientific basis. In the midst of all these varying definitions of what it means to be mentally ill, however, there is one factor that remains a constant in both Esther's definition and medical ones, and that is the experience of mental suffering or anguish. In defining "madness" for the recent compilation, *Keywords in Disability Studies*, Sander L. Gilman notes that although definitions of mental illness are always in flux, "psychic pain was and remains a litmus test for madness" (114). This experience of anguish also seems central in marking people whom Esther identifies as sharing her mental state, as we see most clearly in the way she responds to seeing Joan Gilling's scarred wrists when the two women are placed in the hospital together, saying, "For the first time, it occurred to me Joan and I might have something in common" (199). Joan's self-harming behavior illustrates to Esther that Joan is experiencing psychic pain similar to her own, and serves as a point of connection between the two. It is this definition of mental illness, as a designation of psychic pain, that Esther appears most invested in as she looks for community among fellow patients, case studies, and gossip papers, and it is therefore this definition that I will be focusing on for this paper.

In defining mental illness as a condition involving pain, I am purposefully deviating from popular feminist portrayals of female madness as rebellion, which literary scholar Elizabeth Donaldson has noted have become an "almost monolithic way of reading mental illness within feminist literary criticism" and which she rightly fears "may limit our inquiry into madness/mental illness" (101). As I plan to illustrate, it is the psychic pain Esther feels, rather than any romantic ideas of rebellion, that isolates her from regular forms of community in which the expression of negative feeling is often met with indifference, hostility, or denial. While this isolation furthers her distress, it also encourages her to envision different forms of community that might better incorporate pain. Recognizing the legitimacy of feeling bad as a way of connecting with others can open up new readings of *The Bell Jar* that see the novel not just as a *bildungsroman* about a young troubled girl, but rather as a text that is very much involved in the project of imagining different, more inclusive, forms of community.

FINDING A PLACE TO BE IN PAIN: COMMUNITY IN GOSSIP PAPERS

From the very first pages of the novel, it is already clear that Esther is in mental anguish, but the messages she receives from her community about the social consequences of showing pain or illness greatly deepen her distress. For example, when Esther is required to participate in a photoshoot and suddenly begins weeping, she looks up to find that everyone, including her boss, the photographer, and her friends, has abandoned her, leaving her feeling "limp and betrayed" (100). When Jay Cee finally comes back to the room where Esther has been crying "after a decent interval with an armful of manuscripts," the message she brings is clear: to be a part of this community you have to smile and be productive, and if you let your pain get in the way of your work, we will disappear. This command to get better and be productive appears elsewhere in the novel, most notably in Esther's visit to her father's grave, where she recounts,

> I had never cried for my father's death. My mother hadn't cried either. She had just smiled and said what a merciful thing it was for him he had died, because if he had lived he would have been crippled and an invalid for life, and he couldn't have stood that, he would rather have died than had that happen. (167)

This passage comes directly before Esther's most successful suicide attempt, and illustrates that in the eyes of Esther's mother at least, the only acceptable options in illness are to get better quickly and be productive, or to die. As Spandler and Anderson note in their recent volume on mental illness, "In an age dominated by recovery, it is not acceptable to have enduring mental health issues" (23). This attitude toward illness is evident in many scenes throughout the novel, including when Esther's mother praises her for "deciding" not to be like the "awful dead people" in Dr. Gordon's asylum (145–46), when her nosey neighbor insists that she get dressed and be productive, and when her friends fail to recognize her pain. Esther eventually internalizes this attitude toward illness herself, and prior to one of her suicide attempts she hears voices repeating over and over, "You'll never get anywhere like that" (146–47). Esther feels that she has to constantly be "getting somewhere," or she might as well be dead. In her productivity-focused community, there is simply no time or space for her to focus on her pain, let alone share it with another person. Feeling isolated, Esther turns to textual figures in books and newspapers to find examples of the "hundreds of people like [her]" whom she believes are too far hidden from her "in a big cage in the basement" of an asylum for her to gain communion with in person (160).

Unable to deny her pain and act the cheery part that everyone apparently expects of her, Esther begins to look for examples of other people who are in mental distress to discover a place where she can belong, but what she finds proves grim. In looking through "scandal sheets" for the stories of tragedies and suicides that are left out of the *Christian Science Monitor*, she comes across an article about a man who has been saved from jumping off a ledge. She studies his picture intently, saying, "I felt he had something important to tell me, and whatever it was might just be written on his face" (136). Esther's belief that the man in the newspaper has "something important to tell [her]" is particularly interesting considering that much earlier in the novel Esther decides that the successful women she knows *do not* have anything important to tell her (6). Unfortunately, however, whatever lessons the suicidal man has for her go unlearned, as the paper does not tell her why the man was on the ledge or what happened to him once he left it, disappointing Esther and offering her no help with her own pain. Later, after Esther has received a painful and ineffective dose of shock treatment, she comes across another scandalous headline that depicts a successful suicide. Esther identifies with the woman in this second article even more strongly than she had with the suicidal man, comparing the photo of the woman with her own and finding them to be virtually identical (146), seemingly confirming that the only viable option for someone with her mental condition is death.

Aside from these scandal sheets, Esther also searches through abnormal psychology books for representations of people like herself and identifies with "the most hopeless cases" (159). She quickly becomes disinterested in any literature that does not involve mental illness, stating "everything I had ever read about mad people stuck in my mind, while everything else flew out" (155), and she desperately searches these texts hoping to find people like her. Unfortunately, however, these works of literature, like the scandal sheets, also frequently conclude with the death of the mentally ill person, and consequently her momentary identifications with other people (however remote or fictional) who share her pathology only heighten her sense of distress and isolation. Unable to find a safe place and community among real people or textual ones, Esther makes one final attempt at imagining a place where she might find acceptance and a sense of belonging outside of the graveyard. Desperate to find a community that can accommodate her in her mental distress, Esther looks to institutions as a place where sharing pain with others might be possible.

Dangerous Places: Institutions as Last Hope for Community

Finding her friends, family, and coworkers unsympathetic to her psychic pain and the texts she reads to be of little solace, Esther looks for other places where she might at least be allowed to stay and be tolerated, if not accepted, when her pain becomes too much for her. She first contemplates entering a monastery, explaining that she believes living as a nun would allow her to "concentrate on [her] sin" (a sin that she has earlier identified as her desire to commit suicide) in a way that will "take up the whole of [her] life" (164). She feels that having a designated role to play in this regimented community would allow her to harness mental energy that might otherwise be occupied with attempting to act cheerful when she is not. She quickly dismisses this idea, however, because she is "pretty sure that Catholics wouldn't take in any crazy nuns" (165), and so she looks to other total institutions that have less stringent requirements of their members, like the Deer Island Prison she visits. Prisons, unlike nunneries, will take on anyone regardless of their mental state, a fact that appeals to Esther. As Esther illustrates in her visit to Deer Island Prison, desperation can make even these institutions look attractive as places of possible escape from the isolation of living with a mental illness in a community that only values health. When she arrives at the prison, she describes the buildings as looking "friendly" rather than frightening, and when she learns that sometimes "old bums" purposefully get themselves arrested in the winter so that they will have a warm place to stay with plenty of food to eat, she replies, "That's nice" (150), giving the reader a sense that she wishes that she had a similar place to escape to. It is worth noting that Esther mentally connects both the nunnery and prison to memories of her father, desperately searching for an alternative to the fatal consequences of his inability to "get better" without being completely isolated.

The last institution Esther looks to, and the only one she ever actually enters, is a mental institution, but this institution is so frightening to her that she initially chooses suicide over voluntarily committing herself. Although an asylum might seem a more natural place than a prison for Esther to turn to in her mental distress, when she imagines herself there, the dangers involved in attempting to find a safe place to be in pain become all too apparent. After thinking to herself that she should just "hand herself over to the doctors," she remembers "Doctor Gordon and his private shock machine" and realizes, "Once I was locked up they could use that on me all the time" (159). Esther is also concerned that staying in a psychiatric facility long enough for her to work through her mental illness will impoverish her family, a fear that later proves warranted. Esther reports that her mother has told her that, "I had used up almost all her money" (185) after she is involuntarily committed following an almost fatal suicide attempt.

Fortunately, Esther is "rescued" from the crowded state facility and potential bankruptcy by Philomena Guinea,[2] Esther's rich scholarship donor who pays for her to stay at a private hospital based on the McLean

Hospital where Plath herself once stayed, an incredibly prestigious facility that frequently housed rich and celebrity patients (Beam 1–3). Likely as a result of Esther's placement in such a distinguished private hospital, abuses are not as common in *The Bell Jar* as they are in other American asylum novels like *The Snake Pit*, *One Flew Over the Cuckoo's Nest*, and *Woman on the Edge of Time* that depict vindictive nurses, painful shock treatments, and mind-numbing lobotomies. While readers still get a sense that this type of mistreatment is prevalent in the state institutions that Mrs. Guinea has allowed Esther to avoid, Plath chooses not to dwell on these abuses and instead focuses on highlighting the possibilities for community that a place like an asylum could potentially illuminate, even while acknowledging that the structure of the asylum and the biases of some of its inhabitants can make the actual formation of this community difficult.

Connection Through Pain: Forming New Communities in the Asylum

An asylum's isolation from the outside world puts patients at a high risk for abuse because they are physically unable to escape any negative situations they might be placed in, but it also creates an environment that is ripe for questioning relationships that are normally taken for granted on the outside, and perhaps for imagining new modes of community as well. According to sociologist Erving Goffman, one of the characteristics of an asylum is that an inmate "comes into the establishment with a conception of himself made possible by certain stable social arrangements in his home world," arrangements that are then stripped from him through a "series of abasements" that initiate "some radical shifts in … beliefs that he has concerning himself and significant others" (Goffman 14). Although it goes without saying that there is much to criticize about the abasements that occur in the asylum, these changes in social status can provide a lens through which asylum patients might begin to better view and critique the hierarchical relationships that typically structure society. This is not to say that hierarchical relationships do not exist within the asylum, as the relationships between inmates and staff are obviously extremely hierarchical, but the basis of this hierarchy does not lie in the traditional factors like socioeconomic status, blood ties, educational achievements, or even shared interests that might form the basis of relationships on the outside. The poorest working-class nurse has a higher standing within the asylum than the richest and most educated society woman in her charge. Without traditional markers to determine their rung on the social ladder, inmates are left to find new ways of relating and building communities in which shared humanity and mental illness are often the only bonds holding people together.

When Esther first enters Caplan, a wing of the private hospital, she is still apprehensive that her mental state will prevent her from being able to have any form of relationship or community with the women there because they will see her as "stupid" and not worth associating with. She is immediately suspicious of Valerie, the first patient she meets there, because it looks to Esther like "there's nothing the matter with her" (188) and she is afraid she will reject her when she sees how "bad off" she is. It is clear that Esther is still viewing herself and others according to the hierarchy communicated to her by her mother, colleagues, and others, a hierarchy in which being mentally different is "bad" and something "normal" people should avoid. It is only when Esther sees Valerie's lobotomy scars that she is able to accept that she might actually want to be friends with her, but perhaps because of Esther's apprehension about Valerie's seeming "normality," the two are never as close as Esther eventually becomes with Miss Norris.

Miss Norris is exactly the sort of person many "better people" would like to leave behind for the sake of maintaining some form of hierarchy in which they can view themselves as being more "sane" and "normal." Even the kindly Valerie tells Esther that "Miss Norris shouldn't be in Caplan, but in a building for worse people called Wymark" (192), but Esther is not so willing to cast Miss Norris off. Miss Norris, as a mute and seemingly unresponsive patient, is perhaps the closest representation of what Esther believed she would become before she attempted suicide and entered the asylum, when she feared her body "would trap [her] in its stupid cage for fifty years without any sense at all" (159). The fact that Esther is mesmerized by Miss Norris and that they sit together in "sisterly silence" (191) might therefore reflect Esther's desire to have a community inclusive enough to accommodate her even in this state of unresponsiveness that she believes she is headed toward. Although Esther's status at the hospital seems to be higher than Miss Norris's based on Esther's accumulation of privileges, she still desires to form a "sisterhood" with her that is predicated on their shared mental illness. Esther watches over Miss Norris, refusing to take walks or play badminton to spend more time "simply to brood over the pale, speechless circlet of her lips" (193).

The relationship between Esther and Miss Norris in the novel is apparently not an uncommon one within mental institutions. In *Asylums*, Goffman describes a relationship in which "A patient, often himself considered by others to be quite sick, would take on the task of regularly helping a certain other patient who, by staff standards, was even sicker than his helper" (279). Goffman himself is rather baffled by this type of relationship because "to the occasional observer the relationship was one way" (280), but in *The Bell Jar* this silent communion with another person in psychological distress is presented as being almost more beneficial to Esther, the "helper," than it is to Miss Norris. Because Esther has not yet experienced a reaction to her insulin therapy, the fact that the staff believes she is improving can only be attributed to the time she is spending time with Miss Norris. Although the lack of traditional measures of friendly exchange has made the relationship between the two women easy to ignore for readers focused on Esther's movement toward a "cure," Esther's constant attendance to Miss Norris and her refusal to take advantage of her own privileges in order to avoid leaving Miss Norris alone illustrates that she believes that Miss Norris is someone who is "worth" spending time with and a good companion for Esther in her psychic pain. Their relationship ends suddenly when Miss Norris is sent to Wymark and Esther is moved to a better room, but in moving the two women up and down in the ward hierarchy structure on the same day, Plath forces her reader to at least acknowledge who must get left behind for Esther to "progress," and how a more inclusive community might be able to incorporate someone whose effect on Esther has been nothing but positive.

Before Esther has time to react to the loss of Miss Norris, she gains a new companion in Joan Gilling, a girl she knew in college, and the relationship the two girls build together is one that is clearly molded on shared pain. Just as Esther had read about suicides in the paper, Joan read about Esther's suicide attempt during a time when she was struggling to find the resources she needed to deal with her own mental anguish, and she immediately felt a connection to Esther's psychic distress and eventually attempted suicide herself. Esther is initially suspicious of Joan, but when she sees the "reddish weals upheaved across the white flesh of her wrists," she immediately recounts, "For the first time, it occurred to me Joan and I might have something in common" (199).

Joan's scarred wrists, as a proof of her mental pain, catapult her in Esther's eyes from someone Esther knew only at a "cool distance" (195) to her closest companion in the asylum, at least for a time.

Esther's companionship with Joan is perhaps one of the more complicated relationships in the novel, which I will argue illustrates the limits of community in a place that depicts wellness and positive affect (or at least the appearance of it) as the highest of goals. Although the women attempt to form a relationship that can be accommodating of pain and mental distress, the hierarchical asylum structure that they are both submitted to ultimately turns their relationship into one based on expectations for behavior and achievement that Esther has spent a majority of the novel avoiding. The communion that Esther originally feels with Joan over their shared pain begins to deteriorate once Joan moves on to Belsize, the wing of the hospital from which "people [go] back to work and back to school and back to their homes" or, in other words, leave the community of the mad (204). Once in Belsize, relationships become less about sharing in each other's pain and more about competing for privileges and claims to wellness. When Joan moves on to Belsize before Esther does, Esther complains, "Joan had shopping privileges, Joan had town privileges. I gathered all my news of Joan into a little bitter heap... Joan was the beaming double of my old best self, specifically designed to follow and torment me" (205). As a vision of her "old best self," Joan is no longer someone with whom Esther shares a sense of mental anguish, and when Esther herself moves on to Belsize against her will, any sense of community she felt in the asylum disappears as she realizes that the women there are uninterested in communing with someone who still shows signs of mental anguish. Joan treats her "…cooly, with a slight sneer, like a dim and inferior acquaintance" and Esther is sure that the other women are laughing at her and "saying how awful it was to have people like me at Belsize and that I should be at Wymark instead" (206). Since this is something that Valerie actually *did* say about Miss Norris, Esther's fears are perhaps a reflection of her continued sympathy toward someone she still feels to be a peer in this experience of mental anguish. She feels isolated at Belsize and once again pressured to "achieve" in order to prove that she "belongs" in this community of women, while with Miss Norris she was able to just be with another person without worrying about their expectations.

The system of rewards and privileges that the hospital has set up encourages both Esther and Joan to see each other as competitors in the quest for wellness rather than as fellow sufferers, motivating them to put their best faces forward and hide their mental distress. This creates exactly the kind of relationship based on an exchange of achievements for affection that Esther was working so hard to avoid outside of the asylum, and ultimately leads her to reject Joan as a companion. This rejection, in which she tells Joan "I don't like you. You make me puke" (220) is predicated in the text by a page-long digression in which Esther silently compares Joan to other "weird old women" like Jay Cee, Philomena Guinea, and the minor character of the Christian Scientist who tells her she can will herself to wellness, about whom Esther claims "they all wanted to adopt me in some way, and, for the price of their care and influence, have me resemble them" (220). Esther's relationship with Joan has turned into the same type of relationship she has with her mother, Buddy, and Jay Cee, in which her pain is overlooked by someone who would rather imagine her as being happy, and affection is predicated on certain expectations of behavior. This type of relationship is no longer viable for Esther, and shortly after Joan again proves her inability to share Esther's pain by poorly responding to a potentially life-threatening emergency (during which Esther feels she must hide the true cause of her bleeding in order to get Joan to help her), Plath brings the relationship to an abrupt end with Joan's sudden suicide in one of the book's most dramatic departures from autobiographical fact,[3] rejecting as she does so the curative narrative that Joan represents.

Conclusion

In her book *Feeling Backward: Loss and the Politics of Queer History*, Heather Love asks of people who seem to lack or refuse the agency generally required for creating a communal identity, "Is it possible that such backward figures might be capable of making social change? What exactly does a collective movement of isolates look like?" (147). This is the question I have been attempting to answer as I have traced Esther's relationships with women who have been involuntarily confined with her at the hospital, and at first glance the answer seems bleak. By the end of the novel, Joan is dead, Miss Norris has long since been locked away in Wymark, and Esther has said goodbye to Valerie with the hope that she will never see her again. With all of the relationships Esther has spent so much time cultivating now at an end, it becomes easy to see the novel as ultimately rejecting the possibility of a community of the mentally ill.

This, however, is an oversimplification of the ending of the novel. Esther never actually rejects Miss Norris, but is physically brought away from her by nurses at the asylum, and it is also the asylum structure that drives a wedge between Esther and Joan by submitting them to a system of privileges and punishments that turns their relationship into a competition over who can "beat [the other] through the gates" (225). While the asylum has made it possible for Esther to find people like herself and imagine a community that is inclusive enough to incorporate them all, its abuses and constant focus on rewarding the appearance of wellness is also what makes this community difficult to maintain. Having been deprived of her free will at this asylum and forced to compete for "freedoms" that would normally be afforded to her automatically, it is no wonder she is eager to leave, but that does not mean that Esther is willing to write off her mental illness, or the relationships she has formed through it.

When Esther's mother urges her to think of her mental illness as a bad dream, Esther responds by saying, "To the person in the bell jar, blank and stopped as a dead baby, the world itself is the bad dream. A bad dream. I remembered everything… Maybe forgetfulness, like a kind snow, would numb and cover them. But they were part of me. They were my landscape" (237). In this statement, Esther is refusing to let go of even the worst memories that have shaped her in exchange for a more cheerful relationship with her mother. Although both her mother and Buddy, representatives of "normal" hierarchical familial relationships, do show up at the end of the novel, it is important to keep in mind that Esther is not going home with either of them.[4] Esther is instead leaving the asylum to return to the dormitory and her peers at the college, whom she claims are in many ways similar to the women she has met in the asylum. She asks near the end of the novel, "What was there about us, in Belsize, so different from the girls playing bridge and studying in the college to which I would return? Those girls, too, sat under bell jars of a sort" (238). Esther's experiences building relationships in which people can openly share their mental distress have taught her to see even "mentally healthy" people as isolated from a fuller experience of community that might be possible in a society that was better equipped to allow them to lift their bell jars and share some of their pain/"sour air" with others.

Unfortunately, although Esther's experiences in the asylum have opened her mind to different visions of community, the structure of this asylum has made these relationships of shared pain and distress difficult to preserve. It is unclear when, if ever, she will be able to find a community that she can belong to again, especially given the fact that most people who share her mental distress are locked away or dead. Her lack of options for close relationships becomes even more clear at the end of the novel when she tells the reader, "Dr. Nolan had said, quite bluntly, that a lot of people would treat me gingerly, or even avoid me, like a leper with a warning bell" (237). The overall message about community for the mentally ill seems to be that it is difficult to find, and even more difficult to maintain, but that does not mean that Esther, or Plath, has given up on it.[5] If Esther's attempts to form a community come up short in this novel, she and Plath offer one last way of reaching out to others in pain through the text of *The Bell Jar* itself. After scouring books and newspaper clippings to find other mentally ill people she might be able to relate to, often to little avail, Esther offers her own story to others as a detailed exploration of what it means to be mentally ill. Unlike the figures in the scandal papers whose brief descriptions provide little information on, for example, "why Mr. Pollucci was on the ledge, or what Sgt. Kilmartin did to him when he finally got him through the window" (136), Esther attempts in her story to provide as many details as she can about the consequences, opportunities, and insights that can arise out of an experience of mental distress. Although she does not have all of the answers, her account brings mental illness out of the shadows and allows "readers to come closer to the problems and lessons of depression that Plath never learned" (Adamo 200).

Since the publication of *The Bell Jar*, the textual community of the mentally ill, housed in both memoirs and works of fiction, has expanded to offer even more insight into how we might create communities that can accommodate mental difference. No longer limited to the brief articles on suicide and "hopeless cases" that Esther found when she looked to texts for comfort, authors writing within the last several decades have been able to draw on a wide array of novels and memoirs that provide more promising options for mentally ill people, including *The Bell Jar* itself. Multiple authors have cited *The Bell Jar* as a forerunner to their own work and have even used the novel to better understand their own conditions. For example, the authors of the memoirs *The Noonday Demon* and *The Quiet Room* both compare their mental states to Esther's descriptions in *The Bell Jar* (Solomon 66; Schiller 17). The young adult novel *It's Kind of a Funny Story* and memoirs *Girl, Interrupted* and *Darkness Visible* also explicitly reference Plath as a person who wrote about and experienced a mental illness similar to the one their books describe, and *The Savage God*, a detailed account of suicide by Plath's friend Al Alvarez in which he also tells the story of his own suicide attempt, was inspired by Plath's writings and death. Even popular culture has picked up on the influence of Plath's novel in creating a mad community and identity. In her chapter, "*The Bell Jar* and other Prose," Janet Badia writes that *The Bell Jar* has developed a reputation for having a cult following among readers who are often depicted in popular culture as sharing in some sort of mental distress. The novel, as Badia notes, has appeared in the hands of depressed women in movies like *10 Things I Hate About You* and popular TV shows like *Gilmore Girls* and *Family Guy*. While these representations are often tongue and cheek, the fact that the mere presence of the novel in a film or show can provide such a clear symbol to the audience of a certain type of identity illustrates the novel's reach.

All this is not to say that community with and through mental illness is always easy to find. As almost anyone who has experienced mental distress can attest, many of the challenges Esther faced in creating community still persist for people whose mental states have been heavily pathologized. In the memoir *Willow Weep for Me*, for example, one woman's copy of *The Bell Jar* is confiscated when she is in a psychiatric ward because her doctor does not think it is a "suitable piece of literature 'for someone like [her]'" (Danquah 228), indicating an enduring belief that connections with others should be based in positive affect and healing rather than shared mental distress. This is perhaps why the textual community that Plath contributed to has become so important. Many contemporary authors see themselves as a part of this community and view literature as a way of reaching out to others like themselves. In the contemporary memoir, *Prozac Nation*, for instance, Elizabeth Wurtzel purposefully quotes from a wide range of literature on depression from Edith Wharton's *The House of Mirth* to Susannah Kaysen's *Girl, Interrupted* and calls *The Bell Jar* one of "the great classics of depression literature" (360). Wurtzel states that books like *The Bell Jar* were an inspiration to her in her goal of writing a memoir to "reach other people and touch a little bit of their loneliness" (359), a project that she sees *The Bell Jar* participating in. In another memoir about depression, *Where the Roots Reach for Water*, Jeffery Smith provides a nearly ten-page-long bibliography of books on depression and mental illness, including *The Bell Jar*, that aided him in writing his own memoir, claiming that "since my childhood, books have had everything to do with the turns my story has taken; perhaps never more so than in the months narrated in this memoir" (281). This statement illustrates that he sees his book as participating in a literary tradition that can influence the outcome of his and other peoples' stories or, in other words, that he can create a community of contact through writing. In drawing together a wide range of texts on suicide and mental illness, Smith and Wurtzel's memoirs create a sort of cannon of texts about mental illness, demonstrating that whatever obstacles Esther encountered in finding a community of mental illness, the literary community that Sylvia Plath joined and helped to shape when she wrote Esther's story is alive and well.

Notes

1. I have chosen to use the term "mental illness" from a range of terms, including mental disability, madness, and my personal favorite, psychosocial disability. Although I do not think that it is the best term, it is the most widely used term for psychic distress and therefore often the most convenient for communicating what I mean to people outside of disability studies field. For an in-depth analysis of the various terms used to describe mental illness, see Margaret Price's excellent analysis in the introduction to *Mad at School: Rhetorics of Mental Disability and Academic Life*.
2. The character of Philomena Guinea is based on Sylvia Plath's actual benefactress, Olive Higgins Prouty, who endowed the scholarship Plath received at Smith College and provided financial assistance after Plath was involuntarily committed for attempted suicide.
3. The woman on whom Joan is based, Jane Anderson, was very much alive at the time Plath wrote the novel. See Pat Macpherson, *Reflecting on The Bell Jar*, 80–83.
4. Esther has invited Buddy with the sole intention of "renouncing him" (218), and the reason Esther's release from the asylum has been delayed until the beginning of her school term is specifically so she can avoid staying with her mother (225).
5. Plath herself remained close to some of the people she met in the hospital, continuing to write letters to her therapist and Jane Anderson, the model for Joan in the novel.

Works Cited

Adamo, Melissa. "The Murkiness of *The Bell Jar*: Questions of Genre and Depression." *Critical Insights: Sylvia Plath*, edited by William K. Buckley. Salem Press, 2013, pp. 176–203.

Ahmed, Sara. *The Promise of Happiness*. Duke University Press, 2010.

Badia, Janet. "*The Bell Jar* and Other Prose." *The Cambridge Companion to Sylvia Plath*, edited by Jo Gill. Cambridge University Press, 2006.

Beam, Alex. *Gracefully Insane: The Rise and Fall of America's Premier Mental Hospital.* Public Affairs, 2001.

Bennett, Paula. *My Life, a Loaded Gun: Female Creativity and Feminist Poetics.* Beacon Press, 1986.

Bonds, Diane S. "The Separative Self in Sylvia Plath's *The Bell Jar*." *Women's Studies: An Interdisciplinary Journal*, vol. 18, no. 1, 1990, pp. 49–64.

Boyer, Marilyn. "The Disabled Female Body as a Metaphor for Language in Sylvia Plath's *The Bell Jar*." *Women's Studies*, vol. 33, no. 2, 2004, pp. 199–223.

Budick, E.M. "The Feminist Discourse of Sylvia Plath's *The Bell Jar*." *College English*, vol. 49, no. 8, 1987, pp. 872–85.

Bundtzen, Lynda K. *Plath's Incarnations: Woman and the Creative Process.* University of Michigan Press, 1983.

Coyle, Susan. "Images of Madness and Retrieval: An Exploration of Metaphor in *The Bell Jar*." *Studies in American Fiction*, vol. 12, no. 2, 1984, pp. 161–74.

Danquah, Meri. *Willow Weep for Me: A Black Woman's Journey Through Depression, A Memoir.* Norton, 1998.

Donaldson, Elizabeth J. "The Corpus of the Madwoman: Toward a Feminist Disability Studies Theory of Embodiment and Mental Illness." *NWSA Journal*, vol. 14, no. 3, 2002, pp. 99–119.

Donofrio, Nicholas. "Esther Greenwood's Internship: White-Collar Work and Literary Careerism in Sylvia Plath's *The Bell Jar*." *Contemporary Literature*, vol. 56, no. 2, 2015, pp. 216–54.

Ehrenreich, Barbara. *Bright-Sided: How the Relentless Promotion of Positive Thinking Has Undermined America.* Macmillan, 2009.

Farland, Maria. "Literary Feminisms." *The Cambridge History of the American Novel.* Cambridge University Press, 2011, pp. 925–40.

———. "Sylvia Plath's Anti-Psychiatry." *Minnesota Review: A Journal of Committed Writing*, no. 55–57, 2002, pp. 245–56.

Ferretter, Luke. *Sylvia Plath's Fiction: A Critical Study.* Edinburgh University Press, 2010.

Gilman, Sander L. "Madness." *Keywords for Disability Studies*, edited by Rachel Adams, Benjamin Reiss, and David Serlin. New York University Press, 2015, pp. 114–19.

Goffman, Erving. *Asylums: Essays on the Social Situation of Mental Patients and Other Inmates.* Anchor Books, 1961.

Love, Heather. *Feeling Backward: Loss and the Politics of Queer History.* Harvard University Press, 2007.

Macpherson, Pat. *Reflecting on The Bell Jar.* Routledge, 1991.

Perloff, Marjorie. "'A Ritual for Being Born Twice': Sylvia Plath's *The Bell Jar.*" *Contemporary Literature*, vol. 13, no. 4, 1972, pp. 507–22.

Plath, Sylvia. *The Bell Jar.* 1971. Reprint. Harper Perennial, 2006.

Price, Margaret. *Mad at School: Rhetorics of Mental Disability and Academic Life.* University of Michigan Press, 2011.

Schiller, Lori, and Amanda Bennett. *The Quiet Room: A Journey Out of the Torment of Madness.* Grand Central Publishing, 2008.

Smith, Jeffery. *Where the Roots Reach for Water: A Personal and Natural History of Melancholia.* North Point Press, 1999.

Solomon, Andrew. *The Noonday Demon: An Atlas of Depression.* Simon and Schuster, 2014.

Spandler, Helen, and Jill Anderson. "Unreasonable Adjustments? Applying Disability Politics to Madness and Distress." *Madness, Distress, and the Politics of Disablement*, edited by Helen Spandler, Jill Anderson, and Bob Sapey. Policy Press, 2015.

Wagner, Linda W. "Plath's *The Bell Jar* as Female *Bildungsroman.*" *Women's Studies*, vol. 12, no. 1, 1986, pp. 55–68.

Wagner-Martin, Linda. *Sylvia Plath: A Literary Life.* Palgrave Macmillan, 2003.

Whittier, Gayle. "The Divided Woman and Generic Doubleness in *The Bell Jar.*" *Women's Studies*, vol. 3, no. 2, 1976, pp. 127–46.

Wurtzel, Elizabeth. *Prozac Nation: Young and Depressed in America.* Riverhead Books, 1995.

CHAPTER 5

Writing Madness in Indigenous Literature: A Hesitation

Erin Soros

Note: The following essay contains descriptions of colonial violence and sexual abuse of a child. This material is described elliptically, not graphically. It is also written in discrete sections that can be read together or apart. I have not included subtitles, even though these would help anchor the reading, because I'm working precisely with disorientation, hesitation, and the unspoken or even unspeakable, which are perhaps best symbolized by the humble asterisk and its surrounding absence.

There is something helpless in being a witness.

I have committed this opening line to memory. It begins Stó:lō writer Lee Maracle's *Celia's Song*, or rather it begins the novel after the dedication, which is written to all those children who were "removed from our homes and who did not survive residential school." So we encounter a profoundly troubling form of witnessing: the acute helplessness at and through death. *Celia's Song* is dedicated to those who cannot read it—or at least those who can never read it in this current time that we think we share. But who is this "we" I have so casually posited?

E. Soros (✉)
Toronto, ON, Canada

The homes were those of Indigenous families. Indigenous children were the ones taken away, whose lives were lost. The telling here is both from and to a very specific collectivity. And yet settlers can read these words, even read them aloud, as if recalling oral history that is not our own. What happens then to reference, to meaning and its vulnerable, transitory presence, when I recite the opening words from this novel, my voice alone, or shared? What sense can I make? Or what occurs at the very edge of sense? For sometimes the way the opening line works in my memory seems almost akin to madness: with each recitation I emphasize a different syllable, as if the sentence were a length of beads I were caressing, pausing to tug gently on one singular bead, cool and smooth under forefinger and thumb, then the next bead, the next. *There* is something helpless in being a witness. There *is* something helpless in being a witness. There is *something. Helpless.* In *Being.* A *witness.*

There's the rub: already I have introduced a foreign element, for in my own tradition, a tradition I've left, the beads would form a rosary like the one I held the night before we buried my beloved maternal grandmother. And in recalling that specific sensuous memory linking me to my lost kin, I've left Maracle's story, have I not? I have betrayed it, in the sense of violating a trust and the sense of giving away a secret, for this rosary that comforted me represents part of the colonial apparatus inflicted on those very children within the residential school. How then can I hold this novel, let it work on my corporeal sense-making, with and against what my body knows?

I have promised to write an essay about madness in Indigenous literature. My writing will both honor this promise, and break it. This essay will be an act of literary witnessing, and a meditation on how my witnessing can only quite helplessly fail. When I spoke to Cherokee professor and writer Daniel Heath Justice at the conference of the Native American and Indigenous Studies Association, I raised a tentative concern about my including an essay on Indigenous writing in this anthology on literatures of madness. Justice was sitting in an information booth with a question mark above his head. I teased him about being NAISA's Yoda. His response was simple, and wise: before he even heard the various reasons for my hesitation, he told me to trust it. Immediately I considered pulling the essay, yet when I spoke to the editor Elizabeth Donaldson about my reluctance, she expressed such respect for my questions, and such commitment to the topic—to my work and to that of the Indigenous writers I wanted to address—that I felt apprehensive about letting her down.

I was torn between my wish to share the compelling insight found in the novels of a writer of such daring and skill as Lee Maracle and my sense that my knowledge of Stó:lō culture is inadequate to do so. I was torn between my excitement at the interdisciplinary attunement an essay on Indigenous writing would demand, and a sense of the inadequacy of my academic training. I was torn between my desire to promote Indigenous authors to an interdisciplinary and international audience, and my longing to speak directly with Indigenous readers, young and old, who may or may not be the intended audience of this publication. To situate the novel, I would need to outline Canadian colonial history.[1] To grasp the meaning of the visionary states the novel depicts, I would need to consult elders and other Indigenous knowledge-keepers. To respect the insight shared, I would need to depart from my own scholarly frameworks and gain at least some fledgling ability to listen to and speak with traditions that are yet unfamiliar. I needed more time. I needed a second Ph.D. No, I needed to leave university training itself behind. What I needed, I decided, was to immerse myself in oral history. I needed ten brains. My editor extended the deadline; she extended it again—and then a third try, each extension working mysteriously away at the form this work would take, until through these various steps forward in time I finally came to propose a work that would be not an analysis but what I will call a hesitation.

*

We clear our throats to signal an interruption in our thoughts, or the attempt, often uncomfortable, to signal the interruption of another's. This phlegmy non-word, uttered once or twice, has come to signify a sly gesture that we disagree, that we have insight that someone else lacks. On occasion we will catch our own words with an unexpected cough that is perhaps a bit louder than we could have intended, the force of our body temporarily usurping our language. I remember the coughs in church, sometimes used to hush boisterous children or hide their inappropriate remarks, sometimes erupting into the service unbidden, like a corporeal confession of sins that urges the cougher to slide along the pew, apologetic to rustling bodies, and up the aisle, out of the intimate shameful listening range of others.

Donna Haraway encourages us to "stay with the trouble," not to flee from or to hide our unease with the very catches in our thinking. Her work imagines what it means for humans to live with animals as companion species, so her conceptual trouble has that specific shape. Yet trouble occurs whenever we try to bridge disciplines, when we find ourselves caught at the cusp of our intellectual and cultural frameworks. Trouble arises when we aim to surpass the limits of our academic training, when we see this training as itself bound in colonial ideologies and practices and try instead—is it possible?—to begin learning from those speaking from what have been deemed alien traditions but are in fact knowledges most profoundly linked to the land on which we think. For many of us, trouble lurks even when we simply have what might be a new exciting idea, like a work of writing, and we flounder at how to express it, and yet the conception nudges itself forward, sometimes even gleefully, as if independently, through the very structure of the given.

To think the possible, to imagine the not-yet—is this not also a form of madness?

When I read Tuscarora writer Alicia Elliott's lyric essay "A Mind Spread Out on the Ground," I am with a troubled, and troubling, mind, one that is struggling with depression, but is also valiantly struggling with the definition of the word, and hence the definition of what precisely has to be faced. Elliott takes us through a *Mind Over Mood* Depression Inventory checklist, which "could double as an inventory for the effects of colonialism on our people":

> Sad or depressed mood? Check. Feelings of guilt? Check. Irritable mood? Considering how fast my dad's side of the family are to yell, check. Finding it harder than usual to do things? Well, Canada tried to eradicate our entire way of being, then forced us to take on their values and wondered why we couldn't cope. Definite check. Low self-esteem, self-critical thoughts, tiredness or loss of energy, difficulty making decisions, seeing the future as hopeless, recurrent thoughts of death, suicidal thoughts? Check, check, check. (53)

Her answers lead not to a medical interpretation of Indigenous suffering, but rather to a devastating critique of what her people have had to survive, what their minds and bodies continue to resist. She concludes her essay with a call for ceremony that acknowledges collective loss while it brings new awareness to the beauty of Indigenous people, languages and songs. Elliott is an author reaching for new conceptions of both mental unwellness and renewal—and yet this movement toward the new is also a movement toward the traditional, toward the Mohawk understandings held within the language. We learn not of a vanished past, but a possible future.

One compelling aspect of the essay is how it holds us first against the colonial trouble before we have any access to potential release. She describes the early times of North American settlement, when 'Indians,' as Indigenous people were then called, were assumed to be Satan-worshipers, the devil himself depicted as Native. What she is suggesting here is that the Native person was defined as somehow at the liminal edge of the human, the almost-not human. In this realm, I would argue, the Native is by extension also the almost-not sane. Elliott's historical recounting reminds me of the word "bushed," a term my father taught me, which he learned as a boy in a coastal British Columbian logging camp. "Bushed" refers to someone who has been in the woods too long, who has become crazy with and through the wilderness. My father did not use the term "going Native," but I felt the sense was there: someone white had become too close to the land. That way madness lies.

I could lead from this anecdote about my father's vocabulary into the anthropology of shamanism, the European fascination with visions and ceremony, simulacra and event, voices and prophecy, herbs and drums and sweat. Or I could present archival records of the discursive force involved in banning ceremonies such as the potlatch and in creating residential schools, these colonial techniques of violence that contributed to stripping Indigenous people of their land while coding their culture as somehow outside of culture.[2] Or I could describe contemporary settler media coverage of mental health crises within Indigenous communities: as Elliott cogently articulates in her essay, suicide and self-harm are the leading cause of death for Indigenous people under the age of forty-four. To address madness in Indigenous literature is to encounter these colonial troubles: the ways whiteness associates Indigeneity, and in fact through traumatic rupture has *produced* Indigeneity, as itself on the exterior cusp of reason. The first words of my essay, the title "Writing Madness," refer quite simply to the topic I am trying to address—the writing of madness in Indigenous literature—but the words capture as well the historical and contemporary proliferation of so much colonial writing that researches Indigeneity as pathology, as insanity, as outside all that is deemed reasonable, all that is white. This colonial framing is deeply symptomatic, can itself be diagnosed a form of madness—to be more specific, a writing madness.

My examples of this madness vary from colonial conceptions of "savagery" to psychoanalytic understandings of the "primitive" to our now ostensibly more progressive era in which settler attempts to critique suffering caused by colonialism can themselves reinforce Eurocentric ways of understanding. In a crucial letter to communities published in *Harvard Educational Review*, Unangax̂ professor Eve Tuck calls on scholars and advocates to stop creating "damage-centered" research on Indigenous and marginalized peoples. By "damage-centered," she means work that focuses specifically on suffering: the addictions, the physical and mental health crises, the intergenerational violence that can afflict groups who experience collective trauma and ongoing oppression. She fundamentally questions the benefit of this research and the belief that such detailing of suffering will bring about change. Instead of the static narration of damage, which helps create a fixed construction of a wounded self and community, Tuck builds on the formulation of Gilles Deleuze to suggest that researchers foreground "desire" based research. What agency exists within the community? What do the members hope to experience, to feel, to create? How are they moving and making and sharing even or especially through trauma—as interdependent, desiring subjects? When I read Tuck's work, I am inspired to return to Indigenous literature, for in this poetry and fiction and non-fiction exists testimony not just of intergenerational trauma and isolated suffering, but also of deep kinship, surprising humor, sexual and romantic desire, psychological insight, ceremonial healing, sustained and collective decolonial resistance. And the language itself is desiring, the writing a force of beauty and longing and sensuous intelligence as our fingers flip from page to page. "If you have something hard to say," Lee Maracle asserts, "Use beautiful words."[3]

When Alicia Elliott speaks of Mohawk understandings of depression, she uses two beautiful words. One is wake'nikonhrèn:ton: the mind is suspended. Another is wake'nikonhra'kwenhtará:'on: the mind is spread out on the ground. She initially stumbles on the latter, having heard that the approximate English translation is something akin to a mind fallen to the ground, and it's her sister who corrects her. Her sister is studying Mohawk and is teaching her daughters. She is the first to speak the language since it was beaten from their paternal grandfather in the residential school system. So these words that are new to Alicia Elliott and her sister also constitute a profound return—to a time that is arriving, and that is still yet to arrive, this possible future that the shared articulation of these words hold. Depression has made this narrator go deeper, into her past, and into her kinship, and through this kinship into her own potential. Here the Mohawk tongue is embodied language, given through love. Her sister's translation of the word is a corporeal one: Elliott captures how her sister clarifies the translation by stretching her arms out, as if to rest them on the ground, as if the body knew the meaning—the lowness, sprawledness, stretchedness—as if we can only understand it truly if we were to be in this intimacy with her Tuscarora sister, as if the page is sharing something tender and specific and true while simultaneously creating a vivid picture of what we cannot see.

*

If we are speaking with someone in a face-to-face encounter, those of us who communicate using aural mediums are accustomed to the ways the sensuous world interrupts our words, the consequent hesitations made necessary by the bark of a dog, call of a child, whistle of a pot, screech of car tires, siren of an ambulance, even the sound of cicadas or chickadees or squirrels: the mechanical and animal environment inform aural human dialogue in ways they sometimes seem not to shape our encounter with the page. If a written form indicates these momentary ruptures, it does so only by capturing their absence: we don't hear the interruption, but can only imagine it.[4] Likewise, when we are writing, lost in our own thoughts, we might not experience the subtle but helpful nudge of a foot under the table—hint that we should shift the path of our conversation—or even the gentle tap of a finger on a shoulder, to indicate that someone else would like to join our talk.

My thinking here—this extended hesitation to write on the work of Lee Maracle—is bracketed by conversations I had yesterday morning with Jeffrey Ansloos, a Cree professor and psychologist, and a conversation I had today with John G. Hampton, a curator and artist of Chickasaw and mixed-European ancestry. Ansloos spoke about Indigenous mental health, specifically in relation to youth suicidality, and Hampton spoke about an Indigenous art exhibit, "In Dialogue," that is currently showing at U of Toronto's Justina M. Barnicke Gallery. I can present some of their insights, but I can't capture the open quality of their faces or the care with which they communicated, for these were expressed in physical ways—I can describe these attributes, as I'm trying to do, but there is an indelible loss in this reporting, these black marks on a white page. Moreover, and perhaps more significantly, I am unable to capture how these men might have shielded themselves when speaking within a settler university setting—I was attuned to eye contact, for example, and to when and potentially why Ansloos looked away. But I couldn't grasp how these men would have spoken differently had they been talking to a Cree listener or one of Chickasaw heritage. I can tell you that at one point in the conversation with Ansloos, I echoed and extended the insights he shared: suicide can be a form of agency for youth living within colonialism, indeed a kind of resistance, even as it remains a tragedy for the family and community. Ansloos nodded, listening, hesitating immediately when I used the word "tragedy." He interrupted this contextualization, taking the time to correct my usage. The tragedy, he made clear, is colonialism.[5]

In the current Canadian context, much attention is paid to the loss of Indigenous life through suicide, but not to the deadening power of the settler state itself. Where does the real madness lie?

When Hampton spoke about the show he curated, I noted not just his historical expertise, and aesthetic enthusiasm, but also his own hesitations. At one point, he told me and my colleagues something he did not want repeated beyond the room. I put down my pen. We all nodded in agreement. I felt his trust in us as listeners, and the valuable momentary bond we shared, hearing what we alone were to witness. This article will include such gaps: gestures toward a past that I cannot report and toward a future I have not yet encountered. It is my intention to create a hypertext website that will situate and extend the thinking of this essay, so that those reading it will be able to link to some of the Indigenous texts I reference. I am embarking on this work so international readers can become more fluent in the texts of the writers noted here—consulting their words and not necessarily trusting my own—but I am building this hypertext also because it enables me to include collaborative oral forms: insight from elders, from youth, and from those who might not read these words, from those who would like their research shared in mediums that reach their own communities. It enables me also to continue creating this essay, with and through the insight of others, to invite critique and dialogue, and to encourage readers of this anthology to learn from these new initiatives—and so to imagine here on the page a future that none of us have yet been able to inhabit.

This hypertext will be a living library of sorts. It will contextualize the work of Lee Maracle and other Indigenous authors in ways an essay alone cannot. It will, I hope, record my continued learning from Indigenous elders and other knowledge keepers. The process of learning from elders involves moments of pedagogical doubt or even refusal—on their part, on my own.[6] Elders may feel reluctant to share sacred wisdom with someone outside their community. They may generously disclose insight—and then ask that the information not be communicated with others. They may wish to voice lessons in their own terms, through oral or written means or through collaborative forms. Finally, they may teach me with patient guidance, but meet a lapse in my ability to grasp what they mean. In other words, my disciplinary training may in fact preclude sincere understanding. Any consequent writing that emerges from these interviews will attend then not just to knowledge, but to its limit. It will join settler scholarship that highlights the ethical complexity involved in learning from and writing about cultures whose artworks and stories have been stolen. It will also make space for thinking new forms of pedagogical relationship. As an act of cultural translation, it will represent both the reception of an offering and offering itself.

So this essay as it stands is both an independent work, and a link to a potentially unending series of conversations. The hypertext will be a collaborative effort, while this current text is an individual, single author endeavor, with all the associated frustrations and pleasures. And even as I stumble in this writing, even or especially as I consider the ways that settler scholarship is always deeply problematic, I believe an accounting in detail of this particular trouble is also of value. Here I would turn to one of the images that Hampton noted this afternoon:

> Uneasy
> with
> the com
> fort of com
> plexity

These words, which Haida artist Raymond Boisjoly sketched with a beer can on the wall of an exhibit—crammed in the corner as if the artist had almost been crowded out of the scene—reveal how saying that something is "complex," or perhaps noting valiantly that one sees trouble, is not enough. Hampton suggested that the Indigenous artists in the show do more than nod at such complexity: they explore it deeply, sometimes painfully, in its devastating and enabling nuance. I pause here then to think about the very complexity of working in a written form on Indigenous understandings of madness, when enforced literacy was one element of colonialism, when children were abused physically and sexually as they were taught the English language and the written word.[7] Some survivors will still not have books within the home. This is the complexity, this legacy of brutal literacy, a writing madness situated within larger and terrifyingly intimate forms of colonial violence that compelled children against their will to abandon their parents and their stories. Imagine what they lost: smell of a mother's hair, sound of a father's voice, the interruption of a baby crying, yap of a wolf, touch of a grandmother. They gained the page, and eventually the vote, and as Lee Maracle recounts in *Celia's Song*, those in the village stopped listening and speaking with each other.

*

Alone in her kitchen, the title character of *Celia's Song* prepares to begin her Thursday night ritual of sorting the mail and paying the bills when she is interrupted by a vision. Or perhaps it would be more correct to suggest that her attending to the bills is the interruption: Celia immerses herself in what seems to be an imaginary world and is often reluctant to leave it. She is grieving the loss of her young son through suicide: she has always been a dreamer, someone who retreats from her community to tend her imaginary findings, but at this point in her mourning the effort to stay grounded in her everyday life is simply too painful. If her visions do not return her son, they at least offer comfort: animate memories of her ancestors. Yet at the beginning of the novel she witnesses a horrible storm on the sea, and the sight of a two-headed sea monster slipping free from its place on the front of the longhouse and into the tumbling ocean. The serpent had been guarding the house beneath which bones are buried, but as humans have stopped singing to honor these bones, the serpent has also betrayed its contract. This cessation of singing was not voluntary on the part of the Indigenous community, but the result of colonial rule that banned such forms of communication and ceremony. The two-headed serpent that Celia sees can be read in several ways: as a "delusion" that she alone can witness (and this word "delusion" is explicitly and repeatedly used to describe what Celia envisions); as a creature evidenced by scientific data (which is suggested in the second chapter, when settler scientists also detect and record this strange sight); as traditional knowledge (Maracle has spoken of learning the Stó:lō teachings of the two-headed serpent); as a manifestation of bipolar disorder (Maracle has suggested that the two heads can represent the two poles of depression and mania—and the prevalence of the disorder within Indigenous communities); and finally as the collective psychological legacy of colonialism.[8] What makes the two-headed serpent resonant as a figure is how the novel fundamentally refuses to simplify its status. Even as Celia is called "delusional" we are invited into her delusion: we too see the serpent, both its loving if complacent "loyal" head and its destructive if energetic "restless" head. We come to anticipate and dread the effects of "restless" on the human characters as he slips into their bodies and minds, causing irreparable harm: only spiritual and physical destruction will feed him.

Those cognizant of Sigmund Freud's theories of the death drive may nod in recognition at this description of the effects of "restless." Yet I hesitate to apply a psychoanalytic vocabulary to this text. As settler scholar David Gaertner argues in his reading of the Haisla and Heiltsuk novelist Eden Robinson's *Monkey Beach*, when analyzing an Indigenous story we might best attend to the psychological theories presented in the work itself—and in relation to a book's specific cultural paradigms—before we try to integrate critical models with colonial heritage: "To begin from the assumption that psychoanalysis always can be smoothly immigrated into an Indigenous text is an act of literature nullius, an erroneous belief that a given book is not populated with its own systems of knowledge and hermeneutics" (47). What *Celia's Song* presents through the two-headed serpent is precisely a system of knowledge and hermeneutics, yet this system exists at the cusp. The other people in the Stó:lō village cannot see the serpent, and they dismiss Celia's gift. Celia does not even bother to communicate what it is she has seen. When her nephew Jacob witnesses his ancestor in his own vision, he decries that he is "too goddamned sane for this" (177). Here sanity constitutes a rejection of what his ancestor's return could teach him. As Michi Saagiig Nishnaabe scholar, writer, and artist, Leanne Betasamosake Simpson articulates to the Indigenous readers of her collection of Nishnaabeg creation stories, "Through the lens of colonial thought and cognitive imperialism, we are often unable to *see* our Ancestors. We are unable to *see* their philosophies and their strategies of mobilization and the complexities of their plan for resurgence" (15–16). *Celia's Song* reveals that the emergence of such strategies and plans can come to the fore precisely through the teachings that appear in visions. The characters grow and contribute as they begin to trust what they see and so to organize their community based on this learning. The journey is not from madness to sanity, but rather from individual vision to collective transformation.

Celia's nephew Jacob plays the primary role of leading the village toward revitalization of tradition—and this revitalization involves attending to a sight he wishes he did not witness. One evening when he is walking on the edge of his village, he comes upon a scene of sexual violence enacted on a child. Or does he? As with Celia's visions, the status of what he sees is uncertain. The details are specific, visceral, yet Jacob himself takes responsibility for seeing this event as if the gruesome sight were evidence of his fantasy life and not the scene of a crime.[9] When he later comes to understand that this violation did in fact take place—that his cousin had been brutally raped—he struggles to determine if he saw a warning of this crime or the crime itself. In fact, here the novel again refuses to clarify the ontological status of a vision. Jacob himself does not understand quite what he saw: "What if he had seen it before it happened? What if he was not some madman, but had been shown something? What if he had seen it in the flesh, the drama unfolding as it happened, and he had done nothing?" (140). Only when Jacob retreats to the mountains on the advice of his uncle, where he listens to the teachings of the animals and the guidance of his ancestor, is he able to attend with respect to what he has learned. Emerging in his consciousness is not an assertion of the terrible vision's ontological status—its falseness or its truth—but rather the urgent awareness that he must take action in response. He doesn't prove to himself or others what the vision is, or even how to define the voices he hears on the mountain. Instead, he allows himself to be taught by what he does not quite understand, and he now knows what he must do.

Jacob walks back downhill to his community and he finds that his relatives have begun genuinely speaking to each other as they struggle to take care of the violated girl. Even Celia is engaged, participating and giving helpful instruction. Jacob has his own instruction to share: he urges his elders to help him rebuild the longhouse. This rebuilding represents not just a return to traditional protocol—and to collective forms of renewal and celebration and health—but also a call to justice. For into this sacred space, into a gathering of song and dance, steps the man who abused the child. He too is dancing, and is lost in his own visions, terrible scenes of the abuse he experienced in the residential school system that led him in turn to abuse others, and he keeps dancing, his visions of trauma giving way to the presence of his ancestors dancing with him as he dances his way into their redeeming arms and out of the living world. Ultimately, what Jacob has gained through his traumatic and confusing witnessing is not a static form of knowledge, but something animate, relational, generative: here with his response and its consequences we are not in the realm of true or false, sane or insane, but something else, something both more vulnerable and more forceful, a knowing that creates as opposed to defines, a doing that undoes.

*

"*You know what to do with the story now*" (269). This statement concludes *Celia's Song*: the entire work has been framed, and frequently interrupted, by the voice of Mink, shape shifter and witness. In fact, it is Mink who opens the novel with the words "There is something helpless in being a witness": it is Mink who inevitably sees what humans do to each other and who cannot directly intervene (1). In *Celia's Song*, Mink is the prime seer of reality, the keeper of knowledge, indeed the teller of the tale. The story is both Mink's testimony and offering. Now this wise creature says the story is finished—and yet we are also at a beginning. "*This is all I am committed to tell*," Mink asserts, departing the characters and leaving us to make of the story what we will (269). Our collective interpretation will become an elemental part of its meaning, and so the referential status of the story quivers like the branches of a tree as Mink slips past.

Yet "interpretation" seems too static a word. As Mink insists, we must consider what we might *do* with this story, and not just what the story makes us think. The act of making meaning with Indigenous stories is precisely that: a making. The story is not independent of the unfolding of a life, but coexists with it, ultimately shaping its outcome. In the hands of a Stó:lō youth or adult, I imagine Lee Maracle's narrative of the two-headed serpent will possess a transformative energy. The traditional tale will signify not through interpretation alone, but through what forms of political action and cultural renewal and restorative justice become possible through its sharing. Alicia Elliott turns to Mohawk words in order not just to transform her own understanding of depression but also to envision collective recommitment to her community's language and ceremony: "Things that were stolen once can be stolen back" (54). The Michif[10] and Nishnaabe writer Kai Minosh Pyle juxtaposes traditional stories with her contemporary narrative of mental suffering and she brings Anishinaabemowin words for "craziness" together with the clinical diagnoses that she has herself encountered. She does not romanticize her isolation and pain—her sense of dislocation from others—but nor does she surrender her meaning to a settler medical model. What emerge are new questions and possibilities:

> If we revitalize our language, how will we talk about mental illness? How do we want to treat people with mental illness within our culture? There are things we bring with us from the past, things we come from in the

present, and things we imagine for the future. We are creating the next world, one thought, one action, one movement at a time. (22)

When Pyle reads a sacred story of a woman who is unable to recover from the loss of her husband, Pyle discovers not a practice of diagnosis and treatment of a sick individual, but rather a lesson in how a community learns to wait for the insight that can emerge from prolonged grief. In Pyle's story-within-a-story, the tree that shelters the widow as she mourns eventually gives her the knowledge to peel off its skin and use it to create baskets. The widow brings this knowledge back to her community, just as Jacob returns with the awareness that his village must rebuild the longhouse. Pyle attends respectfully to this tale's lineage: she doesn't just give the citation—*Centering Anishinaabeg Studies* (Doerfler et al.)—but also records the particularities of oral transmission. It was told by Anishinaabe elder Ignatia Broker to Kathleen Dolores Westcott, who then recorded it in an essay co-authored with Eva Marie Garroutte. The telling of the story is also a telling of relationships. And the act of healing involves not diagnostic and reductive treatment, but rather an attention to the lessons in liminality itself. The widow learns at the very border of the human. The tree speaks. The tree teaches the widow how to return to her community with something she can offer not despite but because of what she has emotionally endured. As with Maracle's novel, the experience of "hearing voices" is not symptom but is itself part of the healing. And the path back from isolation involves less the work of conceptual understanding than the art of creating, and recreating, with others. In turn, what occurs through Pyle's own retelling of traditional tales is less an analytical refutation of clinical terms than an artistic reshaping of their power, as if Pyle were holding a kaleidoscope and rotating it so that a new image is formed by the shards.

As I retell these stories, traditional and contemporary, sacred and literary, I'm aware of my own responsibility in reforming them. On the same page that Maracle closes her novel with Mink's apparent trust in her readers, she also presents a warning. Judy, the white woman who lives with her Stó:lō partner in the village, gets something wrong. She refers to Raven as a "he." "Raven is a she," Rena corrects her—stifling a laugh—and Judy asserts with some self-irony that "I am never going to get it right" (269). The novel ends by establishing this limit to understanding. Throughout the text, we witness those who are not of the community struggling to comprehend its ways. Another non-Indigenous character, a white doctor romantically involved with one of the women in the village, has vowed that he will leave "white town" and come live with her, to embrace her village's emergent practices of being and knowing and healing, even at a risk to his career. When the community members decide to treat the violated girl without bringing her to the hospital—the threat that she will be taken away hovering over their care—the doctor chooses to aid their efforts. He uses his clinical knowledge, yet follows their lead, and comes to learn of their traditional techniques. He does not presume to understand, only to join with others, simultaneously using his medical training and betraying it. I find in these non-Indigenous characters—their commitments and their stumbles—a challenging model for reading Maracle from a non-Indigenous perspective. Such reading involves stepping away from the professional confidence that comes with one's academic training within settler traditions—leaving "white town"—while also retaining awareness of one's status as an outsider. It involves attending to one's own errors and cultivating the ability to correct them. And it involves developing relationships—through and beyond the page. For a settler scholar to grapple with this novel and its portrayal of visionary states involves not simply analyzing individual scenes and situating these scenes in dialogue with the work of other Indigenous writers and artists and storytellers, but also continuing to contextualize these pages within the work of activists and community leaders who are recreating Indigenous spaces, languages, and traditions. Such learning and accountability constitute not a singular act of criticism but an ongoing commitment to the kinds of collective transformation that *Celia's Song* begins to envision. The covers of this novel can be closed, but its teachings are still finding their shape.

*

Acknowledgements Thank you to the challenging, generous brilliance of all my teachers—a role expansively defined. Your thinking animates my own.

Notes

1. For an overview of Canadian colonialism and Indigenous sovereignty, see *Indigenous Writes: A Guide to First Nations, Métis and Inuit Issues in Canada*, by Métis legal scholar Chelsea Vowel. This book is accessible to a generalist audience and provides a helpful reference list for each theme addressed.
2. For an extended analysis of the banning of the potlatch, and the contradictions within colonial "reason," see *The Potlatch Papers*, by settler scholar Christopher Bracken.

3. Lee Maracle has said this sentence or similar statements in several contexts, most recently at the Indigenous Literature Studies Association, noted below, and on her twitter account. I am using here the wording I transcribed while listening to public dialogue at ILSA.
4. My thinking about the potential losses arising with the written word, and the terrible violence associated with the colonial teachings of English, developed over seven years working as a literacy coordinator in collaboration with Indigenous leaders at such programs as Vancouver's Urban Native Youth Association and the Vancouver Aboriginal Friendship Centre Society. This thinking has been extended and enriched through conversations with Métis writer and scholar Warren Cariou and through his own writing such as his "Who is the Text in This Class? Story, Archive and Pedagogy in Indigenous Contexts."
5. For an extended analysis of how Indigenous youth resist colonialism's effects, see Jeffery Ansloos, *The Medicine of Peace: Indigenous Youth Decolonizing Healing and Resisting Violence.*
6. For an extended analysis of refusal as decolonial resistance, see *Mohawk Interruptus: Political Life Across the Borders of Settler States* by Kahnawake Mohawk anthropologist Audra Simpson.
7. Note that alphabetical forms of recording are but one form of literacy. Diverse Indigenous practices of inscribing existed before colonial contact, challenging a fixed binary between oral and written storytelling. See *Why Indigenous Literatures Matter* by Cherokee writer and scholar Daniel Heath Justice.
8. My understandings of *Celia's Song* have been enriched by private and public conversations with Lee Maracle, noted below, in which many themes recur and overlap.
9. This reflection on sexual abuse invokes for me the lessons I learned listening to survivors as a rape crisis counsellor in the Vancouver's Downtown Eastside. The ethical requirement to honor and protect their stories creates another essential gap in this text. I cannot cite names or give quotations or describe what I have vicariously witnessed, but I want to recognize here that my theorizing is intrinsically linked to the spoken insight of women in crisis.
10. I have used the words Indigenous writers use themselves to describe their identities and nations. Note that Michif is Métis in the Métis language Michif. Thank you to Kai Minosh Pyle for her timely lessons.

Works Cited

Ansloos, Jeffrey. "Manitou: Indigenous Health, Healing and Futurity." Presentation, Ontario Institute for Studies in Education, 2017.

Ansloos, Jeffrey. *The Medicine of Peace: Indigenous Youth Decolonizing Healing and Resisting Violence.* Fernwood, 2017.

Boisjoly, Raymond. "In Dialogue." Justina M. Barnicke Gallery, University of Toronto, 2017.
Bracken, Chris. *The Potlatch Papers*. University of Chicago Press, 1997.
Cariou, Warren. "Who Is the Text in this Class? Story, Archive, and Pedagogy in Indigenous Contexts." *Learn, Teach, Challenge: Approaching Indigenous Literatures*, edited by Deanna Reder and Linda M. Morra, Wilfrid Laurier University Press, 2016.
Doerfler, Jill, Niigaanwewidam James Sinclair, and Heidi Kiiwetinepinesiik Stark, eds. *Centering Anishinaabeg Studies: Understanding the World Through Stories*. Michigan State University Press, 2013.
Elliott, Alicia. "A Mind Spread Out on the Ground." *Malahat Review*, vol. 197, Winter 2017, pp. 47–54.
Gaertner, David. "'Something in Between': *Monkey Beach* and the Haisla Return of the Return of the Repressed." *Canadian Literature*, vol. 225, Summer 2015, pp. 47–63.
Hampton, John. Curator talk. "In Dialogue." Justina M. Barnicke Gallery, University of Toronto, 2017.
Haraway, Donna. *Staying with the Trouble: Making Kin in the Chthulucene*. Duke University Press, 2016.
Justice, Daniel Heath. *Why Indigenous Literatures Matter*. Waterloo: Wilfred Laurier P, 2018.
Maracle, Lee. *Celia's Song*. Cormorant Books, 2014.
———. Presentation to research group, "Decolonial Disruptions: Indigenous Literatures of Turtle Island." Centre for Indigenous Studies, University of Toronto, 2017.
———. Private conversation after Katherena Vermette's reading of *The Break*. Indigenous Education Week, Centre for Indigenous Studies, University of Toronto, 2017.
———. Public discussion. *Indigenous Literary Studies Association conference, Ethics of Belonging: Protocols, Pedagogies, Land and Stories*. Stó:lō Nation, Chilliwack, 2017.
Pyle, Kai Minosh. "Autobiography of an Iceheart." *Prism International*, vol. 56, no. 2, Winter 2018, pp. 11–22.
Simpson, Audra. *Mohawk Interruptus: Political Life Across the Borders of Settler States*. Durham: Duke UP, 2014.
Simpson, Leanne. *Dancing on Our Turtle's Back: Stories of Nishnaabeg Re-creation, Resurgence and a New Emergence*. Arbeiter Ring Publishing, 2011.
Tuck, Eve. "Suspending Damage: A Letter to Communities." *Harvard Educational Review*, vol. 79, no. 3, Fall 2009, pp. 409–27.
Vowel, Chelsea. *Indigenous Writes: A Guide to First Nations, Métis and Inuit Issues in Canada*. Highwater Press, 2016.

PART II

Mad History

CHAPTER 6

"Is the Young Lady Mad?": Psychiatric Disability in Louisa May Alcott's Fiction

Karyn Valerius

Generations of readers have imagined Louisa May Alcott as Jo March, the boyish teenager she immortalized in *Little Women* (1868). Despite many similarities including Jo's literary ambition and love of the theater, an irreverent sense of humor, and a "quick temper, sharp tongue and restless spirit," Alcott's life was necessarily more complex than the juvenile novel she modelled after her family (*Little Women* 39). As readers of her journals and letters know, Alcott wrestled with despondent moods throughout her life. This struggle, together with her family's poverty, shaped her sense of self and her vocation as a writer and informed the fiction she wrote for adults. While feminist studies of Alcott's life and work abound, relatively little attention has been paid to how she wrote about mental health.[1] In this chapter, I explore how a disability studies analysis that prioritizes representations of mental health and illness might complicate and enhance established feminist readings of her fiction.

Psychiatric disability is a recurring feature of Alcott's self-consciously literary efforts as well as the many commercially motivated thrillers she published anonymously or under a pseudonym.[2] This discussion focuses on three texts that invite readerly identification with female characters

K. Valerius (✉)
Hofstra University, New York, NY, USA

variously described as mad, moody, melancholy, or insane: an anonymous sensation story titled "A Whisper in the Dark" (1863), Alcott's first published novel *Moods* (1865), and the autobiographical novel *Work* (1873). Read together, these texts map the intricate intersections of psychiatric disability and gender inequality in the lives of nineteenth-century women. While "Whisper" works at untangling the knot of mutually denigrating associations between madness and femininity, *Moods* and *Work* develop alternative narratives to represent women's experiences with disordered moods and suicidal despair.

"Slowly Coming Out of the Slough of Despond"

Alcott's sympathetic literary depictions of psychiatric disability grew from her lived experience navigating the "Slough of Despond," as she called the potent mixture of negative moods and emotions resulting from the interaction between her gloomy disposition and life's difficult circumstances (*Journals* 69).[3] In her journals, which begin in 1843 when she was ten years old and continue with some interruptions until her death in 1888, Alcott sketches a portrait of herself as an intrinsically moody person laboring to achieve equanimity.[4] Writing on her thirty-third birthday in 1865, she muses, "It was a wild, windy day very like me in its fitful changes of sunshine and shade" (*Journals* 145). During the lean years before the commercial success of *Little Women*, Alcott mentions poverty, waged labor at jobs she disliked, and the constraints of nineteenth-century womanhood as sources of discontent intensified by her despondent moods. For instance, in an entry written when she was seventeen, Alcott characterizes herself as a "wilful [sic], moody girl" and describes managing her unruly temperament as a demoralizing task:

> My quick tongue is always getting me into trouble, and my moodiness makes it hard to be cheerful when I think how poor we are, how much worry it is to live, and how many things I long to do I never can... So every day is a battle, and I'm so tired I don't want to live, only it's cowardly to die until you have done something. (*Journals* 61–62)

In this passage and others like it scattered throughout her journals, Alcott faults her moods even as she links emotional distress to economic insecurity and frustrated ambition. She identifies her temperament as a significant difference and a disadvantage that put her at odds with the world and raised obstacles on the route to becoming "a truly good and useful woman" (*Journals* 61).

Alcott faltered in her battle with herself and the world in the autumn of 1858. She experienced a crisis set in motion by the death of her sister Elizabeth in March followed by the engagement of her sister Anna in April. She responded to both events as losses (*Journals* 89). Perhaps the alternatives represented by each sister—death or marriage—made it difficult to imagine an acceptable future for herself. That June an opportunity to act in a theater in Boston briefly excited Alcott's "hopes for a new life, the old one being so changed now" (*Journals* 90). This intriguing possibility of a career on the stage fell through, and she returned to Concord and housekeeping for her parents. In need of money and a sense of purpose, Alcott went to Boston again in October to find work and failed (Matteson 240). Loneliness, grief, pressing economic need, and the world's indifference overwhelmed her, and Alcott considered suicide. As she admitted in a letter to her family, she went to the Mill Dam to drown herself but resisted that impulse (*Selected Letters* 34).[5] Instead, she renewed her determination to "take Fate by the throat and shake a living out of her" (*Journal* 90).

The next month, Alcott reflected on her "fit of despair" (as she called it) as a signal moment in her maturation as a person and a writer (*Journal* 92):

> The past year has brought us the first death and betrothal,—two events that change my life. I can see that these experiences have taken a deep hold, and changed or developed me. Lizzie helps me spiritually, and a little success makes me more self reliant. Now that Mother is too tired to be wearied with my moods, I have to manage them alone, and am learning that work of head and hand is my salvation when disappointment or weariness burden and darken my soul. (*Journal* 91)

In this passage, Alcott distills the central conflicts of her life and examines them in relation to one another. She recognizes the transforming effects of grief and expresses a new appreciation for the restorative power of work as a remedy for despair, an insight she would revisit as the premise of her novel *Work*. The self-knowledge that followed from her suicidal crisis confirmed for Alcott her vocation. The role of professional writer not only solved the material problem of how to support herself and her family, it also addressed the existential problem of imagining an alternative to marriage as the route to a mature adult identity. Embracing her painful crisis at the Mill Dam as a catalyst for her fiction, Alcott observed optimistically, "I feel as if I could write better now—more truly of things I have felt and therefore *know*. I hope I shall yet do my great book, for that seems to be my work, and I am growing up to it" (*Journal* 92, emphasis in original).

ICONIC MADWOMEN: "A WHISPER IN THE DARK"

"A Whisper in the Dark" foregrounds the relationship between gender inequality and the denigration of mental illness by putting several nineteenth-century narratives of women and madness into conversation. A lively homage to *Jane Eyre* (1847), one of Alcott's favorite novels, "Whisper" answers Charlotte Brontë's dehumanizing treatment of Bertha Mason, "the madwoman in the attic," with sympathetic counterexamples (Gilbert and Gubar xi).[6] Sybil, the feisty seventeen-year-old orphan who narrates "Whisper," recounts her harrowing experience of wrongful confinement to an asylum and the subsequent deterioration of her mental health. Alcott complicates this conventional Gothic narrative by incorporating a second madwoman, an unnamed patient who Sybil eventually learns is her mother. This woman exemplifies the Romantic (and romanticizing) narrative in which a woman "goes mad" with grief after the death of a loved one (Gamwell and Tomes 109–111; Showalter 11–14). The interaction between these figures and their implied contrast to Brontë's "fearful and ghastly" madwoman dramatizes the co-construction of gender and mental illness within nineteenth-century understandings of female madness (Brontë 242).

"Whisper" delivers a stark analysis of gender inequality in the tradition of Mary Wollstonecraft's *Maria: or, The Wrongs of Woman* (1798), as Elizabeth Keyser has argued (Keyser 4). At the opening of the story, Sybil has left her governess for the custody of her uncle, who is her legal guardian. She initially looks forward to this change and to romance since, she explains, "Madame guarded me like a dragon and I lived the life of a nun" ("Whisper" 39). As the story progresses, Sybil moves from one form of confinement to another. She resists her uncle's plan to control her inheritance by refusing to marry his "winsome" son Guy, only to find herself incarcerated ("Whisper" 37). During a heated confrontation with her uncle about the arranged marriage, Sybil loses her temper. The family physician Dr. Karnac witnesses her outburst, prompting him to ask, "Is the young lady mad?" ("Whisper" 46). In response to this suggestive question, the two men collude, and with the cooperation of the household staff, they lock Sybil in her room, drug her, and remove her to an asylum, where she becomes "a melancholy wreck" of her "former self" ("Whisper" 53). As Sybil's mental health declines, she becomes fascinated with the movements of the patient on the floor above her. This woman, later revealed to be Sybil's mother, covertly communicates with Sybil, urging her to escape. In the end, Sybil does escape only to reunite with Guy, willingly entering the marriage she had originally resisted. This marriage achieves a conventional happy ending, but Sybil's compliance also underscores her lack of freedom, as Keyser proposes (Keyser 9). The apparent inevitability of marriage, the abuse of medical and legal authority by the very men entrusted with her care, Sybil's mistreatment at the asylum, and the reality that she has nowhere to go when she runs away all speak to the forces arrayed against her.

The relationship between the framing narrative of Sybil's wrongful confinement and the embedded story of her "melancholy mad" mother demonstrates the circular logic by which the gendering of madness as a "female malady" disempowers women ("Whisper" 57; Showalter 3). The nineteenth-century association of madness with women followed from the binary construction of gender as it dovetailed with the longstanding definition of reason in opposition to both madness and emotion. The familiar identification of men with reason and women with emotion aligned women also with madness, informing the pervasive belief that women's presumed innate emotional tendencies made them more vulnerable than men to mental illness (Gamwell and Tomes 109; Radden 48). Sybil's mother epitomizes the definition of woman as the irrational sex. She is an iteration of the grief-stricken madwoman who at once pathologizes and elicits admiration for feminine devotion. Her story also confounds emotion and mental illness. According to Sybil, "My mother had been melancholy mad since the unhappy rumors of my father's death" ("Whisper" 57). The causal relation between grief and melancholia (or depression) posited here reflects the similarity between them as forms of sadness as well as the range of subjective states historically designated by the term *melancholy*, which span from "ordinary sadness" to moods and dispositions to mental disorder (Radden 14).[7] Although sympathetic, the romanticizing narrative of female madness represented by Sybil's mother reinforces gender inequality. It also aids and abets the plot against Sybil, despite her mother's well-intentioned efforts to encourage Sybil's escape.

The sexist double standard at the core of nineteenth-century understandings of female madness traps Sybil, as a comparison of Sybil and Guy reveals. Sybil describes herself as a "frank, fearless creature, quick to feel, speak, and act" and as someone "ruled" by "capricious moods," and her "hot temper" surfaces at several crucial moments ("Whisper" 33, 42, 45). Likewise, Guy is "impetuous and frank" ("Whisper" 35). He is affected by moods, as Sybil observes his transformation in a conversation with her: "Bitter was his voice, moody his mien, and all the sunshine gone at once" ("Whisper" 38). His father calls him a "hothead," and Guy warns Sybil not to tease him because, he says, "I'd rather you didn't see me in a rage" ("Whisper" 38, 42). Both young people erupt in anger, but after his "stormy scene" Guy disappears into the rainy night without consequences, while Sybil's "fit of anger" precipitates her confinement ("Whisper" 45, 47).

The flexible definition of madness as a form of irrationality and the imprecision of language also work to Sybil's disadvantage. When Karnac asks "Is the young lady mad?" both meanings of the word "mad" resonate ("Whisper" 46). Sybil *is* angry, and she concedes that her volatile behavior might have resembled madness:

> I have no doubt I looked like one demented, for I was desperately angry, pale and trembling with excitement, and as they fronted me with a curious expression of alarm on their faces, a sudden sense of the absurdity of the spectacle came over me; I laughed hysterically a moment, then broke into a passion of regretful tears, remembering that Guy was gone. ("Whisper" 46)

While Karnac manipulates the confusion of intense emotion and pathology for his own ends, Sybil insists on the authority of her felt experience, appearances notwithstanding. Responding to the condescension of the household staff who have witnessed her "fit of anger," Sybil wonders "Did they never see anyone angry before?" ("Whisper" 47, 48). Sybil's question challenges Karnac's interpretation of her behavior and emotional state, distinguishing between righteous anger and madness. Later, when Sybil disputes the explanation given her for her institutionalization, she demands: "How can I be ill and not know or feel it?" Her caregiver Hannah responds: "You look it, and that's enough for them as is wise in such matters" ("Whisper" 50). Karnac and her uncle discredit Sybil by exploiting the mutually reinforcing exchange that genders madness and pathologizes feminine emotion. They suggest Sybil is mad and then subject her to mistreatment that undermines her mental health, confirming their "diagnosis." Their use of the asylum to punish and control Sybil both presumes and enforces the gendering of madness evident in Sybil's mother's story.

At the same time that "Whisper" illustrates the relationship between female madness and the oppression of women, it responds to the derogatory representation of psychiatric disability in Brontë's *Jane Eyre*. As "mental illness incarnate," Bertha Mason is a frightening spectacle (Donaldson 26). Demeaning descriptions of Bertha's physical appearance combine with her imputed moral depravity and her violent and destructive behavior to vilify her. Described as being nearly Rochester's equal in size and strength and compared to a vampire and a beast, Bertha is characterized as unwomanly, unnatural, and inhuman (Brontë 242, 250). The narrative denies her a voice and positions her not as a betrayed wife but as an obstacle to Jane and Rochester's marriage.[8]

The story's multiple allusions to *Jane Eyre* establish an explicit relationship between the two texts, but Alcott's story parts ways with Brontë's frightening depiction of Bertha Mason, offering instead sympathetic portrayals of Sybil and her mother.[9] Sybil's first person narration encourages readers to identify with her. Unlike Bertha, Sybil is feminine and attractive. She describes herself as "a little figure, slender, yet stately," with "blond hair, wavy and golden" and "a blooming, dark-eyed face, just then radiant with girlish vanity and eagerness and hope" ("Whisper" 34). Once she is institutionalized, Sybil's subsequent remarks on her increasingly haggard appearance and shaved head, and her revelations of her emotional distress and disordered behavior elicit readerly fear and concern on her behalf. Likewise, her mother's inconsolable grief invites sympathy and compassion rather than fear. Despite Sybil's very human flaws—she is vain and has a bad temper—she does not deserve the brutal treatment she receives. While *Jane Eyre* sets Jane and Bertha in competition with one another, Sybil and her mother attempt to cooperate, modelling the very same compassionate identification with the misfortune of another that the narrative seeks to cultivate in readers. Finally, in *Jane Eyre* Bertha burns down Rochester's estate, ending her confinement and her life, while in "Whisper" an explosion caused by one of Karnac's laboratory experiments sets fire to the asylum. Incompetence, or perhaps simply luck, rather than feminine fury facilitates Sybil's escape.

"Whisper" exposes how madwoman narratives that devalue women as the irrational sex also stigmatize psychiatric disability. While Gothic narratives of wrongful confinement often protest the mistreatment of women and Romantic narratives of the grief-stricken madwoman reproduce assumptions regarding the irrationality of women, neither of these narratives necessarily contests the denigration of psychiatric disability.[10] By incorporating versions of both the Gothic and the Romantic madwoman and drawing a comparison with Bertha Mason, "Whisper" alters the dynamic. Alcott's story engages these three figures simultaneously to address the mutually derogatory associations between madness and femininity.

THE "CHAMELEON SELF": *MOODS*

If in "Whisper" Alcott "adopts and adapts" narratives of female madness, in the novels *Moods* and *Work*, her most ambitious projects, she draws from her own experience to create alternatives to madwomen.[11] As in "Whisper," both novels counteract stigma by eliciting sympathetic identification with flawed but appealing female characters as they grapple with disordered moods and suicidal despair. In *Moods*, Alcott does not use the term "mad" to describe the protagonist Sylvia Yule, a young woman "perplexed and burdened" by "mental ills" who marries the wrong man (*Moods* 86). Instead, Sylvia's friends and family characterize her as "freakish" and "capricious" (*Moods* 18, 57, 110, 227). Her "mixed & peculiar character" is specifically described as organic, innate, and explicitly compared to a physical disability or illness: her mental ills are like being "blind, a cripple, or cursed with some incurable infirmity of body" (*Selected Letters* 110; *Moods* 179). Sylvia's mental maladies are somatic and not primarily socially produced; they exist independently of sexist oppression, and as the daughter of a wealthy, indulgent father, she does not face paternal or economic pressures to marry. *Moods* isolates Sylvia's fluctuating moods and impulsiveness as her primary source of conflict to foreground their impact on her life apart from aggravating factors like poverty, abuse, or an arranged marriage.[12]

The description of Sylvia's "chameleon self" as alternately "overflowing with unnatural spirits or melancholy enough to break one's heart" suggests bipolar disorder or manic depression (*Moods* 175, 22). When Sylvia learns that Adam Warwick, the man she desires, is unattainable because he is engaged to someone else, she "turned to pleasure for oblivion":

> Those who knew her best were troubled and surprised by the craving for excitement which now took possession of her, the avidity with which she gratified it, regardless of time, health, and money. (*Moods* 102)

In the wake of her failed romance, Sylvia goes on a manic binge. She shops; she hosts parties; she attends balls, masquerades, and concerts. She goes to the theatre to indulge in tragedies. These manic pursuits, however, are not sustainable:

> This lasted for a time, then the reaction came. A black melancholy fell upon her, and energy deserted soul and body. She found it weariness to get up in the morning and weariness to lie down at night. She no longer even cared to seem cheerful, owned that she was spiritless, hoped she should be ill, and did not care if she died to-morrow. When this dark mood seemed about to become chronic she began to mend, for youth is wonderfully recuperative, and the deepest wounds soon heal even against the sufferer's will. A quiet apathy replaced the gloom, and she let the tide drift her where it would, hoping nothing, expecting nothing, asking nothing but that she need not suffer any more. (*Moods* 102)

In keeping with the familiar rhythm of bipolar disorder, Sylvia cycles from excitement and energetic activity to depression and apathy. Soon after, she seeks out Geoffrey Moor, a friend and suitor whose marriage proposal she previously rejected because of her attraction to Warwick. Giving in to a "craving for affection" and "a strong desire to fill the aching void her lost love had left," she agrees to marry him (*Moods* 106).

The treatment of marriage in the novel is inextricable from the issue of Sylvia's "mental ills." First, Sylvia's temperament is attributed to her parent's ill-considered marriage (motivated by money and ambition):

> If ever a man received punishment for a self-inflicted wrong it was John Yule. A punishment as subtle as the sin; for in the children growing up about him every relinquished hope, neglected gift, lost aspiration, seemed to live again; yet on each and all was set the direful stamp of imperfection, which made them visible illustrations of the great law broken in his youth. (*Moods* 83)

Thus, according to a well-worn trope that attaches shame and moral failing to disability, the sins of the father cause Sylvia's mental condition. She literally embodies the "conflicting temperaments" of her incompatible parents: "These two masters ruled soul and body, warring against each other, making Sylvia an enigma to herself and her life a train of moods" (*Moods* 84). Her parent's marriage was a "sin," not only because it made them unhappy and perhaps caused Sylvia's mother's premature death, but also because it has negative consequences for their children.

Moods argues that it is unwise to marry someone you do not love, but it is equally unwise for incompatible lovers to marry for passion. Geoffrey Moor, the man Sylvia does marry, is a good match for her. She initially seeks out his friendship because she feels his "serenity" can minister to her volatility. However, she harbors a secret passion for Adam, which dooms their marriage. When Sylvia asks Faith, a more mature woman who befriends her, whether she should leave her husband Geoffery for Adam, Faith argues that Sylvia should not be with either man. She should not remain married to Geoffrey because she does not love him, and she should not pursue Adam because their temperaments are incompatible. Marriage to either man will make Sylvia unhappy. Furthermore, Sylvia herself is constitutionally unsuited for marriage:

> There are diseases more subtle and dangerous than any that vex our flesh; diseases that should be as carefully cured if curable, as inexorably prevented from increasing as any malady we dread. A feeble will, a morbid mind, a mad temper, an evil heart, a blind soul, are afflictions to be as much regarded as bodily infirmities. Nay, more, inasmuch as souls are of greater value than perishable flesh. Where this is religiously taught, believed, and practised, marriage becomes in truth a sacrament blessed of God; children thank parents for the gift of life; parents see in children living satisfactions and rewards, not reproaches, or retributions doubly heavy to be borne, for the knowledge that where two sinned, many must inevitably suffer. (*Moods* 179)

According to Faith, Sylvia's mental disease should prevent her from marrying, primarily because of the risk of "increasing… any malady," or passing her illness to her children. Perhaps due to her own experience as the embodiment of her own parent's missteps, Sylvia responds: "thank God that I have no child to reproach me hereafter, for bequeathing it the mental ills I have not yet outlived" (*Moods* 179). Here Alcott describes Sylvia's illness as a congenital legacy that would necessarily be bequeathed, but also opens up the possibility for cure or recovery: the ills are "not yet outlived."

Like the double bind that Sybil faces in "Whisper," in *Moods* Sylvia has no satisfying options. Her mental disability seemingly obligates her to avoid marriage but at the same time leaves her without a path to a satisfying life. Sylvia is ultimately a tragic figure, whose romanticized death at the end of the novel seems more meaningful than her life. Her story demonstrates that marriage as the end and purpose of a woman's life is too narrow and harms some women who cannot or should not comply with this norm.

DEPRESSION AND RECOVERY: *WORK*

Alcott began writing *Work* while she was still revising *Moods*, and she continued to revise *Work* for a decade before finally publishing it in 1873. Her working title for the manuscript, "Success," hints that she imagined this effort as an answer to *Moods*, which she described as "odd, sentimental & tragical" (*Selected Letters* 101, 103, 104). While *Moods* uses the marriage plot as a vehicle to examine the damaging effects of Sylvia's moods, *Work* uses Alcott's life trajectory as its narrative form. The most explicitly autobiographical of the three texts discussed here, *Work* can be read as a narrative of depression and recovery. It has an episodic structure that reflects the vicissitudes of Alcott's life: first the heroine Christie leaves home in search of independence, and then the novel describes the ups and downs of her various careers as domestic servant, actress, governess, companion, and seamstress.[13] Midway through the novel, Christie, like Alcott, contemplates drowning herself following a year in which "[h]er heart was empty and she could not fill it; her soul was hungry and she could not feed it; life was cold and dark and she could not warm and brighten it" (*Work* 146). After a bystander interrupts her, Christie finds help among supportive friends and eventually achieves peace of mind and a full life that includes marriage and parenthood as well as community and meaningful work as a suffragette.

Previous critics have tended to read Christie's potential suicide as the result of her failure to support herself financially. But in fact, Christie's working life includes both successes and failures. As Alcott writes, Christie "suffered a sort of poverty which is more difficult to bear than actual want, since money cannot lighten it and the rarest charity alone can minister to it" (*Work* 146). Christie's despair results in part from her recognition of the way capitalism distorts human relationships. Either her employers humiliate and degrade her, or they fail to respect employer/employee boundaries. For instance, Christie receives an unwelcome marriage proposal from a member of the family where she works as a governess. She also leaves her last position as a seamstress because her employers believe that paying a paltry wage gives them moral authority over a worker's life: when her friend Rachel is fired for being a fallen woman, Christie resigns in solidarity. The third-person narrator of *Work* describes the despair resulting from these unfulfilling work experiences:

> It is not always want, insanity, or sin that drives women to desperate deaths; often it is a dreadful loneliness of heart, a hunger for home and friends, worse than starvation, a bitter sense of wrong in being denied the tender ties, the pleasant duties, the sweet rewards that can make the humblest life happy; a rebellious cry against God who, when they cry for bread, seems to offer them a stone. (150)

Fortunately, despite these setbacks and obstacles, Christie's search for satisfying work is ultimately successful.

While the heroine's averted suicide is only one episode in her narrative, it is highly significant because it is a turning point. After nearly taking her own life, Christie starts over. Even though she still struggles economically in the second part of the novel, she thrives emotionally because she now combines work with meaningful relationships. In *Work*, we see a shift in emphasis from what we might call a diagnostic narrative of the causes of madness—the grief, abuse, and biological inheritance described in "Whisper" and *Moods*—to a narrative of recovery focused on how to live. *Work*'s recovery narrative obtains even in the face of a realized suicide, that of Christie's friend Helen. Christie was hired to care for the invalid Helen, who had depression, and subsequently grew close to her and her family, who had a history of insanity. After Helen kills herself, heartbroken Christie leaves to find another job, but not before advising Helen's sister, Bella, to focus on caring for her at-risk brother:

> I have read many books, thought much, and talked often with Dr. Shirley about this sad affliction. He thinks you and Harry may escape it, if you will.... You are like your mother in temperament and temper; you have self control, strong wills, good nerves, and cheerful spirits. Poor Harry is

willfully spoiling all his chances now; but you may save him, and, in the endeavor, save yourself. (*Work* 124–125)

When Christie is reunited with Bella at the end of the novel, the specter of madness still looms over the family: Bella's other brother Augustine "is melancholy mad: very quiet, very patient, and very kind to every one but himself. His penances for the sins of his race [family] would soon kill him if mother was not there to watch over him. And her penance is never to leave him" (*Work* 431–432). But the good news is that Bella has followed Christie's advice and cared for her brother Harry as he has successfully completed medical training. Bella, however, now fears for her own sanity, because her caregiving and support of Harry has ended and she no longer has purpose in her life: "I'm afraid I shall get melancholy,—that is the beginning of the end for us, you know" (*Work* 433). Yet Christie has new advice, a new prescription, for her friend. She urges her to turn her attention to women like herself: "Dress up their minds in their best; get them out into the air; and cure their ills by the magnetism of more active, earnest lives" (*Work* 439). These women will become Bella's "patients," as she works to improve their lives and, by extension, society itself (Fig. 6.1).

Work concludes with an image of an idealized postbellum feminist utopia, in which a community of women join together to create better conditions for future generations: "With an impulsive gesture Christie stretched her hands to the friends about her, and with one accord they laid theirs on hers, a loving league of sisters, old and young, black and white, rich and poor, each ready to do her part" (*Work* 442). Hepsey, the run-away slave Christie worked with during her short stint as a domestic, sits prominently in the foreground to the right, and her dead husband's retired Union cap and sword hang with his portrait on the back wall. Ruth, Christie's small daughter, sits in the center. The child "spread her chubby hand above the rest: a hopeful omen, seeming to promise that the coming generation of women will not only receive but deserve their liberty, by learning that the greatest of God's gifts to us is the privilege of sharing His great work" (*Work* 443). In this way, purposeful work and meaningful relationships are not just a bridge across the slough of depression for an individual; they are also the basis of the nation's recovery from the wounds of the Civil War.

Fig. 6.1 "Sisterhood," from Louisa May Alcott's *Work*

Conclusion: Minerva Moody

In an 1868 letter to her mother, Alcott playfully referred to herself as "Minerva Moody" (*Selected Letters* 113). In doing so, Alcott was naming a persona she crafted for herself as an alternative to both the madwoman (in her Gothic, Romantic, and attic varieties) and the Romantic man of genius, a figure that celebrated melancholy as a mark of creative power but which excluded her by virtue of her gender.[14] As she wrote in an 1864 letter to publisher James Redpath, apparently in response to a compliment he paid her: "people musn't talk about about 'genius'—for I drove that idea away years ago & don't want it back again. The inspiration of necessity is all I've had, & it is a safer help than any other" (*Selected Letters* 103). "Minerva Moody" signals Alcott's hard won understanding of herself as a moody woman with a modest talent. Her short fiction and novels, as well as her letters and journals, reflect her lived experience with volatile moods and depression. Attending to this dimension of Alcott's work complicates established readings of her fiction, which challenges reductive associations between madness and femininity and posits alternative, more affirmative narratives of women's experiences with disordered moods and suicidal despair.

Notes

1. Notable exceptions include Schnog, Matteson, Douglas, and Gamwell and Tomes. Schnog discusses *Moods* as an example of a novel in which moodiness is embraced as resistance to cheerfulness understood as a regulatory norm for women. She does not, however, discuss Sylvia's moodiness in relation to mental illness or disability. Matteson's biography comments that Alcott's "most significant writings for adults, the works into which she was to pour the greater portion of her true self, were to return frequently to the spectre of depression, inherited madness, and suicide" (213). Douglas mentions Christie's depression in *Work* and Gamwell and Tomes discuss Helen Carroll from *Work* as a nineteenth-century literary example of inherited insanity. To date, there has been no sustained examination of disability in Alcott's work.
2. The plots of "Love and Self Love" (1860), "The Freak of a Genius" (1866), and *A Modern Mephistopheles* (1887) involve suicide. The heroine of "A Nurse's Story" (1865–66) is the caregiver to an "insane" daughter of a wealthy family, and the plot revolves around the family secret of inherited insanity. In *A Long and Fatal Love Chase* (unpublished during Alcott's lifetime but written in 1866), the heroine's mental health deteriorates after she is forcibly confined to an asylum by her bigamist husband. I am using the term "psychiatric disability" in this context because it helpfully avoids the nineteenth-century tendency to conflate mental illness with developmental and intellectual disabilities.
3. This is consistent with philosopher of psychiatry Jennifer Radden's discussion: "Moods are a particular way of experiencing, rather than a particular experience" (14).
4. According to Matteson, Alcott's "struggles with emotional control were a frequent source of profound distress to herself and her family during her years of growing up" (306). Matteson asks whether Alcott might have been manic depressive and concludes that we can't know (305). My purpose is not to retroactively diagnose Alcott, as tempting as it might be, but to reclaim Alcott for a feminist disability studies approach to psychiatric disability by foregrounding how she wrote of her own experience and how that private writing relates to her fiction.

5. Alcott wrote: "Last week was a busy, anxious time, & my courage most gave out, for every one was so busy, & cared so little whether I got work or jumped into the river that I thought seriously of doing the latter. In fact did go over the Mill Dam & look at the water. But it seemed so mean to turn & run away before the battle was over that I went home, set my teeth & vowed I'd *make* things work in spite of the world, the flesh & the devil" (*Selected Letters* 34, emphasis in the original).
6. My discussion here is indebted to Donaldson's analysis of *Jane Eyre*.
7. Radden discusses both the similarities between grief and ordinary and pathological varieties of melancholy and the differences between them: "The normal effects of adverse life experiences, such as oppression or the death of loved ones, are often indistinguishable from the effects of depressive disorder. Yet these forms of suffering are marked by morally relevant differences: such conceptual boundaries must be affirmed and maintained" (20–21).
8. Brontë's portrayal of Bertha Mason is consistent with Garland-Thomson's observation regarding conventional literary depictions of physical disability: "representation tends to objectify disabled characters by denying them any opportunity for subjectivity or agency" (11).
9. On Alcott's relationship to Brontë across her oeuvre, see Doyle. Keyser discusses allusions to *Jane Eyre* in "Whisper" (4, 8, 12).
10. My discussion is informed by historian Douglas Baynton's argument: "While historians have not overlooked the use of disability to deny women's rights, they have given their attention entirely to gender inequality and not at all to the construction and maintenance of cultural hierarchies based on disability" (24).
11. Doyle uses the combination of the terms "adoption" and "adaptation" to capture Alcott's pervasive use and revision of Brontë (24). I'm adopting and adapting Doyle's phrase here.
12. In an 1865 letter responding to a reader, Alcott somewhat defensively affirmed her purpose: "The design of *Moods* was to show the effect of a moody person's moods upon their life, & Sylvia, being a mixed & peculiar character, makes peculiar blunders & tries to remedy them in an uncommon manner" (*Selected Letters* 110). Alcott similarly affirmed her purpose in her preface when she published a revised version of *Moods* in 1882. There she described her novel as "an attempt to show the mistakes of a moody nature, guided by impulse, not principle" (*Moods* 225).
13. See Edelstein on Alcott's "interest in refiguring the trajectory of the female life narrative" (527).
14. On gender, melancholy, and genius, see Radden 17–18, 47, 190. See also Sofer's discussion of Alcott as one example of "U.S. women writers," who she argues "self-consciously examined and revised the two models of authorship available to them: the popular female author and the romantic male genius" in the years between 1860 and 1880 (32).

WORKS CITED

Alcott, Louisa May. *The Journals of Louisa May Alcott*, edited by Madeline B. Stern, Joel Myerson, and Daniel Shealy. Little, Brown, 1989.
———. *Little Women*. 1868. Edited by Valerie Alderson. Oxford University Press, 1994.
———. *Moods*. 1865, 1882. Edited by Sarah Elbert. Rutgers University Press, 1991.
———. *The Selected Letters of Louisa May Alcott*, edited by Madeline B. Stern, Joel Myerson, and Daniel Shealy. Little, Brown, 1987.
———. "A Whisper in the Dark." *Louisa May Alcott Unmasked: Collected Thrillers*, edited by Madeline Stern. Northeastern University Press, 1995, pp. 32–58.
———. *Work: A Story of Experience*. 1873. Schocken, 1977.
Baynton, Douglas. "Disability and the Justification of Inequality in American History." *The Disability Studies Reader*, 4th ed., edited by Lennard J. Davis. Routledge, 2013, pp. 17–33.
Brontë, Charlotte. *Jane Eyre*, Norton Critical Edition, 3rd ed., edited by Richard J. Dunn. W. W. Norton, 2001.
Donaldson, Elizabeth J. "The Corpus of the Madwoman: Toward a Feminist Disability Studies Theory of Embodiment and Mental Illness." *The Madwoman and the Blindman: Jane Eyre, Discourse, Disability*, edited by David Bolt, Julia Miele Rodas, and Elizabeth J. Donaldson. Ohio University Press, 2012, pp. 11–31.
Douglas, Ann. "Mysteries of Louisa May Alcott." *New York Review of Books*, vol. 28, September 1978, pp. 60–65.
Doyle, Christine. *Louisa May Alcott & Charlotte Brontë: Transatlantic Translations*. University of Tennessee Press, 2000.
Edelstein, Sari. "Louisa May Alcott's Age." *American Literature*, vol. 87, no. 3, September 2015, pp. 517–545.
Garland-Thomson, Rosemarie. *Extraordinary Bodies: Figuring Physical Disability in American Culture and Literature*. Columbia University Press, 1997.
Gamwell, Lynn, and Nancy Tomes. *Madness in America: Cultural and Medical Perceptions of Mental Illness before 1914*. Cornell University Press, 1995.
Gilbert, Sandra M., and Susan Gubar. *The Madwoman in the Attic: The Woman Writer and the Nineteenth-Century Literary Imagination*. 2nd ed., Yale University Press, 2000.
Keyser, Elizabeth Lennox. *Whispers in the Dark: The Fiction of Louisa May Alcott*. University of Tennessee Press, 1993.
Matteson, John. *Eden's Outcasts: The Story of Louisa May Alcott and Her Father*. W. W. Norton, 2007.
Radden, Jennifer. *Moody Minds Distempered: Essays on Melancholy and Depression*. Oxford University Press, 2009.

Schnog, Nancy. "Changing Emotions: Moods and the Nineteenth Century American Woman." *Inventing the Psychological*, edited by Joel Pfister and Nancy Schnog. Yale University Press, 1997, pp. 84–109.

Showalter, Elaine. *The Female Malady: Women, Madness and English Culture 1830–1980*. Pantheon, 1985.

Sofer, Naomi Z. "'Carry[ing] a Yankee Girl to Glory': Redefining Female Authorship in the Postbellum United States." *American Literature*, vol. 75, no. 1, March 2003, pp. 31–60.

CHAPTER 7

The Snake Pit: Mary Jane Ward's Asylum Fiction and Mental Health Advocacy

Elizabeth J. Donaldson

When it was first published in 1946, Mary Jane Ward's *The Snake Pit* was an instant success. Chosen as a Book of the Month Club title, the autobiographically-based novel about Ward's experiences as a psychiatric patient in a state mental hospital sold hundreds of thousands of copies even before being made into an Academy Award winning feature film. The extraordinary success of the book and the film catapulted Ward into fame and helped to garner public support for reforms in psychiatric institutions. Yet most people today don't realize or remember that after her stint in Hollywood, Ward took to the road as a speaker for the National Mental Health Foundation, visiting state mental hospitals and lecturing to lay people and to healthcare professionals about the importance of the patient experience and the responsibility of the community to care for people with mental illnesses. This chapter examines the close and productive relationship between Ward's fiction writing and her experiences as a psychiatric patient and mental health advocate beginning with *The Snake Pit* in 1946 and including her final published novels, *Counterclockwise* in 1969 and *The Other Caroline* in 1970. While Ward's *The Snake Pit* had great success in its day, its popularity has not been lasting.

E. J. Donaldson (✉)
New York Institute of Technology, Old Westbury, NY, USA

And Ward's later novels have been completely neglected by critics and are largely unknown. However, Ward's life and her books are an untapped, important resource for disability scholars of mental health. Using archival evidence from the Mary Jane Ward collection at Boston University, in this chapter I place *The Snake Pit* in both biographical and historical context. Furthermore, I argue that *Counterclockwise* can be read as a sequel to *The Snake Pit*; this overlooked novel about Ward's relapse and hospitalization reflects significant social and cultural changes in psychiatric care and is part of a lost history of Ward's influential mental health advocacy in the 1950s. This chapter seeks to rescue Ward from this relative obscurity and to reclaim her as an important voice in a disability studies history of asylum literature and of mental health advocacy in the US.

Patient #19706: Fiction and Lived Experience

For Mary Jane Ward, the sudden success of *The Snake Pit* was a welcome surprise. And Ward's publisher, Random House, was quick to promote her seemingly overnight transformation from unknown mid-West housewife to acclaimed author. A stock story that circulated through many local papers touted her rags to riches tale with the headline, "$10 Recipe to $100,000 Book": "Mary Jane Ward of Evanston, Ill., was informed by the Book of the Month Club that her novel 'The Snake Pit' had been picked for the April choice. She will receive $100,000 in royalties. Her first published work was a recipe for beef sausage loaf, for which she received ten dollars" (*The Winnipeg Tribune*, 14 February 1946, p. 18). Yet stories like these glossed over some of the trickier details. Unlike the stereotypical casserole-making housewife, Ward was a full-time writer with two published novels already under her belt, and *The Snake Pit* was an autobiographically-based book about her experiences as a psychiatric patient in a state mental hospital.

Ward's personal papers contain very few official documents—beyond the paper trail of her admission and discharge dates—regarding the hospitalization that formed the basis for *The Snake Pit*. Ward and her husband were living in New York City, pursuing creative careers and quickly spending their way through their savings, when she became ill. Ward was first admitted to Bellevue Hospital as a psychiatric patient on May 27, 1941. A committal hearing was held on June 3, and two days later Ward was transferred and admitted to Rockland State Hospital, about 45 minutes north of the city; she was patient #19706. Rockland was a typical large state institution of this time: it was similar to a small, self-contained village, sitting on over 550 acres, with its own power station and farmland. Underground tunnels connected buildings for easier access during winter months, and doctors and nurses lived in on-campus housing. Ward left Rockland State nine months later when she was paroled in the custody of her husband on February 22, 1942 (Mary Jane Ward Collection, Box 6, Folder 21; hereafter cited as MJW Collection). The official hospital documents in her archives say nothing about her diagnosis or her treatment.

The novel *The Snake Pit* tells the story of protagonist Virginia Cunningham's year-long hospitalization in Juniper Hill, Ward's fictional representation of Rockland State. While Ward admitted to having a nervous breakdown and to being hospitalized, she also insisted that her book was fiction, especially in the early days of its publication. "Her Book Not Autobiography," a headline in a local paper claimed. But ultimately the autobiographical basis of the book was difficult for Ward to deny, and press reports made this connection in ways that were not always kind. The headline, "She Was Going Crazy—And She Knew It," typified this sort of sensationalized coverage (Martin). Ward's somewhat cagey early public statements may have been attempts to protect herself from having to deal with the stigma that comes along with being diagnosed with a serious mental illness. Some of the questions that she would have to field from reporters were misguided and potentially hurtful, and she was very mindful about how journalists characterized her in newspaper and magazine stories: she diligently collected these articles in large scrapbooks, which are now part of her archival collection.

The novel's autobiographical basis also made her especially vulnerable to criticism about the work itself, which Ward initially had a difficult time placing with an agent and publisher. In his letter rejecting the manuscript, literary agent Ivan Van Auw wrote: "It seems to me if you are going to write a book of this kind subjectively, the reader must be sympathetic toward your principal character. Unfortunately my own feelings were composed more largely of irritation than of sympathy" (MJW Collection, Box 4, Van Auw to Ward, 10 January 1945). Since the principal character, Virginia, was based on Ward herself, this rejection was even more personal and cutting. Van Auw not only disliked the book: he disliked her.[1] One year later, however, Virginia Cunningham/Mary Jane

Ward found a much more receptive audience at Random House. Van Auw's imprudent rejection of the best-selling manuscript became a legendary cautionary tale in publishing, one which Ward herself told with relish, though she kindly omitted identifying the guilty literary agent by name.

Another factor that contributed to Ward's efforts to downplay the non-fictional aspects of the book was her memory loss during her illness. The book is "more fantasy than fact," Ward stated in an interview. "I realized I was writing about a place that lived only in the mind of my protagonist," she continued: "Juniper Hill from tubs to tunnel was built and peopled by a mind that was blacked out—so the accuracy is unreliable" (Woods 65). She had no recollection of the first several weeks of her hospitalization or the period immediately preceding her breakdown (Martin 8), and this sort of memory loss and disorientation were recurring features of the severe episodes of her illness.[2] According to one interview, Ward was initially diagnosed with catatonia, believed to be a form of schizophrenia at the time (Lensing). However, Ward's episodic symptoms would likely be interpreted as major depressive disorder or bipolar disorder today, and problems with memory are likewise associated with those conditions. Ward, furthermore, had a history of depression in her extended family. Her cousin, Ross Lockridge, was also a writer with mental illness—he died by suicide in 1948, just when his highly regarded novel *Raintree County* was topping the best-seller list.

Despite what Ward said about the book being fiction in early interviews, Virginia Cunningham is clearly a very thinly veiled version of Ward herself. Both are writers who have published two novels, both have moved from Evanston, Illinois to New York City, and both are married to a kind, supportive husband. Both have a history of social activism. Before her breakdown, Virginia Cunningham was busy attending meetings for social causes, when she was not battling insomnia and worrying about money. Mary Jane Ward was immersed in activist work as well and, during the wartime paper shortage, typed the manuscript of *The Snake Pit* on the back of old letterhead for The Council for Democratic Action, an Evanston group that organized for social justice (MJW Collection, Box 1). But perhaps the most important similarity is that both women may be considered "unreliable" narrators who nevertheless tell the truth, despite memory loss and disorientation.

Madness Reconstructed: Memory Loss, Narrative, and Politics in *The Snake Pit*

As Catherine Prendergast once wrote, "To be disabled mentally is to be disabled rhetorically" ("On the Rhetorics of Mental Disability" 57). A diagnosis of schizophrenia or severe mental illness can undermine a person's authority to speak: "If people think you're crazy," Prendergast writes, "they don't listen to you" (57).[3] Moreover, the features of an illness itself can be rhetorically disabling: Ward faced the problem of telling a story that she could only partially recall. Yet Ward took this problem—"a mind that was blacked out"—and embraced it: her lapses of memory become a source of suspense and a driving force of the plot in *The Snake Pit* (Woods 65).

In the novel, Virginia Cunningham's memory loss and disorientation are key elements of the story from the very beginning. The reader struggles, as does Virginia, to understand what is happening. *The Snake Pit* begins mid-conversation. "Do you hear voices?" a man asks:

> "Of course," Virginia responds. "I hear yours." ... He was something of a pest, this man, but she could think of no decent way to get rid of him. You could tell he meant well and so you tried to play the game with him, as if with a fanciful child.
> "You can make water say anything," she said. That should appeal to the childish fancy that leaped from pebble to pebble, dancing in the sun, giggling in the sparkle.
> And now the water rushed from the quiet pool of his voice to a stone-cluttered bed uneasy for fishes. The song of the brook soared to a rapid soprano and his voice was changing him into a small boy. Dreadful. She tried not to look, but at last her eyes turned irresistibly and, with horror, saw him a girl. She suspected him of magic and now she knew. (3)

The rush of water signals a collapse in time, as Virginia moves abruptly, and unconsciously, from a conversation with her psychiatrist in his office to a conversation with a fellow female patient on an outdoor bench.

Whatever has happened between these two conversations is lost, and Virginia struggles to make sense of her situation and to overcome her disorientation in both place and time. She doesn't know where she is or how she got there, and as the novel progresses she explores several different possible explanations. At first, she thinks she is in a city park, resting after running errands, but mysteriously without her pocketbook and in an old dress she would only wear for housecleaning, never out in public. Then she toys with the idea that she is on a picnic tour of a city zoo organized by her "True Trotskyite" friends (20).[4] And later she muses that she is at a training school for delinquent girls as part of her research for "a novel with Social Significance" (25), and then, finally, that she is in a prison to observe and gather material for a prison novel. The prison explanation gains hold, and as her doctor prepares her for electroshock therapy the next day, she becomes convinced that they are planning to execute her:

> What had you done? You wouldn't have killed anyone and what other crime is there which exacts so severe a penalty? Could they electrocute you for having voted for Norman Thomas [the Socialist Party presidential candidate]? . . . Dare they kill me without a trial? I demand to see a lawyer. And he—he always talking about hearing voices and never hearing mine. . . . If I say I demand a lawyer they have to do something. It has to do with habeas corpus, something in the Constitution. But they and their smooth talk, they intend to make a corpus of me—they and their good mornings and how are you. (43)

Despite her confusion about where she is and why, Virginia the writer still has her wit and her faculty for word play: "they intend to make a corpus[/corpse] of me." And she maintains her political consciousness and sense of justice, pointedly criticizing the doctor for his misplaced focus on hearing imaginary voices while never hearing hers.

Virginia's use of language ultimately rescues her from this confusion of place, albeit in a surprising way. Later in the afternoon, Virginia realizes she is without her eyeglasses and begs an attendant to help her find them: "'I really think if I'm without them much longer I'll go crazy.' She hadn't spoken loudly but the word, that last word, bounced from one wall to another" (50). Ironically, the word "crazy" breaks the spell and pulls Virginia out of what she now sees was a "prison fantasy" (50). Her casual use of a clichéd expression—"I'll go crazy"—reverberates and rings true. The word bounces from wall to wall as hyperbole meets hard reality. From this point on, she knows that she is in a psychiatric hospital: "Around you in the washroom were women who were shut up with you, women who were far more wretched than criminals. I was trying to glamorize it. What it is, is the one thing I cannot take. I could face the prospect of blindness, of cancer, but this, no. Never this" (51). She is the unlucky winner of the disability lottery: "I am one of them" (54).

Although Virginia might recognize herself here as "one of them" and although she later develops friendships with other patients and nurses, there are limited opportunities to engage in the sort of communal political activities that have helped to define her life outside of the asylum. Her political ideals are, furthermore, recontextualized in the psychiatric hospital setting. For example, in a previous scene a fellow patient, Rosa, disrupts mealtime by delivering a loud and passionate speech in her native Italian. Virginia doesn't understand the language but recognizes Rosa's non-verbal performance and her "magnificent gestures" as a spirited imitation of Mussolini (47). As the attendants join forces to carry Rosa out of the dining hall, Virginia is inspired to take the stage:

> Now for the first time in history we are alone. Now my speech. Ladies! Now is our chance to organize. Unless we organize we are lost. Are we going to continue to accept this oppression? United we have strength. Let us organize. Can we sit here and let them do God knows what to Comrade Rosa? . . . . The speech was clear in her mind. It was somewhat adapted from Helene [her friend in the Communist Party] but she felt in general it was not communistic. She prepared to rise. (48)

But before she can stand, the attendants return and regular order is restored. This scene, which occurs right before Virginia realizes she is in a psychiatric hospital, suggests that political passion and madness are related, a familiar Joan of Arc trope. But the fact that Virginia is so moved by Rosa's speech is somewhat surprising. Previously, Virginia has been careful to distance herself from the extremes of communist thinking: she recalls how she reacted with dismay when she was unwittingly photographed in front of a "Defend the Soviet Union" sign at an Evanston banquet (20). And even now she wants to avoid saying words that are too "communistic" (48). She is wary of ideologues like her friend Helene and the True Trotskyites. But Rosa's deluge of incomprehensible words nevertheless stirs something in Virginia, despite the fact that she can recognize Mussolini and the pattern of fascist thinking that lies beneath them. Comrade Rosa's speech is contagious—a mad pathological babble that threatens to undermine rational political ideals.

Virginia's social consciousness is an important part of the novel: throughout the story she tries to remain consistently true to her political ideals and to her sense of justice, despite the challenges of environment and illness. This is perhaps best illustrated by her experiences in Ward 8:

"In Ward Eight was a spirit of co-operation Virginia had never noticed elsewhere" (192). Here everyone shares their belongings, including the treasured packages and gifts they receive from visiting family members. But, even in this most idyllic ward dynamic, all is not well. All of the women still wanted to get out: "If you had wanted to be in Juniper Hill, Ward Eight would have been a good place to be. None of the ladies, however, wanted to be at the hospital. Whatever their troubles had been outside they were anxious to get back to them and with one exception they all knew where they were and approximately why" (192). That one exception is Tamara. She is tall, muscular, and intimidating. She wears a fur coat that she refuses to take off and she claims to be a Russian countess, although her sister visits in a maid's uniform. Virginia is constantly warned by the nurses to stay away from Tamara, who is believed to be violent. The other women on the ward shun her: "Tamara had five operations on her head, said the ladies, and was hopeless. They were very snobbish about hopeless cases and they blamed Tamara for being hopeless. Their attitude about hopeless insanity was very like the attitude outside. They hated Tamara for being insane" (193). But Virginia sees hope: "there might be a chance for Tamara if someone were to bother to follow up an operation with a little post-operative care" (193). When Virginia plays the piano, Tamara sits next to her, enjoying the music: "Tamara smiled at her and said, 'Thank you so much, my friend'" (194). When a concerned nurse pulls Virginia away from the piano, she is nevertheless relieved: "'Sometimes a sick animal knows more about how another sick animal should be treated,' said Virginia. But to tell the truth, she was not unwilling to go away from the dangerous patient" (194). Virginia's willingness to be pulled away from comrade Tamara hints at some of the barriers that prevent her from realizing her ideals in this environment. "Sick animals," like Virginia and Tamara, surely do know best. But in the ecology of the psychiatric ward, they are not in the position to do much about it, despite any mutual recognition of suffering.[5] Soon afterwards, Virginia experiences an intense episode of paranoia that evolves out of another patient's efforts to befriend her, and when she regains awareness she is no longer a part of the Ward 8 community.[6]

Virginia's abrupt and unwitting movement from one ward to another is a recurring and significant pattern in *The Snake Pit*: for example, a chapter might end in one ward with a small crisis moment, and then the next chapter will begin mid-conversation in a different ward, with

Virginia wondering where she is and how she got there. While these moments are similar to the collapse in time at the start of the novel, it's important to note that Virginia maintains her awareness that she is in state mental institution: she just doesn't know exactly where she is in the system or whether or not she is progressing, or getting any better. At Rockland State, wards are organized numerically: Ward 1 is quite often the last stop before a patient is released, while the more severely ill patients are housed in higher number wards. However, Virginia's movement among the wards is anything but a neat linear progression toward good health: she starts in Ward 3 and then moves to 1, then 2, then 5, then 12, then 8, then 14, and then, finally, to the snake pit, Ward 33. Despite Virginia's disorientation, the novel itself has a clear and simple continuity of time and place: one year in Juniper Hill. We begin here and end here. Virginia is eventually granted release, but we never actually see her leave and we don't learn anything about her subsequent life. In the final pages, Miss Sommerville, a former psychiatric nurse turned patient, erases Virginia's name from her mock roster: "She held the book out to Virginia. 'See. You're gone'" (278).

GOING MAD IN PUBLIC: POSTWAR CULTURE AND PSYCHIATRY

The Snake Pit's success pushed Mary Jane Ward into the public eye, especially after the novel was adapted into a feature film starring the popular actress Olivia de Havilland. Under the direction of Anatole Litvak, the film took certain liberties with the plot of the original novel—the screen version of Virginia Cunningham was more of a muddled housewife than a muddled socialist writer, and the novel's references to Virginia's communist friends and her social justice work were scrubbed from the film. The film also added a tidy Freudian explanation for Virginia Cunningham's illness—an unhealthy attachment to her father and guilt over the death of her fiancé. In the film, Virginia is released because she is cured. In the novel, Virginia is released primarily because her husband is moving out of state. (And this is actually what happened—Edward Quayle, Ward's husband, moved back to Illinois, and out of the service area of the New York State mental health system. So Ward was paroled to his custody and moved away with him.)

The film takes a rather chaotic, almost surreal plot and makes it more orderly. But the film is hardly an antiseptic version of the novel. It does attempt to faithfully depict the treatments that Ward writes about—notably hydrotherapy, or the tubs, and Ward's experiences of electroconvulsive therapy (ECT). The film's depictions are significant because they opened up the psychiatric patient experience to a wider audience, who previously had limited, if any, knowledge about the closed world of institutional mental healthcare. The film helped to shape public thinking about mental illness, and perhaps one of the most significant ways it did that was through de Havilland's compassionate portrayal of Virginia Cunningham. The film was a critical success and de Havilland, already a full-fledged movie star at the time, earned an Oscar nomination for Best Actress in a Leading Role. While the film was gritty, the cast was glamourous, and it didn't hurt the cause to have good-looking people like de Havilland cast as psychiatric patients.

The Snake Pit, however, was just one element in a new national conversation about the care and treatment of patients with mental illness. One of the major factors contributing to this discussion was the employment of large numbers of conscientious objectors (COs) in state hospitals during the war. At the time of Ward's hospitalization at Rockland State, large state medical institutions faced a staffing crisis as doctors and nurses also left for war work. Psychiatric aides—the backbone of the day-to-day custodial care for the hundreds of thousands of patients in these institutions—left for higher paying positions. In order to fill the pressing need for more attendants, about 3,000 conscientious objectors—people who refused to serve in the military for moral or religious reasons—were placed in state mental hospitals under the Civilian Public Service (CPS) program (Sareyan 14). These men, and often their wives who accompanied them as workers, had a substantial effect on the future of mental healthcare in the US.

Conscientious objectors brought compassion, a commitment to social justice, and an outsider's perspective to the insular environment of these large institutions. They reached out to their patients, and after the war they reached out to the public to raise awareness about the conditions in state psychiatric hospitals. They shared information with each other, they organized, and some of them also remained in the field of mental health even after the war ended. They formed an organization within CPS called the Mental Hygiene Program and starting in 1944 published a monthly newsletter, *The Attendant* (Sareyan 132–33). These newsletters offered practical suggestions about how to improve interactions with patients. Some suggestions were as radical as simply calling the patients by their names: for example, when an attendant asked, "Mr. Edwards, would you please do this for me?" the formerly uncooperative patient would comply, noting that it had been "some time" since any one had addressed him by name (Sareyan 133). But perhaps the most lasting contributions of the CO-led Mental Hygiene Program were its collection of data from COs working in state mental hospitals and its expansion into a national advocacy organization. The Mental Hygiene Program became the National Mental Health Foundation (NMHF), which in turn funded and published Frank Wright's book *Out of Sight, Out of Mind* (1947), a sweeping exposé of life in state institutions, which was based on material and testimony from over 1,400 surveys of COs working as attendants (Taylor, Steven 139; Sareyan 19–20). The NMHF acted as a clearinghouse for data about state mental hospitals, providing information for journalists and researchers (Sareyan viii). Albert Deutsch drew on this material for his ground-breaking and influential book on state mental hospitals, *The Shame of the States* (1948). NMHF data were also used as source material for Albert Maisel's stirring photo-essay "Bedlam 1946" published in *Life Magazine*.

The postwar conversation about mental health care took place at a historical moment of deep moral reflection regarding society's obligations to relieve the suffering of vulnerable people. *Life Magazine*'s "Bedlam 1946" visually evoked comparisons to Nazi death camps: in one photo, desperately thin, naked men with shaved heads idle along the stark walls of a hospital day room (Maisel 105). And the accompanying text explicitly reinforced this connection to the brutality of the recent world war, calling for the end of "concentration camps that masquerade as hospitals" (Maisel 118). It's worth noting, however, that while "Bedlam 1946" expresses a sense of deep moral outrage that these "concentration camps" exist in the American heartland, the essay does not highlight the mutual culpability of American eugenic thinking in the creation of both camp and hospital.[7]

COUNTERCLOCKWISE: ADVOCACY AND THE ASYLUM

After the flurry of activity surrounding the film's release abated, Ward took to the road as a speaker for local and national advocacy groups, including the National Mental Health Foundation, the very same organization founded by the COs. Ward also served on the NMHF Board of Directors at the same time Eleanor Roosevelt was supporting the group with fundraising efforts (Sareyan 179; Taylor, Steven 325).

And both women were honored in the same year, 1949, by the Women's National Press Club at a gala affair in Washington DC (MJW Collection, Scrapbook D). At this event, Eleanor Roosevelt was named woman of the year. Ward was acknowledged for her work in mental health and was presented an award by President Truman, who had signed the Mental Health Care Act in 1946 creating the National Institute of Mental Health.

During this period, Ward had high hopes about future progress in the care of people with mental illness and she worked relentlessly throughout the late 1940s and early 1950s to cultivate public support. Ward lectured to both lay people and healthcare professionals about the importance of the patient experience and the responsibility of the community to care for people with mental illnesses. Ward visited state mental institutions and spoke at professional conferences to superintendents, doctors, nurses, and aides. She also spoke in hotel ballrooms in smaller cities to local chapters of civic groups founded by concerned citizens. She published articles in local papers and national magazines promoting reforms in state mental hospitals, persuading people to support family and friends with mental illnesses, and fighting against stigma. She was a tireless advocate, visiting over 300 hospitals as part of her work in the mental health movement in the years immediately following *The Snake Pit*'s publication (Sotor D5; MJW Collection, Scrapbook D).

Ward also went on to publish five more novels before her death in 1981. Her last two published novels, *Counterclockwise* (1969) and *The Other Caroline* (1970), return to the topic that made her famous—mental illness. *The Other Caroline* is about a woman in a state mental hospital who believes that her brain has been transplanted in another person's body: her psychiatrist has her type up the "other" woman's journals, in order to help her remember who she is. In *Counterclockwise*, a writer and former psychiatric patient, Susan Wood, has achieved fame and fortune by writing a novel based on her experiences as a patient in a state mental institution. Wood works for a foundation as a mental health advocate until she experiences a nervous breakdown and must be admitted, once again, to a psychiatric hospital. According to Ward's letters, *Counterclockwise* is autobiographical, and *The Other Caroline* is not.[8]

Some of the autobiographical elements of *Counterclockwise* are obvious: Wood and Ward are both former patients, writers, and mental health advocates. But other elements, such as the second breakdown, are less public and more obscure. Evidence from her archives (specifically from correspondence exchanged among Ward, her husband, and her contacts in publishing) reveals that Ward, like Wood, also experienced a second breakdown that resulted in hospitalization. Furthermore, Ward's breakdown was in part precipitated by the strain of her mental health advocacy work. In April 1962, she wrote, "My second breakdown terminated the activities that were literally killing me, . . . and dropping out of all mental health work along with having an unlisted phone . . . have helped a great deal" (MJW Collection, Box 6, Folder 3, Ward to Bennett Cerf, April 1962). The pace of Ward's mental health advocacy work was clearly demanding, emotionally and physically. For example, a schedule from Ward's October 1952 visit to Topeka, Kansas, the original home of the Menninger Clinic, describes a grueling day. Ward began at 10am with a visit to the Winter Veterans Administration hospital, which included various meetings with hospital psychiatrists, nurses, and aides, followed by a luncheon, more meetings, dinner with local civic groups, more meetings, an evening lecture by Ward, and then a reception, ending at 10 pm (MJW Collection, Scrapbook D). There were no real breaks for Ward in this 12-hour period, which was followed the next day by a site visit and even more meetings at the Menninger Clinic, which at this point was well established as a leading educational hub for psychiatrists. Based on what appears, or doesn't appear, in her scrapbooks, this second breakdown and Ward's disengagement with advocacy work occurred in 1955.

In *Counterclockwise*, the main character's breakdown is caused by a combination of two events. First, Susan Wood discovers that a colleague has stolen thousands of dollars in bonds from the nonprofit mental health foundation that they work for.[9] This theft is not reported to the police. The foundation is in the midst of a fundraising campaign, which the bad press would hinder. Furthermore, the thief is a former friend in need of psychiatric care, and so she is spared arrest by the foundation committee. In the novel, the theft is a disturbing betrayal of the mental health movement by one of their own. It illustrates how fragile the movement is, how easily it can be destroyed from within.

The second cause of Susan Wood's breakdown in *Counterclockwise* is a traumatic experience that happens during a hospital tour. This type of visit was a routine component of her work (and of Ward's) for the foundation. However, in *Counterclockwise* something unexpected happens during one of these tours. Wood begins her site visit on a hopeful note: the hospital superintendent shows her the bright and cheery dayrooms of the highest functioning patients, and all seems well. But the superintendent is called to another meeting and leaves Wood in the hands of the head nurse with directions to visit Building 10A, a ward where remarkably the head nurse has never been. Building 10A is hidden not only from visitors but also from almost all of the professional staff. 10A is a repurposed staff housing unit divided into two spaces: an upstairs with one small group of patients and a locked basement with another, separate small group. The main room of the basement space is concrete, with a concrete bench around three sides, and a drain in the floor (*Counterclockwise* 234). It is populated by naked incontinent female patients—women shaved bald to prevent lice infestations, barely recognizable as humans (237). They are the visceral antithesis of Ward's hope for the future. Seeing these women, in these conditions, is what finally breaks Ward's character.

Counterclockwise ends with Susan Wood telling the story of her visit to Building 10A to her psychotherapist. The iteration of this repressed traumatic memory signals the end of the narrative. It's how we the readers, and Susan Wood's psychotherapist, know that she is truly cured: she's finally spoken about the unspeakable. This ending gives us an oversimplified, Freudian-style closure in a way that is somewhat similar to *Snake Pit* the film. Susan Wood is cured and reenters life outside of the asylum, freed from her obligations to the mental health movement due to her precarious health. The women in Building 10A are a memory, but one that supposedly no longer debilitates or haunts Susan Wood; they are left behind, for now.

Conclusion

The group Ward worked with, the National Mental Health Foundation, created by CO psychiatric aides, would later merge with the National Committee for Mental Hygiene, an organization founded in the 1930s by Clifford Beers, another former psychiatric patient and writer who was a tireless public advocate for mental health.[10] In the early 1950s, this combined organization, now known as Mental Health America, created what they hoped would be a lasting symbol: a bell forged out of chains and other discarded metal restraints from US mental hospitals. Decades later, in a letter to her Chicago literary agent, Mary Jane Ward recalled the ceremony that introduced this bell to the public: "I was the one who gave the history of the bell when it was unveiled in the mid-fifties.

It was a thrilling and exasperating time for me. I was the one who had to cope with Clifford Beers' widow while everyone else had a fine emotional time—Karl Menninger couldn't give his speech for crying" (MJW Collection, Box 6, Folder 6, Ward to Roy Porter, February 4, 1975). This image of the sometimes fragile Ward keeping it together while everyone around her became too emotional to function—including Menninger, the professional—is a telling juxtaposition to Susan Wood's breakdown after seeing the women in 10A. But both the private breakdown and the public show of strength were intertwined parts of Ward's advocacy efforts, which evolved in "crip time" (Samuels). Despite sometimes moving counterclockwise, and confronting problems that she had no way of solving, Ward had clear successes and she remained engaged in ways that her health permitted. "Disability and illness," Ellen Samuels reminds us, "have the power to extract us from linear, progressive time." After an extended period of rest and reconstitution, Ward renewed her connections with people in the mental health community in the 1970s and still held hope that the promises of the 1963 Community Mental Health Act—to provide quality community-based care for people with mental illnesses—would one day be realized. Tracing these connections among Beers, Ward, and their allies reveals a persistent, but not always apparent, legacy of advocacy by people with mental illnesses, for people with mental illnesses.

The Snake Pit shows us that a novel about psychiatric disability can exert significant social influence and can act as a catalyst for progress and change. Yet Ward's later novel *Counterclockwise* cautions us with its very title. Despite linear narratives of progressivism and the advance of medical knowledge, illness recurs. Therapies fail. Social movements burn out. As the history of mental health care in Ward's life and work illustrates, progress and change do not follow a straight path forward. The work of disability advocates is ongoing and always incomplete, but we can take strength (and even inspiration) from the setbacks and successes of those like Ward who have come before us. We work in crip time, bending the long arc of history toward disability justice.

Notes

1. Decades later, Ward still remembered the brutal effect this rejection had: "I've had a red face, redder than it was when The Snake Pit was denounced by the Ober agency [Van Auw's employer]. Maybe you doubt

that I took that rejection seriously but I sure did. If it hadn't been for Ed [Ward's husband] the manuscript would never have got out of the house again" (MJW Collection, Box 6, Folder 3, Ward to Bennett Cerf, April 1962).
2. Memory loss is a major side effect of electroshock therapy, which was part of Ward's treatment while at Rockland State, and her memory loss here may be attributed to the electroshock effects. However, during her second major hospitalization, Ward was treated only with psychoanalysis, not electroshock, and seems to have experienced similar memory problems (MJW Collection, Box 6, Folder 3, Edward Quayle to Bennett Cerf, April 1962).
3. Prendergast has largely retracted and revised this earlier statement, calling it a "flawed prognosis, one that underestimated both the schizophrenic rhetor and the psychiatric establishment that has discovered more effective, if always imperfect, medications" ("Mental Disability and Rhetoricity Retold" 66–67).
4. Virginia's engagement with socialist politics is an important theme which I return to later.
5. Sunaura Taylor's *Beasts of Burden: Animal and Disability Liberation* exposes how "the animal body is integral to the ways disabled bodies and minds are oppressed" and reveals the mechanisms that lurk beneath Ward's metaphor here (xv).
6. When Virginia has this episode of paranoia and is relocated, we also learn that Ward 8 is racially segregated: "The doctor . . . had been favorably impressed by her insisting upon going to a ward where there was no racial discrimination. Virginia had no recollection of any such insistence, but since the doctor had been favorably impressed she decided not to question it" (204). Virginia later shares an item of clothing with a "colored girl" in the integrated Ward 12, which gets her in trouble with a white nurse (205).
7. See Snyder and Mitchell's discussion of these "Eugenic Atlantic" connections in *Cultural Locations of Disability* (Chapter 3).
8. Ward asked her friend Millen Brand, who co-wrote the screenplay for the film *The Snake Pit*, if he would be interested in reading her new novel, then titled "The Death and Burial of the Other Caroline": "I think I should tell you that this one falls into the same general category, in my opinion, as *Counterclockwise*. It isn't autobiographical, though" (MJW Collection, Ward to Brand, 17 July 1968).
9. I haven't found any evidence that this incident was based on an event in Ward's life, but it is possible that it was. No one has written a biography of Ward, and Ward's own autobiography, which was titled "Snake Pits Revisited," appears to have been lost. According to letters in her archive,

Ward circulated the manuscript of her memoir to potential publishers in the early 1970s. But there were no takers, and Ward herself did not plan to add any more material to her papers at Boston University at that time: "I don't want some person pawing through them to quote excerpts for a so-called biography, at least not while I'm able to hear about it and read" (MJW Collection, Box 6, Folder 6, Ward to Roy Porter, 13 February 1975).

10. Beers' autobiography, *A Mind That Found Itself*, was first published in 1908, and his collaboration with psychiatrist Adolf Meyer is a foundational chapter in the history of mental health advocacy in the US. Beers' writing and advocacy was pivotal to securing funding for Johns Hopkins' Henry Phipps Psychiatric Clinic, which opened in 1913 under Meyer's leadership (see also Dain).

Works Cited

Beers, Clifford. *A Mind That Found Itself*. Longmans, Green, and Co., 1908.
Dain, Norman. *Clifford W. Beers, Advocate for the Insane*. University of Pittsburgh Press, 1980.
Deutsch, Albert. *The Shame of the States*. Harcourt, Brace & Co., 1948.
Lensing, Mildred. "Why See a Stigma in a Snake Pit?" *The Courier-Journal*, Louisville, Morning edition, 21 June 1951. Mary Jane Ward Collection, clipping from Scrapbook D.
Litvak, Anatole, dir. *The Snake Pit*. 20th Century Fox, 1948.
Maisel, Albert Q. "Bedlam 1946: Most U.S. Mental Hospitals Are a Shame and Disgrace." *Life Magazine*, 6 May 1946, pp. 102–110+.
Martin, Willa. "She Was Going Crazy—And She Knew It." *The Des Moines Register*, 28 April 1946, p. 8G.
Mary Jane Ward Collection. Howard Gotlieb Archival Research Center. Boston University, Boston, MA, May 2016.
Prendergast, Catherine. "Mental Disability and Rhetoricity Retold: The Memoir on Drugs." *Changing Social Attitudes toward Disability: Perspectives from Historical, Cultural, and Educational Studies*, edited by David Bolt, Routledge, 2015, pp. 60–67.
———. "On the Rhetorics of Mental Disability." *Embodied Rhetorics: Disability in Language and Culture*, edited by James C. Wilson and Cynthia Lewiecki-Wilson, Southern Illinois University Press, 2001, pp. 45–60.
Samuels, Ellen. "Six Ways of Looking at Crip Time." *Disability Studies Quarterly*, vol. 37, no. 3, Summer 2017.
Sareyan, Alex. *The Turning Point: How Persons of Conscience Brought about Major Change in the Care of America's Mentally Ill*. Herald Press, 1994.

Snyder, Sharon L., and David T. Mitchell. *Cultural Locations of Disability*. University of Chicago Press, 2006.
Sotor, Nancy. "'Snake Pit' Was Once Rejected: State Hospitals Benefited from Author's Efforts." *The Arizona Daily Star*, April 1973: D5. Mary Jane Ward Collection, Scrapbook D.
Taylor, Steven J. *Acts of Conscience: World War II, Mental Institutions, and Religious Objectors*. Syracuse University Press, 2009.
Taylor, Sunaura. *Beasts of Burden: Animal and Disability Liberation*. The New Press, 2017.
Ward, Mary Jane. *Counterclockwise*. Henry Regnery, 1969.
———. *The Other Caroline*. Avon, 1970.
———. *The Snake Pit*. Random House, 1946.
Woods, Marjorie Binford. "Mary Jane Ward Declares Her Book Not Autobiography." *The Indianapolis Star*, 14 July 1946, p. 65.
Wright, Frank Leon. *Out of Sight, Out of Mind*. National Mental Health Foundation, 1947.

CHAPTER 8

Alcoholic, Mad, Disabled: Constructing Lesbian Identity in Ann Bannon's "The Beebo Brinker Chronicles"

Tatiana Prorokova

QUEERNESS AND DISABILITY IN THE 1950s–1960s

From the viewpoint of psychology and psychiatry throughout the most part of the twentieth century to be queer was considered a "sexual deviation" and "a classifiable mental illness" that required "diagnosis, treatment, and prevention" (Anderson and Holland 4, 6). Gays and lesbians were commonly classified as mentally impaired people, who were responsible for the "perversity" that they desired or practiced. Queerness was viewed as a contagious disease, for gays and lesbians could spoil the body and the mind of a "decent" person, turning him/her into a mentally impaired one, too.

Equating queerness to a form of illness, society labeled lesbians and gays as disabled and interpreted their sexual desires as manifestations of psychiatric and perhaps even of physical impairments. The form of disability assigned to queers in the mid-twentieth century reflects the biased nature of the term "disabled" discussed by activist Mary Johnson:

T. Prorokova (✉)
University of Marburg, Marburg, Germany

© The Author(s) 2018
E. J. Donaldson (ed.), *Literatures of Madness*, Literary Disability Studies,
https://doi.org/10.1007/978-3-319-92666-7_8

"'disabled' is in the final analysis a political or a moral judgement, based not on anything about the individual in question so much as the viewer's own perception and attitudes about the way society should function" (qtd. in Kudlick 767). This period's medical constructs of queerness as mental disability were also reflected in cultural narratives, even in lesbian pulp fiction. Lesbian pulp fiction, and specifically Ann Bannon's "The Beebo Brinker Chronicles," explored the ways society discriminated against lesbians while simultaneously deploying the image of a lesbian as alcoholic, mad, and disabled. Scrutinizing the ways Bannon's novels portray the lives of queers, this chapter argues that in its tragic stories about lesbians "The Beebo Brinker Chronicles" not only skillfully mirrors the image of 1950s–1960s homophobic America but it also raises even more profound questions concerning lesbian identity and disability. Equating queer identity to psychiatric (and in some cases also physical) disability, Bannon's novels censure the ableist and homophobic attitudes that dominated both socio-cultural and medical discourses at that historical moment. "The Beebo Brinker Chronicles" criticizes the politics and morality that surrounded queer and disability discourses in the mid-twentieth century.

Recent disability scholarship examines this interconnection of queerness and disability. Ellen Samuels argues that "disability has more in common with sexual orientation than with race, ethnicity, or gender" (234). According to Carrie Sandahl:

> [S]exual minorities and people with disabilities share a history of injustice: both have been pathologized by medicine; demonized by religion; discriminated against in housing, employment, and education; stereotyped in representation; victimized by hate groups; and isolated socially, often in their families of origin. Both ... are diverse in terms of race, class, gender, sexuality, religion, political affiliation, and other respects and therefore share many members (e.g., those who are disabled *and* gay), as well as allies. Both have self-consciously created their own enclaves and vibrant subcultural practices. (26, emphasis in original)

What connects disability and sexual orientation? The issue is particularly important to examine bearing in mind the cultural and social equation of queerness and madness (or mental disability): "disabled people are routinely infantilized, constructed as helpless and asexual (particularly in the case of motor impairment) or, alternately, as possessed of uncontrollable sexuality (in the case of developmental disability), much like the stereotypical queer, who takes on an identification as predator as well" (McRuer and Wilkerson 10–11). In the 1950s–1960s, promiscuity was strongly associated with gays and lesbians. Same-sex desires were, hence, seen as an uncontrollable hypersexuality. Medical intervention—it was believed—was necessary.

Another important issue that emerges in tight connection with the problems of queerness and/as disability is that of valid sexuality. Samuels argues that "most people with disabilities, like most queers, do not share their identity with immediate family members and often have difficulty accessing queer or crip culture" (234). In turn, Robert McRuer and Abby L. Wilkerson note: "In a backlash to discourses about coming out of the closet, bisexuals, lesbians, and gay men have been told repeatedly to keep it in the bedroom, as if the mere acknowledgement of a non-heterosexual identity were a gross violation of sexual propriety. Similarly, people with disabilities are told in a thousand ways that their sexuality is unseemly, when its existence is not denied altogether" (8–9). But Bannon's powerful lesbian characters complicate this relationship between queerness and disability. Even at their most self-destructive, Bannon's characters are madwomen who offer the possibility of freedom as they rebel against the discriminatory social structures that will ultimately contain them.

The "Golden Age" of Lesbian Pulp Fiction

As a result of a so-called "paperbacking revolution" of the 1950s–1960s, fiction—including a very distinct literary genre, lesbian pulp fiction—became much more easily accessible and affordable for American readers (Foote 170). Having become known as the "golden age" (Barbara Grier qtd. in Keller 388) of lesbian pulp fiction, 1950–1965 were, paradoxically, the years when "lesbianism was mostly invisible in popular culture" and queerness was viewed as a "crime, sin, or illness" (Keller 386).

The first lesbian novel written prior to the "golden age" was arguably Radclyffe Hall's *The Well of Loneliness* (1928), and only a few books that could be classified as lesbian literature were produced between the 1930s and the 1950s. The decades that followed, however, allowed the readers to glimpse into the new, unknown, and strictly forbidden territory of lesbianism, in the times "when a single kiss could make a woman both an outcast and an outlaw" (Seajay 18). Novels like Tereska Torres's *Women's*

Barracks (1950), Vin Packer's *Spring Fire* (1952), Valerie Taylor's *The Girls in 3-B* (1959), and, of course, Ann Bannon's "The Beebo Brinker Chronicles" (1957–1962) outlined a new tradition in American literature. With the help of these authors, lesbianism started to become more visible in fiction.

That visibility was, however, still problematic. In the mid-twentieth century, homosexuality was virtually equated to mental illness. Therefore, although this literature attempted to reflect queer lives, it could not break the free from heteronormativity or the patriarchal society of the time. These literary depictions did try to make their readers aware of the hard lives that gays and lesbians were secretly leading, but it would be wrong to claim that pulps were meant to start a fight for equality. As Julian Carter writes, "as a genre, [pulp fiction] is less interested in social documentation or naturalist representation than in sensationalism" (584). Lesbian pulps did not always authentically portray queer life. Two factors prevented realistic portrayals in lesbian pulp fiction: first, the authorship, and second, the publisher. As Roberta Yusba observes, "The vast majority of these lesbian novels were written by men, designed to fulfill straight men's fantasies" (qtd. in Nealon 748). Male authors depicted lesbianism as an exotic sexual play for an audience of heterosexual men. It is, hence, unsurprising that in the 1950s lesbian pulps were "often pornographic in character" (Hermes 50).

The publisher also played a considerable role in the formation of lesbian characters in these pulps. While it might seem paradoxical that in the times when being gay or lesbian was a sin/crime/disease there were publishing houses that agreed to release lesbian pulps, there is a clear explanation: the publishers were making money. It was, therefore, particularly important to continue to meet the needs of the reader and sell even more books. This also might partially explain why so many of those novels were pornographic: because many of the readers were heterosexual men. The choice of the covers for many of those books—"featuring girls in some stage of sexual vulnerability" (Foote 180)—only reinforces the pornographic nature of the pulps. At the same time, lesbians were a considerable part of the readership too: "Dog-eared copies of books by Ann Bannon, Valerie Taylor, Artemis Smith, and Paula Christian were passed among friends in lesbian communities. The pulps also reached isolated, small-town lesbians who could read them and see that they were not the only lesbians in the world" (Roberta Yusba qtd. in Nealon 748).

In the 1950s–1960s, no one yet recognized how important the wave of lesbian literature was. Pulps, Yvonne Keller writes, were

> a readily available, popular discourse that put the word *lesbian* in mass circulation as never before. Despite the ambivalence lesbian pulps have often evoked, they are important to lesbian studies because their truly impressive quantities helped create the largest generation of self-defined lesbians up to that point, a group of women who would go on to make history as they, alongside others of nondominant sexuality, midwife the largest gay/lesbian/queer movement in the United States to date. (387, emphasis in original)

The role of lesbian pulps as both literary and cultural texts, thus, should not be underestimated, for these novels helped create lesbian identity and community.

Disabling Lesbians in Ann Bannon's Novels

One of the most prominent authors of lesbian pulps was Ann Bannon (Ann Weldy), whose "The Beebo Brinker Chronicles" made her the "Queen of Lesbian Pulp Fiction" (*Ann Bannon* n.p.). The "Chronicles" consists of five books—*Odd Girl Out* (1957), *I Am a Woman* (1959), *Women in the Shadows* (1959), *Journey to a Woman* (1960), and *Beebo Brinker* (1962)—that scholars call "the premier fictional representation of US lesbian life in the fifties and sixties" (Nealon 748). The novels primarily zero in on the lives of three lesbian women—Laura, Beth, and Beebo—depicting the hardships of finding out one's true identity, learning about sexuality, and struggling to survive in heterosexual, patriarchal America in the middle of the twentieth century.

Ann Bannon's "The Beebo Brinker Chronicles" is quite distinct compared to other contemporary lesbian pulps. Suzanna Danuta Walters asserts:

> These pulps are clearly different from the more overtly sexual material that constituted itself as pornography for men, using lesbian sexuality as quite traditional voyeuristic titillation. The Bannon pulps not only distinguished themselves through their female *authorship* but through their female *audience* as well; an audience that was reading as much for pleasure of self-confirmation as it was for the pleasure of the text. (84, emphasis in original)

Bannon's heroines are at times unsure about their desires or, on the contrary, appear sexually promiscuous, willing to get more of what society deprives them of. Yet, in this case, the strong desires for sexual gratifications that these women have are largely employed "not only to keep the plot moving, but also as a way for characters to discover themselves" (Shapiro 14). The process of discovering oneself, however, is not limited only to the discovery of one's sexuality; it arguably also involves the discovery of what lesbianism is and what it means to be a lesbian in the mid-twentieth century America. My contention is that Bannon's vision of lesbians in the 1950s–1960s as mad and disabled is determined by the dominantly homophobic views in the U.S. in that time.

Bannon's heroines strongly associate their lesbianism with their physicality and sensuality; in other words, the readers observe these women "try[ing] to understand the relationship between their bodies and their desires" (Nealon 755). For example, Beebo, who is introduced to the reader as a "big girl," is represented as a "bodily freak" because she looks too boyish for a woman (Bannon, *Beebo Brinker* 4; Nealon 756). The message that the novels try to convey is, therefore, "that Beebo is not typically feminine and hence that she is possibly a lesbian" (Barale 539). A similar difficulty is experienced by Laura who seems to be always unsure about her gender and sexual desires. She is embarrassed that her breasts do not look feminine enough: "Laura's small breasts bothered her. She would fold her arms over them as much to conceal their presence as to conceal their size. She wished that they were more glamorous, more obviously *there*. In their present shape they seemed only an afterthought" (Bannon, *Odd Girl Out* 19, emphasis in original). Yet later she does not understand how she can be lesbian if, in principle, she is an "ordinary" girl:

> And then she looked down at herself, and nothing seemed wrong. She had breasts and full hips like other girls. She wore lipstick and curled her hair. Her brow, the crook in her arms, the fit of her legs—everything was feminine.... She thought that homosexual women were great strong creatures in slacks with brush cuts and deep voices; unhappy things, standouts in a crowd. She looked back at herself, hugging her bosom as if to comfort herself, and she thought, "I don't want to be a boy. I don't want to be like them. I'm a *girl*. I *am* a girl. That's what I want to be. But if I'm a girl why do I love a girl? What's wrong with me? There must be something wrong with me." (68–69, emphasis in original)

Whether describing a stereotypical butch or a stereotypical femme, Bannon always pays close attention to bodily details. The physical appearance of the heroines becomes the key characteristic that helps them understand their sexuality. Yet this attention to the body tends to reduce lesbian identity to physical features: Bannon's characters are still trapped in a heteronormative framework that determines how they read their own bodies.

In *Women in the Shadows* and *Journey to a Woman*, Bannon suggests that the traditional female body and its "privileges" are off limits to lesbians. As Jack considers starting a "normal" life and having a child, he proposes to Laura. Laura, at first, revolts against the idea, as she finds the thought of living with a man and bearing a child simply repulsive. Nonetheless, she soon agrees to play this heterosexual game, gets married, gets pregnant, gives birth, and seems to have a happy family. It is significant that when her first love Beth returns, hoping to be able to restart their love affair, Laura rejects her. She chooses her family over the liaison with Beth. And although it is made explicit in the novels that the marriage and the birth of the child do not turn Laura into a heterosexual woman and she continues to see other women, those relationships are not particularly foregrounded. What is crucial, however, is that by rejecting Beth—the woman whom she first fell in love with and who, in principle, taught Laura who she was—Laura rejects the lesbian future that she had hoped for in college. Laura's motherhood, therefore, transforms her, placing her firmly in a heteronormative narrative. Significantly, events in Beth's life also support the suggested dichotomy of lesbianism and motherhood in Bannon's work. Beth gets married to Charlie and gives birth to two children. Yet it is only after rejecting this heterosexual model of life and shutting down her maternal instincts that she manages to uncover her true sexuality and be in relationships with other women.

Bannon's most dramatic exploration of how the lesbian body disrupts heteronormativity is the character of Vega in *Journey to a Woman*. Vega is the first woman Beth gets romantically involved with after her arrival in New York. Vega has an overtly homophobic mother; she is also deeply troubled by the sexual relationship with her brother Cleve that took place earlier in their lives and stopped when "they both got scared and ashamed when they got a little older and realized it wasn't very healthy for a brother and sister" to be so "abnormally close" (Bannon, *Journey to a Woman* 210). An earlier scene suggests that Cleve might still have an "abnormal" affection for Vega: "He sounded almost jealous.

He sounded almost like a man warning another man away from his wife, not a friend warning another friend of his sister's emotional quirks" (50). All these circumstances undoubtedly make Vega hide her true self. She eventually opens up to Beth, yet realizes that Beth would never be able to truly love her: after an unsuccessful operation related to her tuberculosis, Vega's body is disfigured. During a romantic scene, Vega reveals her fear that Beth would never desire a body like hers:

> Beth couldn't stand it any longer. She rushed toward Vega, but Vega very swiftly and unexpectedly opened her diaphanous dressing gown, holding it wide away from herself so that Beth should see every detail of her white body.
> Beth stopped abruptly, within a foot of her goal, and stared. She made a small inarticulate sound, and Vega searched her face with horrible anxiety, "If you can make love to that," she whispered, "then I'll believe you love me. I'll accept it."
> She was a complex of scars that twisted every which way over her chest, like yards of pink ribbon in snarls. She had no breasts, and the operation to remove her lung had left a bad welt that Beth returned to once or twice with a prickle of revulsion. Even Vega's dainty little abdomen had its share. And the bones, the poor sharp bones without the ordinary smooth envelope of tender flesh that most girls take for granted and even rail against when there's too much. Vega's bones were all pitifully plain and frankly outlined.
> Beth put her trembling hands over her mouth, to stifle her horror, and let the tears flood from her eyes. (Bannon, *Journey to a Woman* 66)

By providing such a graphic image of Vega's disfigured body during this sexual encounter, Bannon explicitly connects lesbian desire and disability. In a society where heterosexuality is viewed as the only norm, lesbian bodies are deviant bodies.

Vega's body is *extraordinary*, and Beth's repulsion at seeing it revealed reflects her ambiguous participation in the larger cultural construction of ableist, heteronormative traditional femininity: Vega's body becomes a "visual assault … a shocking spectacle to the normate eye" (Garland-Thomson 26). Having pointed out "the desire to split bodies into two immutable categories: whole and incomplete, abled and disabled, normal and abnormal, functional and dysfunctional," Lennard J. Davis contends: "Normality has to protect itself by looking into the maw of disability and then recovering from that glance" (129, 48).

Similarly, Rosemarie Garland-Thomson writes, "To be suddenly confronted with a person extraordinary enough to provoke our most baroque stares withers our ready curiosity and we turn away, snuffing out the possibility for mutual recognition" (79). Beth's looking away in an attempt to avoid the disabled queer body is ambivalent yet symbolic in this scene. First, the "whole" body that Beth craves for can be seen as a heteronormative construct. Beth, therefore, while deeply censuring the frames that heterosexual patriarchal America puts her in, dictates similar discriminating rules to the women that she falls in love with. Her non-acceptance of a disabled female body reveals her own hypocrisy toward femininity and lesbianism, for both, according to Beth, can be constructed only by "perfectly shaped" women. Second, Beth's rejection of Vega here can be read as a rejection of the queer disabled body. Beth's verdict concerning Vega is apparent: the disabled woman is not a "real" woman in the eyes of Beth. Beth laments: "Why didn't you tell me? Why did you spring it on me that way? *I could have taken it, if you'd only let me know. If you'd only prepared me a little for it*" (Bannon, *Journey to a Woman* 67, emphasis added). Vega is, however, convinced that Beth is being insincere: "No, what you mean is, you *could have controlled the look on your face*. You could have made up a kind little speech and said it right away, before *your silence spoke for you*" (67, emphasis added).

After the women have had sex, the reader finds Beth tormented by the unexpected yet inevitable end of the relationship that, crucially, Beth fully blames on Vega's physical appearance. While Vega is asleep, Beth is lying next to her, pitying herself for such an unfair outcome: "She [Beth] stared into the night and cursed the unkind fate that had promised so much and delivered so little.... She even went so far as to imagine the young girls in the next few rooms and to wonder if it were possible to see them, to make friends" (Bannon, *Journey to a Woman* 69–70). After the women part in the morning, Beth continues to justify her actions and her rather relieved if not happy reaction to finally being alone: "*Jesus, I wanted to make love to a woman, not a carved-up scarecrow!*" (70, emphasis in original). Beth is not just selfish. She appears to embody a dangerous ideology of discrimination and humiliation of women with physical disabilities.

The scene above comments not only on the issue of disability but also on lesbianism that appears reduced in several ways. First of all, the scene suggests that lesbian love is purely physical, overtly hinting at the promiscuity of lesbians. And Beth's reaction vividly illustrates and supports this viewpoint: "And now, with brutal suddenness, she [Beth] had seen her [Vega's] mutilated body, repellent and pitiable, and she could not find her desire any more. It had dissipated" (68). And although Beth tries to persuade herself that love is not just about the body, she soon gives up: "She had wanted a whole woman, warm and yielding. She had dreamed that her hands would touch the smooth perfumed flesh of a body that knew how to love. It had been a vital part of her desire…" (68). Despite the fact that the women do make love eventually, it is clear that Vega does not interest Beth anymore. Thus, through the portrayal of an impaired lesbian body and its ultimate rejection by Beth, the scene insists that lesbian love is just about sex and body aesthetics. On the other hand, it is plausible to argue that in "The Beebo Brinker Chronicles" Vega metaphorically stands for a general image of a lesbian woman who is vehemently rejected by society. She is not perceived as a true woman because she is lesbian, and it is crucial that she is deprived of her breasts—one of the key body parts that could biologically define her as a woman—which, it can be argued, is a punishment for her disobedience to the traditional social norms. In this way, a lesbian woman becomes equated to a physically disabled woman, as she is, in principle, no "true" woman in a traditional, patriarchal, and heterosexual sense of the word.

MADWOMEN IN "THE BEEBO BRINKER CHRONICLES"

The novels also explore the mental disability of lesbians, often portraying heroines as unstable or mad. For example, during one of the quarrels with Laura, Beth is characterized as a "madwoman": "The water clung to Beth's hair and dripped from her face and for a moment she thought she would explode with rage. But it came to her slowly that she could not get any angrier than she had just been. She hadn't the strength and there was no way to express it without behaving like a madwoman" (Bannon, *Journey to a Woman* 167). As if sensing the equivocacy of the moment, Bannon reassures the reader right away: "She was not that kind" (167). Although some of her actions hint at mental instability, Beth is not truly mad.

Another scene that associates lesbianism with madness is included later in *Journey to a Woman*, when unable to cope with all the hate and betrayal that fills her life, Vega shoots herself. Earlier in the novel, her brother insisted that Vega's mental instability was largely provoked by alcoholism.

Sharing with Beth that Vega cannot "'go to sleep at night without a bottle by [her] bed'," Cleve adds: "'She is sick' ... 'I don't mean the TB, I mean up here', and he tapped his head at the temple" (Bannon, *Journey to a Woman* 52). Vega is ruined by her homophobic mother, jealous brother, declining modeling business, drinking, and, perhaps more importantly than all that, Beth's betrayal. Vega does not "give a damn any more what happens to [her]" (196). Before committing suicide, Vega is determined to kill Beth. Pointing the gun at her ex-lover, Vega confesses:

> "I spit on them [her family] all," Vega said. "Do you wonder why I'm not screaming, Beth?" she added in her voice that was calm with the serenity of madness. "I've done all my screaming, that's why. I did it all at Cleve and Mother. And the doctors, the first few weeks I was in the hospital. There isn't any left in me. Gramp is dead, Beth. And Mother is dying, just like all those neglected cats. Cleve doesn't count, he never amounted to anything. I have only you now. I have your whole future in my hand, here. And it's going to pay for my whole past." She shook the gun back and forth. "I have your life and your death, I have infinite power over you, and nothing, not the tears or begging or hypocritical love or fancy excuses, is going to save you. Nothing." (196)

Vega's attempt to kill Beth is a symbolic action that she has to take to avenge all those who rejected her for her sexual orientation, impaired body, disobedience to the imposed social norms, and being who she is. She is finally depicted as an empowered woman who seems capable of taking the situation in her hands, to be the one who sets the rules. Her ultimate suicide, however, not only reveals her mental weakness and ultimate instability. It also reflects the real situation in 1950s–1960s' America, when a lesbian woman was voiceless. The image of Vega with a gun is an emancipatory—and thus surreal for that time—portrayal that Bannon shatters into pieces at the end of the novel. From an emancipated woman, Vega turns into a symbol of self-destructive power.

The novels also include other more explicit images of lesbian heroines as madwomen and depict mental disability as a result of alcoholism. The problem of alcoholism is entwined as a warning sign throughout the novels as the heroines find out about lesbian bars and start to visit them frequently. Alcoholism as a serious issue is not explicitly discussed in relation to the bars; the bars are, instead, used to introduce the gay bar culture of the 1950s–1960s. Yet it is clear that frequent visits to such bars and heavy consumption of alcohol could lead to alcoholism, which is what happens to Beebo. Through her problem with alcohol, the novels vividly create the image of Beebo as a madwoman. In *Women in the Shadows*, Laura writes about Beebo in her diary: "*Sometimes she's not rational. But what can I do?*" (5, emphasis in original). Already the first pages of the novel describe the aftermath of a party (these seem to happen often in Laura and Beebo's apartment): "Beebo was still hungover from that long night of dreary festivity. Jack was always hung-over, so he didn't count. As for Laura, she had learned from Beebo to drink too much herself, and she was learning at the same time how it feels the next day. *Bad*. Plain bad" (6, emphasis in original). Alcoholism destroys Beebo: she disgusts Laura, who seems to stay with Beebo only because she is afraid that Beebo will do something horrible to herself once Laura is gone. Even more importantly, the scene portrays the dangerous problem of co-drinking, warning that living with an alcoholic might turn Laura into one herself. While Beebo's friends explicitly tell her that she has problems—"You're an alcoholic" (17)—she dismisses them, believing she can control her drinking. As a tall butch with a rather strong body, Beebo stands out as atypically female. And her alcohol use calls further attention to her extraordinary body. Even Laura does not feel comfortable going out with Beebo—particularly so when the latter is tipsy:

> It was true that Laura was ashamed to go anywhere out of Greenwich Village with her… Beebo, nearly six feet of her, with her hair cropped short and her strange clothes and her gruff voice. And when she flirted with the clerks! Laura had been afraid more than once that they would call the police and drag Beebo to jail. But it had never happened. Still, there was always a first time, and *if she had a couple of drinks before they went*, Laura wasn't at all sure she could handle her. (29–30, emphasis added)

Beebo's addiction hurts her relationship with Laura. She becomes paranoid: Beebo does not trust Laura and suspects that she is seeing someone else. Beebo's aggressive behavior that results from her continuous consumption of alcohol pulls the two women apart. Perhaps sensing the problem, Beebo tells Laura that she was attacked by several men who brutally beat and raped her (for being a butch) and then killed their dog Nix. The reader finds out later that Beebo faked the attack and killed the dog herself—"[s]liced him in half with that big chef's knife you had in the kitchen table drawer" (Bannon, *Women in the Shadows* 144). After the fake rape, Beebo continues to put pressure on Laura, blaming her for not being caring enough: "Where the hell have you been? ... I'm sick and miserable, I've just been through hell, and you can't even come home from work to make any dinner for me" (Bannon, *Women in the Shadows* 62). In turn, Laura is irritated that Beebo continues to drink, believing that it is alcohol consumption that ruins their relationship. Beebo skillfully yet basely manipulates Laura, exclaiming: "I can't stay sober if you don't love me" (63). But Laura understands the game now: "You're only saying that to make me feel guilty. To put the blame on *me* instead of on yourself where it belongs!" (63, emphasis in original).

Beebo is clearly a victim of homophobic society; yet she is also portrayed as a victim of herself and her internalized homophobia. Her inability to believe in happiness with a faithful lover drives her crazy and makes her harm herself and those around her. Significantly, having found out that Beebo was paranoid and committed violence only to keep her closer, Laura realizes how much she loves Beebo and how much Beebo needed her when Laura had her doubts concerning their relationship. While for their friends this revelation turns into a shock, as they expect Laura to turn away from Beebo for good, Laura is furious at them for drawing such conclusions. For example, after learning that Beebo killed their dog Nix, their gay friend Jack exclaims: "Damn silly hysterical female. I thought Beebo had more sense than most women" (Bannon, *Women in the Shadows* 146). In turn, Laura responds: "'Just because she's not *like* most women?' Laura cried. 'Jack, you make me furious! The more mannish a woman is, the more sense you think she's got! God! Beebo's *sick*! She's sick or she wouldn't have done it. When I think what she must have gone through, I—oh...' And she wept again, silently and hard. 'She's no damn silly female. You damn silly *man*!'" (146, emphasis in original). Laura's reaction is crucial, as she is literally the only character in the novel who sympathizes with Beebo, for she understands that Beebo has fallen victim to various circumstances. First, it is social judgment, mockery, and violent non-acceptance of her being a butch. It is pivotal that while inventing the story of her fictitious pummeling and rape, Beebo shares with Laura: "I don't know why it didn't happen to me years sooner. Nearly every butch I know gets it one way or another. Sooner or later they catch up with you" (53). She adds: "The goddam sonofabitch toughs who think it's smart to pick fights with Lesbians.

They ask you who the hell do you think you are, going around in pants all the time. They say if you're going to wear pants and act like a man you can damn well fight like a man. And they jump you for laughs... God" (53). While the story is invented in this context, one realizes that what Beebo is saying is far from being fiction for many lesbian women. She then adds, "those bastards followed me right up here and tried to prove what men they are" (53), overtly hinting at rape. Second, Beebo is ultimately an outsider even in the circle of her friends, who either consider her plain alcoholic and mad, or who believe, like Jack, that being a non-feminine lesbian, she is supposed to be as "sensible" as a man. These views foreground the strong influence of patriarchy in the U.S. in the 1950s–1960s on the construction of social behavior, even among gays and lesbians; moreover, it is deeply humiliating to women who are apparently seen by heterosexual *and* gay men as emotionally unstable and unable to control themselves. Finally, Beebo is betrayed by the closest person she has—Laura—who mistakenly believed that alcohol was an annoying rather than dangerous and destructive habit and that the mockery that Beebo had to live with because of her unusual appearance did not cause any emotional pain.

Having realized that alcoholism and multiple other life situations led to Beebo's instability, Laura is the only one who can diagnose Beebo correctly. Unlike Jack who considers Beebo "hysterical," Laura concludes that Beebo is "sick." The difference in interpreting Beebo's condition is pivotal, for while everyone else believes that Beebo is only acting weird, thus reinforcing the *socio-culturally* constructed image of a (lesbian) woman as perpetually mad, Laura is the only one to identify her condition as illness rather than an ordinary behavior of an a priori hysterical and unstable woman. One might speculate that Beebo's desire to remain Laura's lover is her last chance to stay mentally healthy. Yet Beebo's aggression looks similar to domestic violence. Having turned this violence upon herself for the most part (excluding the dog), Beebo appears manipulative and self-destructive, driven by the desire of physical control over a weaker person. Laura's inadvertent pathologizing (or diagnosis) of Beebo, in turn, seems rather dangerous, for it erases the socio-political contributing factors of Beebo's madness, unintentionally reinforcing the image of a lesbian woman as a madwoman.

Through the occasional yet powerful images of physically and mentally disabled lesbian women, "The Beebo Brinker Chronicles" seems to reinforce the concept of deviation imposed by the homophobic society of the 1950s–1960s. Yet the novels also overtly claim that it is exactly because of the homophobic views and unwillingness of society to accept lesbians and gays, provide them with equal rights, and guarantee a normal life, that queer people were unable to organize their lives in a proper way, be happy, and fully accept themselves.

Conclusion

Ann Bannon's "The Beebo Brinker Chronicles" is undoubtedly a valuable contribution to lesbian literature. Through her somewhat naive, at times short-sighted, yet always resolute heroines, Bannon provides her readers with an overview of lesbian lives in 1950s–1960s' America. From the social non-acceptance in smaller towns to the promising life in Greenwich Village, New York, "The Beebo Brinker Chronicles" reveals what it means to fight for who you really are, for your identity, sexuality, and social belonging.

The novels obviously cannot ignore the social tension that existed around the issue of queerness, and, through the portrayal of some of the heroines as alcoholic, mad, and disabled, they reveal the complexity of lesbianism in the mid-twentieth century. Thus, the reader witnesses how one of the main heroines—Beebo Brinker—becomes an alcoholic and almost ruins the life of her partner. Beebo's jealousy that is triggered by alcohol turns into an obsession that transforms her into a madwoman. Another heroine, Vega, is depicted as alcoholic, obsessed, suicidal, and mad. Pivotally, through the depiction of Vega, the novel not only draws the connection between lesbianism and madness, but it also links lesbianism to physical disability. Vega is not only a mentally disabled woman, but she is also a physically disabled one (in both cases, as the novel suggests, *because* she is lesbian). It is symbolic that an operation left her without her breasts (the part of the female body that from a biological perspective signifies female femininity). Vega, therefore, visually becomes "disabled" as a *woman*.

In Ann Bannon's "The Beebo Brinker Chronicles," 1950s–1960s America lesbianism was equated to physical and mental disability. The novels portray lesbians as addicted, alcoholic, and physically or psychologically impaired women. And it is crucial that alcoholism is used as an anchor to explain madness and disability. On the one hand, alcohol becomes the choice of lesbians who, unwilling or unable to cope with social pressures, turn to a bottle to reach peace with themselves and society.

On the other hand, alcoholism inevitably leads to their madness. In the 1950s–1960s, according to Bannon's novels, queer women are disabled by the demands of traditional femininity and heteronormative culture.

Works Cited

Anderson, Joel, and Elise Holland. "The Legacy of Medicalising 'Homosexuality': A Discussion on the Historical Effects of Non-heterosexual Diagnostic Classifications." *Sensoria: A Journal of Mind, Brain & Culture*, vol. 11, no. 1, 2015, pp. 4–15.

Bannon, Ann. www.annbannon.com. Accessed 5 June 2017.

———. *Beebo Brinker*. 1962. Cleis Press, 2001.

———. *I Am a Woman*. 1959. Cleis Press, 2002.

———. *Journey to a Woman*. 1960. Naiad Press, 1986.

———. *Odd Girl Out*. 1957. Cleis Press, 2001.

———. *Women in the Shadows*. 1959. Naiad Press, 1986.

Barale, Michèle Aina. "When Jack Blinks: Si(gh)ting Gay Desire in Ann Bannon's *Beebo Brinker*." *The Lesbian Issue*, special issue of *Feminist Studies*, vol. 18, no. 3, 1992, pp. 533–49.

Carter, Julian. "Gay Marriage and Pulp Fiction: Homonormativity, Disidentification, and Affect in Ann Bannon's Lesbian Novels." *GLQ: A Journal of Lesbian and Gay Studies*, vol. 15, no. 4, 2009, pp. 583–609.

Davis, Lennard J. *Enforcing Normalcy: Disability, Deafness, and the Body*. Verso, 1995.

Foote, Stephanie. "Deviant Classics: Pulps and the Making of Lesbian Print Culture." *Signs*, vol. 31, no. 1, 2005, pp. 169–90.

Garland-Thomson, Rosemarie. *Staring: How We Look*. Oxford University Press, 2009.

Hermes, Joke. "Sexuality in Lesbian Romance Fiction." *Feminist Review*, no. 42, 1992, pp. 49–66.

Keller, Yvonne. "'Was It Right to Love Her Brother's Wife So Passionately?': Lesbian Pulp Novels and U.S. Lesbian Identity, 1950–1965." *American Quarterly*, vol. 57, no. 2, 2005, pp. 385–410.

Kudlick, Catherine J. "Disability History: Why We Need Another 'Other'." *The American Historical Review*, vol. 108, no. 3, 2003, pp. 763–93.

McRuer, Robert, and Abby L. Wilkerson. "Introduction." *GLQ: A Journal of Lesbian and Gay Studies*, vol. 9, no. 1–2, 2003, pp. 1–23.

Nealon, Christopher. "Invert-History: The Ambivalence of Lesbian Pulp Fiction." *Is There Life after Identity Politics?*, special issue of *New Literary History*, vol. 31, no. 4, 2000, pp. 745–64.

Samuels, Ellen Jean. "My Body, My Closet: Invisible Disability and the Limits of Coming-Out Discourse." *GLQ: A Journal of Lesbian and Gay Studies*, vol. 9, no. 1–2, 2003, pp. 233–55.

Sandahl, Carrie. "Queering the Crip or Cripping the Queer?: Intersections of Queer and Crip Identities in Solo Autobiographical Performance." *GLQ: A Journal of Lesbian and Gay Studies*, vol. 9, no. 1–2, 2003, pp. 25–56.

Seajay, Carol. "Pulp and Circumstance." *The Women's Review of Books*, vol. 23, no. 1, 2006, pp. 18–19.

Shapiro, Ellen. "Review: The Politic and the Erotic." *The Women's Review of Books*, vol. 1, no. 9, 1984, pp. 13–14.

Walters, Suzanna Danuta. "As Her Hand Crept Slowly Up Her Thigh: Ann Bannon and the Politics of Pulp." *Social Text*, vol. 23, 1989, pp. 83–101.

CHAPTER 9

Seeing Words, Hearing Voices: Hannah Weiner, Dora García, and the Poetic Performance of Radical Dis/Humanism

Andrew McEwan

On December 29, 1977, a short-lived New York cable TV show composed of readings by contemporary poets called *Public Access Poetry* aired Hannah Weiner's performance of an excerpt from her ongoing series of poems, *Clairvoyant Journal*. Hannah Weiner was an American poet and performance artist associated with a number of avant-garde movements including the Fluxus art and performance group of the 1960s and 1970s, and the Language school of avant-garde poetry that gained prominence in the 1970s and 1980s. In the *Public Access Poetry* recording, Weiner begins her performance by confronting the viewer with a statement about her poetic process: "I see big words. They appear on my forehead, in the air, in space, on the page." Weiner called these linguistic experiences "clairvoyance" and described the writing that came from them "clair style" (*Hannah Weiner's Open House* 122; hereafter *Open House*). For the TV performance, Weiner explains that the "big words" are performed by Sharon Mattlin, the self-critical little words— "that sometimes make nasty comments"—are voiced by Margaret

A. McEwan (✉)
St. Catharines, Ontario, Canada

DeCoursey, while Weiner "reads herself." The three speakers proceed to perform the beginning of the published version of the journal, which starts with an entry dated February 28, 1974: "GO FOR A SAMAHDI / *feel different* // BEGIN / BEGIN WITH ME" (*Clairvoyant Journal* 2/28).[1] Wiener's *Public Access Poetry* performance of mental otherness restages the interruptions of an embodied, non-normative cognitive experience within a poetic community and interrupts the liberal poetics of self-sufficiency, single voicing, and independence. Weiner situates her cognitive poetic experience as both internally and externally plural, with all the interruptions of meaning that this entails.

Thirty-seven years after Hannah Weiner's *Public Access Poetry* performance, the Spanish artist Dora García staged a similar recorded reading of *Clairvoyant Journal* as part of her *Hearing Voices Café* project. *The Hearing Voices Café* forms a part of García's ongoing work to explore the radical disruptions created by outsider voices and aesthetics, which she groups under the project title *Mad Marginal*. García's artist's statement about *The Hearing Voices Café* announces that it "revolves primarily around exchange, research and destigmatization" (*The Hearing Voices Café*; hereafter *Café*). The installation formally ran out of a Hamburg café during October and November of 2014, "as a public meeting place for voice-hearers and their friends, people interested in the phenomenon, and coincidental guests" (*Café*). García writes that the work was formally composed of "detailed information material, a regularly updated newspaper and an audio work." Through such means, *The Hearing Voices Café* staged an interruption in both the normative institutional gallery experience and the regular functioning of the café. The audio work to which García refers is the recording of the multi-voiced performance that she staged of Hannah Weiner's *Clairvoyant Journal*. Through this link, the *Café* places Weiner's "clairvoyant" mental experience within a public space as a performance of the non-normative self as multiple and interruptive in a similar way to Weiner's own performance on *Public Access Poetry*. The blurring of the public and the institutional, the aesthetic, and the social, the artistic vision and the community organization, all contribute to a project of radical exploratory research and multi-modal aesthetic experience. These works perform a critical interruption within liberal humanism from the perspective of mental otherness that does not figure those who experience such states and stigmatizations as poetic tropes, but as co-researchers. In the dialogue García's work forms with Hannah Weiner and other psychiatric outsiders, we may read both her own and Weiner's performances as mutually informing acts of radically resistant mental and aesthetic alterity.

Hannah Weiner's multi-voiced *Clairvoyant Journal* and Dora García's *Hearing Voices Café* question normative linguistic performance and the boundaries of individual subjectivity. Through these textual artistic practices, both Weiner and García stage linguistic disruptions of the clean separations between inside and outside, sanity and insanity, rationality and irrationality, singularity and plurality, and experience and performance that regulate normative mental and aesthetic embodiments. I read these performances in conversation with the critiques of residual liberal humanist subjectivity as proposed by critical disability studies, as well as emergent posthumanisms. Weiner and García's linguistic–aesthetic performances question the status of the liberal humanist subject and gesture toward a performed posthumanism through interruptive multiplicities instantiated by non-normative mental experience and socially stigmatized mental disability. I read posthumanism and disability studies critiques of liberal humanism through Weiner's interruptive performance and García's resistance to the marginalizations of the gallery as institution in order to theorize what I call radical dis/humanism. This concept is informed by Lennard Davis' term "dismodernism," which describes an alternative to both postmodern and humanist identity politics through the consideration of the destabilizing nature of disability as an identity category when productively universalized as a condition of all life (*Bending Over Backwards* 27–32). Tempering Davis' universalization, though, I will employ Daniel Goodley and Katherine Runswick-Cole's notion of "dis/humanism" to think through posthumanism from a critical disability studies perspective. What I am calling radical dis/humanism is the avant-garde performance of an immanent and non-binary dis/humanism within a humanist framework that, following García's reading of the anti-institutional psychiatrist Franco Basaglia, disrupts institutional stasis and demands a redefinition of relations from an outsider and avant-garde perspective.

From Humanism to Radical Dis/Humanism

Interventions within disability studies under the terms of critical disability studies and crip theory have contested the position of the able-bodied and able-minded ideal subject as a model for rights, citizenship, and rhetorical authority. These interventions seek resistant models for rethinking the exclusions of liberal humanism. Nevertheless, the human, as a contemporary regulatory ideal within rights discourse, remains a seemingly inevitable focal point for working toward the pragmatic matters of healthcare, rights, and recognition of disabled persons. While some theorists advocate for a widening of the terms for which bodies count as human within the structure of liberal democracy, many seek alternatives to the very terms of the human and its complicity with violent historical and contemporary exclusions. Theorist Tobin Siebers argues that dominant ableist culture disqualifies certain bodies and embodied minds through the individualization of disabling processes and the naturalization of otherness (*Disability Aesthetics* 23–25). Siebers argues that "disability studies transforms ... basic assumptions about identity, ideology, politics, meaning, social justice, and the body" (*Disability Theory* 1). As such, Siebers' critique of ableism as a dominant ideology that segregates, regulates, and individualizes bodies through the arbitrary hierarchical construction of ability and disability extends to a widespread critique of seemingly "natural" assumptions about what constitutes the "human" as a "social and political actor" (*Disability Theory* 188). Siebers writes that whereas

> The liberal tradition represents citizens as autonomous, rational beings ... a focus on disability provides another perspective by representing human society not as a collection of autonomous beings, some of whom will lose their independence, but as a community of dependent frail bodies that rely on others for survival. (*Disability Theory* 182)

Therefore, disability studies provide a productive way to view and critique the function of the human within liberal humanism from the perspective of those bodies and minds excluded by liberal humanist frameworks for recognizing rights and agency. Significantly, Siebers gestures toward the integral notions of frailty, community, and dependence that disability centralizes as necessary to social and political life. The liberal humanist focus on autonomy and rationality stigmatizes certain types of interdependence through ableist social, political, and physical barriers. Disability centralizes interdependence in opposition to the liberal humanist notion of independence and performs a vital critique of the norms assumed as constitutive of the human.

In relation to Hannah Weiner's poetic work and Dora García's multi-modal aesthetic research of mental and artistic outsider status,

I employ the terms of mental disability studies as a theoretical model with which to interrogate the ableist cultural ideals of the human that both Weiner's and García's work productively problematize. In using the term "mental disability," I follow the work of Catherine Prendergast and Margaret Price, both of whom group a wide range of non-normative mental conditions and states under this category in order to place focus on those groups who experience rhetorical and social disabling based on perceived conditions of the mind. Catherine Prendergast writes that "to be disabled mentally is to be disabled rhetorically" (202). Prendergast groups mental disability through the diminishment of rhetoricity-based speculation upon states of mind. This draws attention to the process by which judgment about mental states socially and politically excludes persons deemed to be non-normative or disabled. Following Prendergast, Price argues that the category of mental disability functions as a relevant coalition not because of any inherent truth to the classifications of mental impairment or of the disabling locations being within the mind, but rather because such groups experience "disempowerment as rhetors" through speculation on mental states (304). In this, Price resists speaking of impairment as a contextually independent condition. With the mind as a commonly conceptualized location of individuality and self-singularity, mental disability provides an especially productive perspective from which to interrogate and resist the normative liberal humanist construction of the human.

As with the above line of critique from disability studies, contemporary and emergent posthumanisms consist of a variety of divergent strands of thought that are united by a shared interest in thinking through the impasse of the liberal humanist subject. In her book *The Posthuman*, Rosi Braidotti argues that, "Post-humanism is the historical moment that marks the end of the opposition between Humanism and anti-humanism and traces a different discursive framework, looking more affirmatively towards new alternatives" (37). This affirmative, generative approach marks much of posthumanism's distinction from the anti-humanism of the poststructuralists. It offers a way to think through anti-humanism to generate new alternatives for the "basic unit of reference" of the human as proposed by humanism. It asks how we can constitute subjects in a way that does not partake in the liberal humanist project of individualism and self-singularity.

Within disability studies, Lennard Davis incorporates posthumanism in his critique of the supposition of the inherent value of working toward a more equitable expansion of the human as a necessity in the project of resistance to ableist culture. In speaking to the dehumanization of severely disabled persons, Davis argues, following Giorgio Agamben, that we may see this exclusion as the basis on which the liberal state, and its notion of the human, is based (*The End of Normal* 29). As disability is excluded so as to constitute the normative human subject, Davis suggests that we face great resistance when we attempt to incorporate abjected bodies and embodied minds within the contemporary liberal human subject necessary for the purpose of leveraging rights. Nevertheless, Davis advocates for the seemingly contradictory position of what he calls "dismodernism," which

> advocates the defining of the posthuman by the inclusion of the abject, bare life, the disabled—in other words, including the imperfect, the interdependent, the non-ideal in the very sphere of the polis. (*The End of Normal* 29)

As such, "dismodernism" proposes a pragmatic process of recuperation in the face of liberal humanism's exclusions. Davis contends that frailty and disability constitute a mode of being for all subjects in certain moments and situations (*The End of Normal* 27). Davis extends this critique by universalizing the experience of disability as constitutive of all life. Through a universalization of disability, Davis attempts to destabilize the humanist subject and the normative body. As such, "dismodernism" resists the incorporation of disability into the liberal humanist subject, though "dismodernism" nevertheless remains a politically limited approach as a result of its universalization.

Similar to Davis' "dismodernism," Daniel Goodley and Katherine Runswick-Cole advocate for "dis/humanism" as a disability-studies-based posthumanism. "Dis/humanism," they write,

> acknowledges the possibilities offered by disability to trouble, reshape and re-fashion traditional conceptions of the human ... while simultaneously asserting disabled people's humanity (to assert normative, often traditional, understandings of personhood). (2)

In this dis/humanism maintains a firm grasp on the specificity of experience of disabled bodies, and the very pragmatic desire for subjectivity under the contemporary terms of the human of liberal humanism.

Goodley and Runswick-Cole assert the twin ambition to also maintain disability's critique of the normative human so as to work toward an ontological reconfiguration of the basis for political relations. Such a pragmatic twofold strategy, they argue, "recognize[s] the ambivalent relationship that disabled people ... have towards traditional notions of the human" (3). This "dis/humanism," with its constituent forward slash, recognizes both the power of the "dis" of "disability" to disrupt the configurations in which it is politically inserted, but also the "human" side, which remains both pragmatically desirable and to some degree bracketed, though available when the socio-political context calls for it (5). They argue that this approach is not "oppositional," but rather "frictional" (5). Goodley and Runswick-Cole base dis/humanism's link to posthumanism in Rosi Braidotti and other posthumanist projects (5–8). They argue that

> What it means to feel human is also a matter of how one is meant to feel as a human in contemporary society. We suggest that, like post-human interventions, becoming dis/human allows us to interrogate the kinds of human currently valued by society: humankinds that are contested and directly contravened by the presence of disability. (8)

With what they describe as an assemblage of the "dis" and the "human" to account for both a critical and an undermining perspective twinned with a pragmatic and normative desire for recognition (11), Goodley and Runswick-Cole offer a form of posthumanism that questions the status of the liberal humanist individual as universal and natural.

In the following discussion of Hannah Wiener's *Public Access Poetry* performance of her *Clairvoyant Journal* and Dora García's *Hearing Voices Café*, I develop a modification of "dis/humanism," which I will call *radical dis/humanism*. The politics of this project, and the addition of the word "radical," derives from García's employment of the radical psychiatry of the Italian anti-institutional psychiatrist Franco Basaglia. In the radical dis/humanism practiced in Weiner and García's work, the problematizing "dis" and the normative "human" compose a poetics of radical multi-voiced interruption. The performances of Weiner and García display dependencies, fatigues, interconnections, resistances, and disruptions from a radical, and even avant-garde, outsider position. They form poetic resistance to ableist exclusions of the supposedly non-normative mind within public space.

Clairvoyant Interruptions

On the first interior page of the original printed version of Hannah Weiner's *Clairvoyant Journal*, the following note appears surrounded by blank white space:

> I SEE words on my forehead. IN THE AIR on other people on the typewriter on the page These appear in the text in CAPITALS or *italics*

As with her introductory statement on *Public Access Poetry*, Weiner stresses the meaning and importance of her method of reproducing her mental and perceptual experience of clairvoyance. In this, Weiner stages a poetics of mental non-singularity, mental otherness, and resistance to both traditional poetic and medical readings of her linguistic "clairvoyance." In an explanation of her experiences, techniques, and theories titled "Mostly About the Sentence," Weiner writes that she began to see words during August 1972 (*Open House* 122). First, she describes, they "appeared singly" (122). The word "WRONG" appeared to her, followed later by two word phrases such as "NO-ALONE" (122). Frustrated by the apparent incompleteness of the phrase "*not* alone," and its isolation from further meaning, Weiner writes that she "got down on knees and begged or prayed please let me see a complete sentence" (123). We may read Weiner's desire for singularity and completion of meaning as a normative desire within the non-normative perceptual experience. The linguistic visions, though, become for Weiner a poetic process to reproduce the experience of an interruptive and multi-voiced self, which in the poem appears as interrupted voices and text. Although such visions were medically codified as psychotic schizophrenia,[2] Weiner resisted the medical and ableist reading of her specific experience and instead employed modes that reproduced her experience as disruptive linguistic performance. I read this as Weiner's staging of radical dis/humanism from an avant-garde and mentally othered position.

Hannah Weiner's project of journaling her experiences in *Clairvoyant Journal* forms what Patrick Durgin has described as a "phenomenologically complex realism" (*Open House* 15), insofar as it seeks to realistically represent her daily experience in which linguistic visions perpetually interrupt her thoughts and perceptions. Weiner characterizes the three consistent voices of the poem as follows: "The capital words, which give instructions, the italics, which make comments, and the ordinary type, which is me just trying to get through the day" (Bernstein and Weiner 146). Such an arrangement figures the perceptual and cognitive experience of the individual as a clearly subdivided assemblage of voices. When performed on *Public Access Poetry*, Weiner presents an alternative way of reproducing non-normative personal experience through her poetic community by employing Sharon Mattlin and Margaret DeCoursey to read two of the voices that constitute her own experience. Nevertheless, Weiner acknowledges that the fixity and sequentiality of the printed page, even with her extensive personal system of transcription, as well as the interruptive performance, are artificial reproductions that solidify and "control" a fluid and changing experience. In an interview with poet and academic Charles Bernstein, Weiner says that *Clairvoyant Journal* is "a daily journal, and it's gone slightly screwy, and is under control when you read it, with three voices, or when you see it, because of the different typefaces" (Bernstein and Weiner 149). In this statement, Weiner articulates the impossibility of accurately performing or transcribing her linguistic clairvoyance for others, and therefore asserts her perceptual alterity, as well as the role of any printing or performance to contain and make legible a radical difference. Nevertheless, Weiner's performances and publishing of her journals indicate the formally disruptive quality of her experience when disseminated within a communicative form. The "screwy" elements of the journal and the performance, which refuse to cohere into containable meaning and easily demarcated significations, suggest an insertion of the disruptive "dis" of disability within the linguistic and performed aesthetic experience of poetry.

Hannah Weiner never accepted the medical interpretation of her condition as schizophrenia, nor embraced the kind of positive and resistant disability identity that disability studies and activism were working toward in her lifetime. As such, I do not propose to promote Weiner categorically as disabled. The reality and performance of her non-normative visions as part of her lived experience, though, present a strong resistance to the dominant liberal humanist and ableist conceptions of mind and human subjecthood. Weiner recognized the alterity of her "clairvoyant" experience of language in relation to normative states of mind. In a statement about her visions, she writes: "I am unusual, as far as I can discover, in having this extensive gift of SEEING language" (*Open House* 64). Further, her descriptions of the terms of "clairvoyance" and her maintenance of its resistant political specificity fit with models of disability activism, even if the terms of such activism were not available to her.

One tempting way of interpreting Hannah Weiner's "clairvoyance" and "clair style" writing is to figure it as a poetic metaphor for the multiple ways in which any person engages with language, their own interior mental experience, and textual composition based on citationality. Such an approach would appear supported by Lennard Davis' "dismodernism," which, as described above, universalizes experiences of disability so as to reconfigure notions of normative subjectivity. One might see Weiner's experience of "clairvoyance" as a usefully elaborated enunciation of the types of thoughts and experiences anyone may experience occasionally, but which are suppressed or disregarded in order to maintain an idea of the self as normatively autonomous and singular. One should remain attentive to the exclusions such a move produces, and the importance, at times, of maintaining an identity category in order to name especially stigmatized embodiments of difference. Eli Clare writes that such identity categories give us "words to help forge a politics" (qtd. in Kafer 15). Although Weiner did not take on the identity categories of disability, her own term, "clairvoyance," provides an identity that she uses to "help forge a politics." Weiner does so primarily through the refusal to universalize her experience. In what would become Weiner's final interview, Charles Bernstein posits the possibility of universalizing her statements about "clairvoyance" when he says: "I thought we all see words, in some sense" (Bernstein and Weiner 158). Weiner quickly rejects this and asserts the alterity of her individual perceptions of linguistic experience:

> No, it isn't the same at all! If you saw words in color across the living room, twelve or twenty feet long, "OBEY CHARLEMAGNE" or something, or saw them every time you moved, you'd realize that it's really visual, and at the beginning it was in color. (Bernstein and Weiner 158–59)

Weiner's rejection of Bernstein's poetic interpolation maintains a resistant alterity. Her experience refuses to provide a generalizable metaphor for poetic inspiration and therefore is not universalizable in a dismodern way. Although "clairvoyance" provides a resistant alternative to liberal humanist normative perceptions and singular autonomy, it also maintains a political specificity for the purposes of pragmatic resistance to its interpolation through metaphor.

Hannah Weiner's three-voice performance on *Public Access Poetry* of *Clairvoyant Journal* presents the multiple embodiment and voicing of her interruptive and radical dishumanist poetics. As shown in Fig. 9.1, during the *Public Access Poetry* reading the three women sit in a row and very little physical movement marks their performance. The performance consists mainly of the oral rendering of Wiener's perceptual linguistic experience. Nevertheless, the visual aspect of the television production places the three voices as embodied poetic elements differentiated through bodies, tone, and affect, and aligned as a singular experience through Weiner's introduction. Interruption prohibits teleological thought or poetic direction and becomes self-critical in performance as the voices comment and address each other. During the reading, the following exchange takes place:

Weiner: How can I describe anything when all these interruptions keep
DeCoursey: *arriving*
Weiner: and then tell me I don't describe well
Mattlin: WELL
DeCoursey: *forgive them*
Weiner: big
Mattlin: ME [pause] COUNTDOWN
Weiner: got that for days and yesterday it didn't stop
Mattlin: GO TO COUNTDOWN GO TO COUNTDOWN
   (3/10 in printed *Clairvoyant Journal*)

Fig. 9.1 Hannah Weiner's *Public Access Poetry* reading of *Clairvoyant Journal*

In this passage, the voices' messages overlap one another, and Weiner's voice remains the most steady as she speaks the words she associates with her own ideas. These words appear to maintain a trajectory of thought, but get off track with the word "big." Further, we can see the different speakers, the different voices, completing Weiner's thought as "the interruptions keep *arriving*" marks a performative moment in which the interruption arrives through a naming of its act of arriving and, simultaneously, completes Weiner's phrase and thereby "arriv[es]" all the more smoothly. As such, thoughts move between voices and form the assemblage of the perceiving and speaking self. This performance foregrounds the interdependence needed to perform the poem and make the "clairvoyant" experience legible for the visual and aural medium of the television. The interdependent and simultaneously interruptive performance controls a radically untranslatable mental experience into a poetics of self that employs community as constitutive of the individual, thereby resisting liberal humanist norms of autonomy. Weiner places her non-normative mental experience of multiple voices within an analogous space of multiple bodies. This invokes community to perform a self's perceptions of self-multiplicity. The inclusion of such a self-multiplicity and radical community dependence within the poetic and political set of relations disrupts and undermines the liberal humanist concept of the subject, and productively imposes a counter ontology from a disability perspective.

Despite the utility of Weiner's poetic innovation in her performance for disrupting ableist and humanist notions of the self and community, one must also remain wary of generalizing Weiner's personal and aesthetic performance of mental otherness. As she tells Charles Bernstein: "how can you not be avant garde if you're the only person in the world who sees words?" (Bernstein and Weiner 127). Weiner's radical dishumanist poetics stem from such resistance to generalization and metaphorization into dominant normative and ableist desires for legibility and universalization, even within avant-garde aesthetics and poetics. She offers an interruption of liberal humanist expectations and interpretations through the performance of the multiplicity of the radical dishumanist self.

The Marginal, the Radical

In an essay in her most recent of four *Mad Marginal* cahiers, the Spanish artist Dora García doubly reproduces Hannah Weiner's division of voices in *Clairvoyant Journal*: "Commands comments, inner monologue: read, recite, write" ("I See Words" 376). García draws upon Weiner as an inspiration for this fourth volume, *I See Words, I Hear Voices*, as is clear from the title. The two sequences offer a rearticulation of Weiner's "BIG WORDS," "little words," and her "own words" as she introduces them in the *Public Access Poetry* performance. Translated into García's project, these words figure as textually engaged performances of "read[ing], writ[ing], recit[ing]" and thereby focus attention on the linguistic engagements that constitute a shared poetics. García's colon that separates Weiner's demarcated voices of "Commands comments, inner monologue," from normative linguistic engagements of "read, recite, write," constitutes the imperfect translation of a dis/humanist poetics ("I See Words" 376). This draws together normative strategies of thought, desire for a universalizing critique, and the radical alterity of the lived experience of mental non-normativity. For García, the project of *Hearing Voices Café* constitutes an interrogation of the languages of internal multiplicity, which she places in relation to such normative institutional frameworks as the fully functioning café and the art gallery. Within her wider *Mad Marginal* project, García stages the voices and words of other artists, readers, and non-institutionally aligned outsider figures as co-researchers and collaborators. García's poetics in the *Mad Marginal* project, and, more specifically, in the *Hearing Voices Café*, draws upon the documentation of converging voices that variously overlap, interrupt, and inform other voices, all of which are both integral to perceptive experience and at the same time socially marginalized.

Britta Peters, the organizer of the "Illness as Metaphor" exhibition in which Dora García staged the *Hearing Voices Café*, writes that the *Café* may have been the "sickest" project of the exhibition, since "in the encounter with people who had been pathologized on account of their tendency to hear voices, the work quite forcefully conveyed the meandering boundary between sick and healthy" (51). In a seemingly dismodernist move, García's introduction to the project situates the *Café* within normative perceptual experience: "The designation 'Hearing Voices Café' actually applies to every well-patronized coffee shop" (*The Hearing Voices Café*). In this, she implies that the social and public space of the café already contains a multiplicity of voices one experiences and variously interacts with. Next, she adds a second level of meaning to the title with the less normative definition that associates "hearing voices ... with the phenomenon of hearing inner voices" (*The Hearing Voices Café*). In the interplay between these two meanings, García allows the aesthetic project to generally provide "a gathering place for people who hear voices" (*The Hearing Voices Café*). García further extends the "voice hearing" aspect of the café through the production of linguistic events and artifacts that constitute the project as a resistant and radical space that centers the marginal social network organized around disability and its normative analogs. These analogs, though, do not constitute metaphorical universalizations, since the various experiences of "voice hearing" are not aligned by García as a shared experience. Rather, the different meanings of the phrase create a community based in shared and specific, normative and non-normative experiences. The audio of García's staging of Hannah Weiner's *Clairvoyant Journal* adds recorded voices of Weiner's "clairvoyant" poetics into the café's aural atmosphere and constitutes yet another voice patrons hear. With voice hearing as a supposedly non-normative perceptual and mental state, García inserts the disruptive "dis" of disability, which deepens the meaning of the everyday experience of overheard conversation, and prompts a consideration of the limits of the self and perception within a public space. Further, this "dis" interrogates the metaphorical limits of "voice hearing" by blending the atypical perception of voices of auditory and linguistic hallucinations, as described in psychiatric language, with the aural experience of normative public life. Nevertheless, the project's introduction of "pathologized" persons into the aesthetic dialogue radically questions the ableist designations of "sick[ness]" within artistic and commercial social gathering places.

Earlier work in Dora García's *Mad Marginal* project draws specific inspiration from the writings of the Italian anti-institutional psychiatrist Franco Basaglia. For García, Basaglia provides the theoretical connection between "radical politics, radical psychiatry, [and] radical art" (García, "Radical Psychiatry" 8). García writes of her interest in the similarity between the "outsider art" produced by Basaglia's patients and mid-century "avant-garde art," both of which were labeled as "degenerate" ("Radical Psychiatry" 8–9). Basaglia himself makes this connection between the avant-garde and the psychiatrically marginalized in a lecture to the psychiatric establishment in London when he quotes a 1925 Surrealist manifesto which was addressed to operators of psychiatric institutions: "Tomorrow morning, when without any lexicon you try to communicate with these men, you will be able to remember and recognize that, in comparison with them, you are superior in only one way: force" (Basaglia, "The Destruction" 1). Elsewhere, Basaglia writes of "madness" as "a voice confused with misery, indigency, and delinquency;

a voice silenced by the rational language of illness; a message ... rendered indecipherable by the definition of dangerousness and the socially necessary invalidation of which it is the object" (*Psychiatry Inside Out* 249). Both the Surrealist revolutionary address to asylum operators and Basaglia's description of how mental disability becomes illegible invoke language and communication as processes by which the violence of mental ableism operates.

Dora García employs Basaglia's work in order to theorize a radical anti-hierarchical aesthetic project that creates networks of voices and co-researchers without privileging the artist. She writes that the institution, both artistic and psychiatric, functions antithetically to radical politics and radical art. In her introductory essay to her *Mad Marginal* project, she defines her terms:

> What does radical mean? Believing or expressing the belief that there should be great or extreme social or political change...
> What is an institution? The best definition for me came from Franco Basaglia: that which resists change.
> It was clear, then: radical and institutional are mutually exclusive. Radical psychiatry, radical politics, radical art: rage against the institution. ("Radical Psychiatry" 14)

As oppositional forces, the institution and radical movement form a framework with which García proposes to interrogate outsider, marginal, and resistant politics and aesthetics through language without tying the project to an oppositional dialectic. Although García doesn't specify liberal humanism as an institution that "resists change," her *Hearing Voices Café* and the broader *Mad Marginal* project focus attention on the outsider bodies and embodied minds left out of the liberal humanist model. The radical focus of this project stems from the repeated performance of resistance to repressive institutional stasis within both the aesthetic and the political. The "institutions" of liberal humanist politics resist anything except superficial change, which only reorients the constitutive exclusions within a current political moment. Radicalism, for García, involves a resistant politics of continual change and critique from non-hierarchical communities and assemblages. She foregrounds the interplay of multiple voices and co-researchers within her *Mad Marginal* project, which perform a poetics of interruption of the singular artistic vision.

As a "sick" project, insofar as it refuses the metaphorization of mental disability and instead performs the interruption of mental outsiderness within the institutional framework, Dora García's *Hearing Voices Café* and her *Mad Marginal* project interrogate alternative political relationships at the margins of the normative. These aesthetics form a radical dis/humanism insofar as they contest the liberal humanist notion of autonomy, independence, singular voicing, and hierarchy, and instead offer change as a political and aesthetic driving force, while also advocating for rights to normative spaces and identities. The *Café* reintroduces Hannah Weiner's multi-voiced poetics into a social and community space as one of many linguistic interrogations of institutional norms. These voices create a radical and productive space in which relationships form counter to the institutional norms of liberal humanist ableism. García's work gestures toward an aesthetics that blends activist community building, grassroots organizing, and public voicing as the elements of the aesthetic work. Such acts develop a multi-voiced project of non-institutional relationships.

Towards a Radical Dis/Humanist Poetics

Read as a dis/humanist project, Dora García's work constitutes a radical resistance to institutional stasis and singular voicing. The voices of the *Hearing Voices Café* and the other *Mad Marginal* collaborations form a nebulous project that, like Hannah Weiner's *Clairvoyant Journal* performance on *Public Access Poetry*, stages public interruptions that resist ableist norms. Both projects express normative desire through an integration within public spaces and the voicing of the desire for legibility within the norm for political and social change. Fitting with Daniel Goodley and Katherine Runswick-Cole's formulation of dis/humanism, these projects entangle normative desire with radical and critical alterity as a resistant positioning of mental disability within linguistic institutions. Both projects, to borrow phrasing from Goodley and Runswick-Cole, "assert[...] disabled people's humanity" and question the terms on which liberal humanism asserts the human (2). These desires and goals remain inseparable within the aesthetic project of multi-voiced interruption. Both Weiner's and García's poetics resist inclusions of marginal and outsider positions that only create new or deferred forms of exclusion by maintaining outsider status within liberal humanism. Such a process takes place in Weiner's resistance to the universalization or metaphorization of "clairvoyance" and García's project of continual change and political resistance through collaborative co-research. Therefore, the slash of "dis/humanism," when viewed from the perspective of these poetics, signifies the twin normative desire and disabled critique, both of which operate within radical dis/humanism as not a binary theory but an interruptive and multi-voiced theory. Radicality may be seen to partake in what Alison Kafer calls the "political/relational model of disability," since this change-oriented approach offers a politically active critique of dominant ableism not as a singular struggle or activist teleology, but as a mode of action and relation (4–10). Weiner and García's work resists institutionalization and singular voicing as an ongoing linguistic practice. Their projects of radical dis/humanism perform interruptions on the fringes of the institutional, whether in poetry, the public medium of television, the café, the art gallery, or medical and psychiatric language. Radical dis/humanism counters liberal humanist ableism with a poetics that performs a community assemblage of interdependent voices. It asserts the radicality of public acts of "see[ing] words," and "hear[ing] voices" (García 363).

Notes

1. Throughout this paper, when quoting Hannah Weiner's texts, I will follow her own technique for notating the various voices in her work as accurately as possible. In addition, as *Clairvoyant Journal* is unpaginated, I will cite each quotation with the journal entry date in which it appears in the Angel Hair Edition of the text.
2. Patrick Durgin writes that Hannah Weiner was diagnosed with "psychotic episodes indicative of schizophrenia" (*Open House* 13) and, further, that her symptoms limited her ability to access and seek care, which likely "precipitated" her death ("Psychosocial" 133). Charles Bernstein too notes that Weiner was diagnosed with schizophrenia ("Hannah Weiner").

Works Cited

Basaglia, Franco. "The Destruction of the Mental Hospital as a Place of Institutionalisation: Thoughts Caused by Personal Experience with the Open Door System and Part Time Service." First International Congress of Social Psychiatry, 1964.

———. *Psychiatry Inside Out: Selected Writings of Franco Basaglia*. Edited by Nancy Scheper-Hughes and Anne M. Lovell. Columbia University Press, 1987.

Bernstein, Charles. "Hannah Weiner." 1997. *Jacket2*, vol. 12, 2000, jacketmagazine.com/12/wein-bern.html.
Bernstein, Charles, and Hannah Weiner. "Interview for *LINEbreak*." *Wild Orchids*, vol. 2, 2010, pp. 141–65.
Braidotti, Rosi. *The Posthuman*. Polity, 2013.
Davis, Lennard. *Bending Over Backwards: Disability, Dismodernism and Other Difficult Positions*. New York University Press, 2002.
———. *The End of Normal: Identity in a Biocultural Era*. University of Michigan Press, 2013.
Durgin, Patrick. "Psychosocial Disability and Post-ableist Poetics: The 'Case' of Hannah Weiner's *Clairvoyant Journals*." *Contemporary Women's Writing*, vol. 2, no. 2, 2008, pp. 131–54.
García, Dora. *The Hearing Voices Café*. thehearingvoicescafe.doragarcia.org.
———. "I See Words, I Hear Voices: On Graphomania or the Obsessive Impulse to Write." *Mad Marginal: Cahier 4: I See Words, I Hear Voices*, edited by Dora García and Chantal Pontbriand. Sternberg Press, 2015, pp. 362–77.
———. *Mad Marginal: Cahier 1: From Basaglia to Brazil*. Mousse, 2010.
———. "Radical Psychiatry, Radical Politics, Radical Art: An Introduction to the 'Mad Marginal' Project." *Mad Marginal: Cahier 1: From Basaglia to Brazil*. Mousse, 2010, pp. 10–21.
Goodley, Daniel, and Katherine Runswick-Cole. "Becoming Dishuman: Thinking about the Human through Dis/ability." *Discourse: Studies in the Cultural Politics of Education*, vol. 37, 2014, pp. 1–15.
Kafer, Alison. *Feminist, Queer, Crip*. Indiana University Press, 2013.
Peters, Britta. "The Hearing Voices Café." *Mad Marginal: Cahier 4: I See Words, I Hear Voices*, edited by Dora García and Chantal Pontbriand, Power Plant, 2015, pp. 48–52.
Prendergast, Catherine. "On the Rhetorics of Mental Disability." *Towards a Rhetoric of Everyday Life: New Directions in Research on Writing, Text, and Discourse*, edited by Martin Nystrand and John Duffy. University of Wisconsin Press, 2003, pp. 189–206.
Price, Margaret. *Mad at School: Rhetorics of Mental Disability and Academic Life*. University of Michigan Press, 2011.
Siebers, Tobin. *Disability Aesthetics*. University of Michigan Press, 2010.
———. *Disability Theory*. University of Michigan Press, 2008.
Weiner, Hannah. *Clairvoyant Journal*. Angel Hair Books, 1978.
———. *Hannah Weiner's Open House*. Edited and introduced by Patrick Durgin. Kenning Editions, 2007.
———. *Public Access Poetry*, 29 Dec 1977. *PennSound*, 2010, writing.upenn.edu/pennsound/x/Weiner.php.

PART III

Mad Survival

CHAPTER 10

"My Difference Is Not My [Mental] Sickness": Ethnicity and Erasure in Joanne Greenberg's Jewish American Life Writing

Gail Berkeley Sherman

The autobiographical novel published by Joanne Greenberg in 1964, *I Never Promised You A Rose Garden*, challenges literary conventions associated with disability narratives by asking readers to expand their ethical inclusiveness beyond apparent boundaries marked by ethnicity, religion, illness, or disability.[1] The novel's performance of Jewish identity in the post-Holocaust United States contests stereotypes and resists ethnic erasure by reframing readers' assumptions about ethics and difference. While the 1977 movie version of the novel lacks such ethnic specificity and hence seems dated, the novel retains its power and significance more than fifty years after publication.[2] The implications of the novel's narrative refiguring of difference are just as relevant in today's climate of xenophobia and fear of the mentally ill as they were in the post-Shoah, nuclear age of 1964. Both the novel's sympathetic portrayal of a mentally ill Jewish protagonist and its mobilization of language to reframe difference contribute to *Rose Garden*'s continuing power and importance. The novel refigures difference as more than a sign of otherness: difference

G. B. Sherman (✉)
Reed College, Portland, OR, USA

© The Author(s) 2018
E. J. Donaldson (ed.), *Literatures of Madness*, Literary Disability Studies,
https://doi.org/10.1007/978-3-319-92666-7_10

as a fundamental marker of humanity. Difference is not a barrier but a precondition to ethical engagement. Throughout *Rose Garden*, readers encounter characters in dialogue, modeling a search for language that enables ethical exchange. Narrative innovations enable the novel's discussion of mental illness to produce a conception of the human that valorizes—rather than diminishes—difference and vulnerability.[3]

Disability, Difference, Language

Rose Garden calls into question conventions of mental illness narratives and stereotypes of Jewish identity to enlarge our ethical perspective on disability and other kinds of difference. The protagonist's assertion, "My difference is not my sickness" (168), is not simply a request that readers see a mentally ill individual as more than her illness; it challenges the binary structure of thought that underlies categorizing human beings as sick or healthy, able or disabled. *Rose Garden* translates its protagonist's plea into an understanding central to disability studies: when we recognize that vulnerability and dependence are common to all human beings, we strip illness (and disability) of its status as separating "normal human beings" from "others." Acknowledging that mental illness, like physical disability, may facilitate an individual's understanding of human vulnerability, *Rose Garden* reveals the vulnerability fundamental to all humans, whether ill or healthy, "mad" or "sane."

The cultural work of *Rose Garden* can usefully be viewed in the context of a tripartite movement in the 1960s to lessen stigma associated with mental illness, to resist medical models of psychiatric disability, and to redefine mental illness as a product of social structures.[4] Yet even when placed alongside novels by "wounded storytellers" that participate in this movement, *Rose Garden*'s innovations in telling the story of the "difference [which] is not [one's] sickness" stand out, as a look at important exemplars through the lens of Arthur Frank's typology of illness narrative reveals.[5] Sylvia Plath's 1963 novel, *The Bell Jar*, for example, narrates the "restitution" to health of a protagonist facing a depression revealed to be rooted in the sexual repression of the American 1950s. Although this popular work's conventional narrative arc destigmatizes mental illness, it exemplifies the limits of Frank's "restitution" plot, reinforcing the binary of health and illness. More radically, in a "chaos" narrative such as Ken Kesey's 1962 *One Flew Over the Cuckoo's Nest*, mental illness allows the narrator to affirm a worldview that inverts dominant social values: in an oppressive and punitive social structure, sanity, not mental illness, is actually "crazy," maintaining the binary structure.[6] Similarly, the quest plot, a common structure found in illness narratives by John Berryman and William Styron, among others, also destigmatizes mental illness, yet fails to question the nature of difference. David T. Mitchell and Sharon Snyder's more recent critical concept of disability as a "narrative prosthesis" not only destigmatizes disability, but also calls binary distinctions into question by acknowledging disability as a constant presence that enables narrative. Extending this concept to mental as well as bodily disability enables us to recognize *Rose Garden*'s expansion of the role disability plays in enabling narrative, linking difference and vulnerability, and inviting readers to participate in an ethics of inclusion.

In narrating the story of the teenage protagonist's hospitalization after a suicide attempt, *Rose Garden* repositions vulnerability, dependence, and difference as markers of the human condition rather than markers of disability. Rather than identifying her as disabled, different, and disturbing, the novel initially introduces the protagonist and other characters as they interact in their social roles—father, mother, girl, daughter. Such naming invites readers in, since we all have mothers and fathers, and are someone's child. Even an initial reading of the opening paragraph reveals how these terms also signal distance among the characters later identified as Jacob, Esther, and their daughter Deborah:

> They rode through the lush farm country in the middle of autumn, through quaint old towns whose streets showed the brilliant colors of turning trees. They said little. Of the three, the *father* was the most visibly strained. Now and then he would place bits of conversation into the long silences, random and inopportune things with which he himself seemed to have no patience. Once he demanded of the *girl*, whose *face* he had caught in the rearview mirror: "You don't know, do you, that I was a fool when I married—a damn young fool who didn't know about bringing up children—about being a *father*?" His defense was half attack, but the *girl* responded to neither. The *mother* suggested that they stop for coffee. This was really like a pleasure trip, she said, in the fall of the year with their lovely young *daughter* and such beautiful country to see. (1, emphasis added)

Language reveals how social roles constrict human interaction: while adjectives render the passing countryside "lush," "quaint," and "brilliant," strain and silence characterize interactions among father, mother, and daughter. By the end of the paragraph, "lovely" and "beautiful" ring hollow after the deceptive observation that traveling to a mental hospital is "really like a pleasure trip." Boundaries created by social roles turn conversational fragments into "random and inopportune things," into demand, defense, and attack.

Verbal violence and euphemistic evasion create a rhetoric that unsettles readers, moving them from identification with common family roles to the possibility of recognizing the hypocrisy those roles can conceal. The passage centers on the image of the "face," repeated throughout the novel; here, the "face" in the car mirror evokes the only direct discourse in the passage, Jacob's defensive response to his daughter's face. This unexpected verbal attack prompts readerly curiosity. By registering Jacob's attack as tacit acknowledgment of his own vulnerability, the novel signals that recognizing vulnerability is key to responding with empathy to the other. Once their empathic curiosity is aroused, readers can welcome Deborah's perspective, even as it reveals an alien consciousness, experienced "on the other side of the wall," in Deborah's fantasy of "the Kingdom of Yr" (4), in which fantastic gods render judgments in a private language, Yri, accessible only to Deborah. Madness is neither valorized nor condemned, but instead registered as different from the familiar world of social roles, in which father, mother, and daughter speak euphemistically, evade each other's demands, and often fail to recognize the difference that underlies ethical engagement as modeled in ongoing dialogue.

Dialogue, initiated by an encounter with what Emmanuel Levinas would term the face of the other, shapes *Rose Garden* and its disruption of conventional arcs of mental illness narratives.[7] As noted above, one such simple narrative structure follows the protagonist's path from disability to triumph. Another common narrative structure about mental illness traces an inversion of values: so-called madness or disability is revealed as sanity or super-ability. In contrast to these structures or that of the linear quest, *Rose Garden* involves readers in an ongoing, open-ended, empathic dialogical conversation. In the afterword to the 2007 edition of *Rose Garden*, Greenberg characterizes all her writing as "a reactive art ... a conversation with the world" (286). Mobilizing direct and indirect discourse and multiple linguistic registers, this dialogic "conversation" calls attention to the cultural specificity of its characters and its context, asking readers to recognize difference as the sign of human vulnerability, and modeling empathic response.

The recognition of human vulnerability is what primarily characterizes psychoanalyst Dr. Clara Fried's responses to Deborah, whom she first encounters in a report consisting of a jargon-filled diagnosis of schizophrenia (10), and only afterward in a face-to-face meeting (19). As Fried peruses "the facts and the numbers" (10) of the report, the novel reveals the violence inherent in it. In contrast to the report's reductive language, the German-Jewish analyst responds in "her native tongue" (12), a phrase literally referring to the German she reverts to: "*Aber wenn wir*... If we succeed ..." (12, ellipses in the original). More importantly, the phrase "native tongue" signals the difference between Fried's language and the objectifying language of the report, her concern for "the person" not "the patient." Using the first person plural ("*wir*"), Fried indicates her involvement in Deborah's struggle for mental health; similarly, the language of Greenberg's novel encourages the readers' empathy for Deborah, the rejection of any sense of absolute otherness. While the foreign language, German, signals otherness, its association with the empathic Dr. Fried helps normalize the reader's response to Deborah's fantasy language, Yri. A foreign language, even the private language of madness, need not be a threat. While language can dehumanize the other, it is essential to empathy, ethical response, and ongoing dialogue.

Throughout *Rose Garden*, empathic dialogue springs from a response to the face of the other. Subtle changes in linguistic register allow the narrative to signal shifts in engagement between characters. In Fried's first verbal exchange with Deborah, for example, recognition of the other registers on each interlocutor's face, communicating an initial acceptance of vulnerability articulated in dialogue:

> [Fried said:] "First I want to tell you that I will not pull away symptoms or sickness from you against your will."
> Deborah shied away from the commitment, but she allowed her *face* a very guarded yes, and the doctor saw it. ...
> "Tomorrow at the same time," the doctor told the nurse and the patient.
> "She can't understand you," Deborah said. "Charon spoke in Greek."
> Dr. Fried laughed a little and then her *face* turned grave. "Someday I hope to help you see this world as other than a Stygian hell." (19, emphasis added)

Puns and shifts in linguistic registers establish the level of intimacy of dialogue between Dr. Fried and Deborah. It takes a moment for the reader to accept the invitation into this intimacy, to understand that, for Deborah, "the nurse," who relies only on the language of her role with "the patient," might as well be speaking a foreign language, the Greek both of the mythological ferryman of the underworld and of the proverbial "it's all Greek to me." In addition, the passage relies on the interaction of facial expression, personal naming, and naming by social roles to alert readers to ethical choices embodied in speech: "Deborah" and "Dr. Fried" share a level of understanding absent from exchanges between "the doctor," "the nurse," and "the patient." Once Fried articulates her recognition of Deborah's vulnerability and Fried's responsibility ("I will not pull away...against your will"), Deborah can respond tacitly through facial expression, and in turn Fried can communicate recognition of her own insufficiency, hence vulnerability ("Someday I hope to help you..."). Two named individuals subtly communicate their difference from each other and mutual dependence, constituting themselves not as able and disabled, but as fully ethical human beings, constituted with responsibility for each other.[8]

For Greenberg, responsibility is the given of the human condition. *Rose Garden* asks readers to question and reject binary categorizations of human beings as healthy or ill, sane or insane, in favor of a more inclusive definition of human beings as revealing their fundamental vulnerability and dependence in their difference from each other. While the presence of sickness or symptoms may determine the degree of human dependence at any given moment, rejecting the binary categorization of individuals allows difference to function as the foundation of ethics. *Rose Garden*'s emphasis on the multiple particularities of historicized bodies anticipates the call by disability theorists Sharon L. Snyder, Brenda Jo Brueggeman, and Rosemarie Garland-Thompson to reject the idea of "a standard, normative body, unmarked either by individual form and function or by the particularities of its history" (2). The novel evokes Deborah's subjection to anti-Semitic attacks as well as her illness to extend its rejection of any "absolute state of otherness" (2); dialogue consistently models the acceptance of human differences as the necessary condition for empathy and indeed ethics.

In the narrative of therapeutic dialogue between Deborah and Fried, the image of the face again signals empathy and ethical response.

Deborah recalls the lies told her by doctors preparing her for childhood surgery for a urethral tumor, "the wrongness inside her, in the feminine secret part" (40):

> [T]hey had said, "We are going to fix you fine now." In the language of the game-playing liars she had understood that they were going to murder her....
> As she told it, she looked at Dr. Fried, wondering if the dead past could ever wake anything but boredom in the uncaring world, but the doctor's *face* was heavy with anger and her voice full of indignation for the five-year-old who stood before them both. "Those damn fools! When will they learn not to lie to children! Pah!" And she began to stub out her cigarette with hard impatience. (41, emphasis added)

What Deborah sees in Fried's face gives both characters access to the imagined self of Deborah's past, the image itself a *mise en abyme* of the function of the novel for the reader: language evoking a child's imagined murder stirs the reader, as it does Fried, to empathy and identification. Here focalizing through Deborah, the narrative asks readers to expand their moral capacity, rejecting "boredom in an uncaring world" and anger. While readers might laughingly dismiss a five-year-old's unrealistic fear of "murder," the narrative pushes them to envision more than an overly sensitive child. Greenberg's narrative juxtaposition of child's memory, teen discourse, and doctor's facial and verbal response invites readers to move beyond indifference to an affirmation of a bond with the other. As the Other speaks, the reader chooses: recognize difference and respond with empathy, or take refuge in "indifference" and accept the death of the Other as well as the self.[9]

While "indifference" rejects the demands of language, *Rose Garden* celebrates the power of language to rename, destigmatize, and render "queer" the difference that binary categorization attempts to solidify and reject.[10] Inside the hospital, Deborah and other residents name themselves, turning clichés into demands to be recognized: "eccentric and strange, ... crazy, bats, nuts, loony, and, more seriously, mad, insane, demented, out of one's mind" (43). In claiming these names, they reject "the euphemisms such as one always heard outside" (43). Describing herself as "crazy," Deborah corrects Fried's validating but skewed idiom, "Crazy as a fruitcake":

> Nutty as a fruitcake.
> Ah, yes, I remember. I hear also someone say 'bats.' What is 'bats'?
> It means bats-in-the-belfry. It means that up in your head, where the bells ring, it's night and the bats are flying around, black and flapping and random and without direction.
> Oh, I will have to remember that one. The Americans capture the feeling of mental illness quite accurately sometimes. (116)

Dead metaphor comes to life as differences within language are revealed. While ironically allowing that Dr. Fried is the "sane" expert and Deborah the "crazy" patient, this dialogue enlists the reader in affirming (as Fried does) Deborah's linguistic and psychological skills, in celebrating the disappearance of "indifference." Wordplay differentiates individuals from each other and demonstrates their mutual dependence. For Greenberg, "indifference" gives way to the pain and joy associated with the recognition of responsibility, the fundamental relationship of self and other, mediated by the face and articulated in language. Such responsibility refigures our notion of what it is to be human, rooting humanity, empathy, and morality in the very differences that have been mobilized to constitute categories such as disability/ability. Greenberg's narrative breaks down the hierarchy of able and disabled, substituting a recognition of all human beings as vulnerable, dependent, and actually or potentially disabled.

When the mentally ill protagonist who insists on calling herself "crazy" asserts that her "difference is not [her mental] illness," *Rose Garden* mobilizes its construction of disability in general, and mental illness in particular, to create a more inclusive ethics.[11] In response to a visiting doctor's "utterly and singularly irrelevant ... icy logic" (168), Deborah utters this "last cry" (168). She insists that her difference—externally, from others, and internally, from parts of herself—is fundamental to her identity as a "crazy" human being who, like all human beings including the doctor and the reader, is different from others, dependent on others, responsible to others, and vulnerable to others' violations of her being. As Dr. Royson fails to hear Deborah's "last cry," the text asks readers to hear her claim, to see her face, to view her with empathy born of their recognition of her differences.

Difference, Stereotypes, Ethnic Erasure

Challenging its readers to enlarge their sense of the human community, *Rose Garden* locates the foundations of xenophobic subjectivity, racism, ethnocentrism, nationalism, and other kinds of supremacist thought in the inability of human beings to recognize their dependence and accept their vulnerability. *Rose Garden*'s cultural work of countering indifference is rooted in twentieth-century Jewish history, experienced by the author through the loss of family members in the Shoah. When I asked her in a recent interview about how she started writing, Greenberg responded, "My father, who was an immigrant, was distraught over what was happening [to Jews in Europe], and I thought I could kind of fix it, so I wrote a letter to Hitler. Hitler never answered, so my good advice went to waste. But I liked doing that; I liked doing that" (Sherman 86). This childhood memory signals the ethical imperative that motivates Greenberg's writing from its earliest beginnings. While giving presence to Deborah's encounters with anti-Semitism, and alluding to Fried's experiences in Nazi Germany, *Rose Garden* also narrates Deborah's self-conscious and appropriately naive discovery of her—and other Jews'—"own form of intolerance" (218):

> I never knew anyone who was not Jewish, and I never gave my last particle of trust to someone who wasn't Jewish. Dr. Hill, the new doctor, and Carla are Protestants, and Helene is Catholic, and Miss Carol has kind of a frantic-Baptist background.... I've been doing something funny in my mind. I've been *making* them Jewish so that they could be close to me.... It's one step more than forgetting that they're gentiles—the ones we were always told betray you in the end. I also have to forget that they're not Jewish, too. (218, emphasis in original)

Intolerance is an inability to accept the Other except by imagining the other as the self, resorting to "indifference." As in Levinasian ethics, *Rose Garden* enacts the belief that difference is not antithetical to moral behavior, but foundational to it; humans develop not by denying difference, but by responding to difference with an empathic acknowledgment of one's own dependence and vulnerability.

Unlike some novelistic representations of madness from the 1960s, *Rose Garden* resists simply inverting the valorization of sanity and insanity in the face of social oppression, or even genocide. On the one hand, Fried both reflects on the "madness" of Nazi Germany, and recognizes that the mental hospital (not the "normal" social world) allows Deborah to counter her own prejudice and develop tolerance.[12] However, charged language topples any simple inversion of values: challenging Deborah to reconstruct her self-image, Fried asks, "Am I crazy or did you make that story up?" (219). What is "crazy" is not the deft psychotherapist, the oppressive world of social roles, or even Nazi Germany, but confusing hatred and murder, believing in an all-powerful rather than vulnerable self. In the novel's account of a second therapeutic discussion of Deborah's belief that she tried, at age five, to kill her younger sister, Fried marshals Deborah's trust in her and an analysis of the facts of Deborah's story to call forth Deborah's assent to the statement that "our would-be murderess is no more than a jealous five-year-old looking into the cradle of the interloper" (220). When she corrects Fried's details ("'Bassinet', Deborah said" [220]), the narrative asserts that Deborah is "back in the room being five again" (220). By returning to the room in her mind, Deborah can recognize that she made up the story of killing the baby because she "hated it enough to want to kill it" (219).

The novel refigures difference as enabling, not obstructing, ethics. Words like "crazy" and "madness" denote not opposed sides of a stable binary, but symptoms of vulnerable humans. Vulnerability underwrites the juxtaposition of paired narratives of discovery: Deborah realizes not only that tolerance is rooted in acknowledging, rather than rejecting, difference (218), but also that madness is rooted in unacknowledged hatred of the other (219). Moreover, Fried, who names genocidal hatred madness, also recognizes that hatred of a vulnerable baby will produce sickness unless the "indifference" to the other is transformed through language that articulates one's own vulnerability. Indifference requires maintaining notions of sanity and insanity that cannot make sense of Deborah's story or of the history of genocide in the twentieth century, and *Rose Garden* employs narrative strategies that persuade the reader to refigure these notions, reject indifference, and affirm the value of difference.

Most emblematically, *Rose Garden* redefines and affirms difference by undoing anti-Semitic stereotypes and resisting ethnic erasure. Whereas Jewish identity is built up in the novel as complex, multi-faceted, even contradictory, the 1977 film version directed by Anthony Page almost programmatically undoes all Jewish references in the novel, from names to historical references. While the erasure of ethnicity was probably intended to make the film more universal, it undoes one of the novel's most important contributions to the discussion of mental illness: its critique of difference and indifference.

By focusing on Deborah's delusional world of Yr, the film exoticizes mental illness and otherness, reconstituting difference as a basis for dehumanization and rejection. Conversely, by refiguring difference as the foundation of—rather than an obstacle to—ethical inclusion, the novel reclaims the performance of Jewishness as contributing to human thriving and culture. Like distinctions of (dis)ability, age, gender, language, religion, or other distinguishing traits, Jewishness functions in the novel as a key signal of difference. Whereas the novel's central characters bear distinctively Yiddish/German names, the film constructs a bland, WASPy "Blake" family; while the California actress Kathleen Quinlan is at best a visually plausible choice for the New York Jewish teenage Deborah, the tall blonde Swedish Bibi Andersson shares with the novel's German-Jewish psychoanalyst Fried—described from Deborah's perspective as "a tiny gray-haired, plump little woman…[a] little housekeeper" (16)—little beyond a non-American accent.

Absent from the film are the novel's references to the Nazis and Hitler (see pages 10, 37, 47, 97 *inter alia*), to the anti-Semitism Deborah experiences at summer camp and at home (e.g., 68, 82, etc.), and to the differences between American and European anti-Semitism (97–98). The impact of this loss in the film becomes clear in considering the novel's closing association of Hitler and the atomic bomb (278); this association actualizes the assertion that genocide, like weapons of nuclear war, threatens all of humanity, not just the immediately identified Other. Unlike the film, the novel resists ethnic erasure, verbal or physical, and in doing so critiques fundamental assumptions about the relations among differences.

The ethnic erasure carried out by the film's casting, dialogue, and visual emphases reveals, by contrast, the novel's innovative mobilization of interactions, often within Deborah, of Jewishness and mental illness, as a narrative strategy that positions the reader to sympathize with the other. Fried's memory of working with a patient in a German hospital, "at a time when Hitler was on the other side of its walls and not even she could say which side was sane" (10), like her reference to "the anti-Semitism of the [summer] camp" (82) recognizes the stereotyped identification of Jews and illness that led step by step to the Nazi killing centers.[13] When a doctor tells Deborah's mother the story of a patient who recovers his sanity, only to be murdered in a concentration camp, the narrative undoes anti-Semitic associations between Jews and illness, and assumptions about sanity and insanity, with excruciating irony:

> I once had a patient who used to practice the most horrible tortures on himself, and when I asked him why he did such things, he said, 'Why, before the world does them.' I asked him then, 'Why not wait and see what the world will do?' And he said, 'Don't you see? It always comes at last, but this way at least I am the master of my own destruction.' ... He got well. Then the Nazis came and they put him into Dachau and he died there. (37)

The doctor explicitly tells Esther this story to counter Esther's denial of her daughter Deborah's illness. This denial conceals not only Esther's specific self-blame for that illness, but also her general inability to accept the feelings of guilt and failure that block access to a fully ethical identity rooted in acknowledging differences, vulnerabilities, and dependence. The doctor claims that his story demonstrates that "you can never make the world over to protect the ones you love so much. But you do not have to defend your having tried" (37). Defense against having tried but failed, through no fault of one's own, conceals a vulnerability that demands recognition.

The doctor's narrative promotes empathy. As the doctor encourages Esther Blau to greater self-knowledge through hearing another's story, the novel's narrative strategies counter discomfort with the mental patient's logic of self-torture. Rather than allowing the creation of a safe distance between self-victimizing patient and sane listener, *Rose Garden* mobilizes historical context, horrific outcome, and the doctor's coda to highlight common human vulnerability in the face of historically varied threats. The novel invites acknowledgment that self-harm is a specific and individual form of the widespread desire for a humanly unattainable control over specific uncontrollable biological, cultural, or historical forces.

Insisting on cultural specificity, the novel addresses anti-Semitic acts in Europe and the United States before, during, and after the Shoah:

> In the time and place where Deborah was growing up, American Jews still fought the old battles that they had fled from in Europe only a few years earlier. And then there were the newer battles, pitched as the Nazis walked through Europe and screamed hatred in America. There were Bund

marches in the larger cities, and flare-ups against synagogues and neighborhood Jews who had ventured out of the ghettoes. Deborah remembered having seen the Blau house splashed with paint and the dead rats stinking beside the morning paper that told of Czech Jews running for the Polish border only to be shot by the "freedom-loving" Poles. She knew much of the hate and had been attacked once or twice by the neighborhood bullies.... (97–98)

Deborah comes to see that part of why "the world is horrifying to her" (97) is that her grandfather, humiliated at the hands of "a long-dead Latvian count" (97), shapes her as his revenge on the anti-Semitism in the world. The Yiddish word with which the novel describes Deborah's symptoms demonstrates the power of cultural memory, and demands that the reader acknowledge its claims: "Like a dybbuk or the voice of a possession, the curse proclaimed itself from Deborah's body and her mouth" (46). For the Jewishly knowledgeable reader, the folkloric figure of the dybbuk embodies the vulnerability of individuals to the haunting demands of the past. To the less knowledgeable reader, "the voice of a possession" may not convey the full animosity of a dybbuk, the soul of someone who has died who enters an individual to carry out unfinished business by any means necessary, but the linguistic choice is significant.[14] "Dybbuk," the only Yiddish word in the novel, defamiliarizes mental illness and reminds readers that what is perceived as madness occurs in a historically and culturally specific setting; most importantly, the use of a Yiddish word unflinchingly demands that readers accommodate the other in their encounter with Deborah Blau. Whereas the novel brings the culturally specific dybbuk into the world of all its readers, the film omits it. The disappearance of the dybbuk in the film emblematizes the film's impoverished communication of Greenberg's design on the reader: as the novel constructs ethnic specificity, it mobilizes differences in language to insist on the ethical imperative to recognize and respond to the specificity of each other's differences.

RESISTING CLOSURE, LEAVING A LEGACY

Rose Garden innovates a complex discourse consonant with a radically inclusive post-Shoah ethics. It stages an encounter with the face of the Other, refiguring the acceptance of difference as the ground of ethics. Layering multiple registers of discourse, reformulating narrative conventions of accounts of mental illness and disability, *Rose Garden* brings readers to an engagement with the otherness of schizophrenia, provoking readers to reject romantic associations between madness and genius, easy inversions of sanity and insanity, and expectations of the triumph over mental illness of "heroic" individuals. Its final pages, while resisting closure, epitomize the work of the novel in bringing the reader to acknowledge the face of the other, and in constructing a model of narrating mental illness that, for good or for ill, has helped enable the explosion of autobiographical writing on mental illness of the last decades. Examining the linguistically and structurally open-ended final pages of *Rose Garden* suggests how its narrative legacy invites continuation today.[15]

The closing pages of *Rose Garden* present the reader with an unprecedented juxtaposition of modes of discourse. Thought, speech, written text, and inner ramblings are signaled by text marked by visual and verbal complexity: italics, capitalization, mathematical symbols, curses, and quoted real or imagined speech appear in no immediately discernable order. Despite the presence of multiple innovations in language throughout the novel with the fantasy language of Yri, nothing quite prepares readers for the challenge of the final pages. The juxtaposition of discursive modes looks chaotic: apparently unrelated assertions march down the page with only typographical differentiation to assist readers in sorting a concatenation of wildly discrepant linguistic registers. Mathematical textbook jargon is interspersed with long bits of schizophrenic inner discourse interrupted by unattributed speech. The discursive plenitude of the closing sequence maps the complexity of human cognitive and communicative modes. These final pages invite the reader to move from confusion to recognition of the implied narrator's non-judgmental representation of Deborah Blau, once again a patient in a mental hospital, focused on the authoritative languages of mathematics and history, enmeshed in the sounds of sane and insane speech, resisting the internal rambling appeals of the gods of Yr:

> *Will you not save us as a shield against your hard rind, Bird-one?*
> *I can't do that anymore. I am going to hang with the world…Full weight.*
> (278, italics in original)

Inner dialogue gives way, in the last lines of the novel, to the cry of a fellow patient, a ward attendant's response, a passage from a history textbook, and, in its last instance of cited utterance, Deborah's speech, in which she repeats out loud her internal resistance:

> I am the secret first wife of Edward VIII, Abdicated King of England! Jenna's going again. Call Ellis; we'd better get a pack ready.
> AND BOTH RAILROAD AND THE MORSE TELEGRAPH MAINTAINED CONTACT INDISPENSABLE TO MODERN INDUSTRIAL SOCIETY.
> "Full weight," Deborah said. (279)

To whom is this repetition of a metaphorical phrase addressed? Not to any internal or external characters interacting in the narrative space of the novel, not to the textbooks Deborah examines, but to the reader. It is the reader whom the novel commands to respond fully to the voice of the other, to define the question to which "Full weight" is an answer, and to unpack the symbolic significance of the phrase.

"Full weight" is an affirmation of dependence on an Other: hanging full weight literally implies that all of one thing can be supported by some other thing. This connotation signals that Deborah can imagine and speak out loud the possibility of trusting the world to take her on in her full identity; it invites the reader to consider the implications of such dependence. In addition, "full weight" also connotes taking on a responsibility, completely; throwing one's full weight into something means taking on risk, accepting vulnerability, tolerating the possibility of loss. "Full weight," in other words, is a linguistic construction that affirms a dynamic relationship offering both promise and threat. It is a metaphor that invites the reader to recognize mutual dependence as the truest marker of human identity; to affirm commonality with those from whom they are separated by barriers of ability, ethnicity, language, religion, or less marked differences; and to see difference as the ground that enables embracing others.

More precisely, however, Greenberg's autobiographical novel ends, not with those two words of affirmation, but with a significant declarative clause: "Deborah said." Rather than simply conveying the content of a character's articulation, these words emphasize the act and the ownership of speech. As Emmanuel Levinas asserts, "language is born in responsibility" (82). While Deborah's speaking signals the character's assumption of an open-ended responsibility, the novel's final image of the act of speech invites further narrative innovation. And, as the words of scholars like Sander Gilman insist, a closer look at representations of disability and ethnic identity is needed to show us how *Rose Garden* and other works enlarge our ethical embrace.

Notes

1. Hereafter, *Rose Garden*. Thanks to my students and colleagues, especially Laura Leibman, Walter Englert, and Ellen Stauder, for their many forms of support.
2. A new edition appeared in 2007; it was recently translated into Korean; reader recommendations are high on popular websites.
3. To demonstrate *Rose Garden*'s reformulation of difference, I mobilize the Levinasian construct of the "face" as "living presence" and expression; as Emmanuel Levinas says, "The face speaks. The manifestation of the face is already discourse" (*Totality and Infinity* 194). Disability theory resonates with the Levinasian assertion that human subjectivity is rooted in the recognition of one's own vulnerability.
4. Trends exemplified in work by Erving Goffman, Abraham Maslow, Thomas Szasz, R. D. Laing, Timothy Leary, et al.; Halliwell's recent discussion is especially useful (231–88).
5. As a pioneering scholar of illness narratives, Arthur Frank identifies three plot types (restitution, chaos, and quest) that structure "testimony" by "witnesses."
6. See also Wilson Kaiser's discussion of Native American cultural specificity as a resource for Kesey's resistance to institutional oppression. Alice Hall (30–58) surveys recent developments in disability studies and literature, without addressing the specific question of narrating mental rather than physical disability. In addition to David Mitchell and Sharon Snyder's pioneering work, this study responds to Michael Bérubé's call for attention to disability's "complex relations to the conditions of narrative" (570).
7. For a relatively succinct discussion of this philosophical concept, see "The Face," in which Levinas' reformulation of relationship between self and Other is especially accessible. To situate Levinasian thought in the context of disability studies, I appreciate Alice Hall's critique of other problematic binaries, like the medical and social models of disability (25–27), as well as her account of empathy (35–36). Hall notes the "'hyper-representation' in life writing in the last twenty-five years" of people with disabilities (130) that I find in part engendered by Greenberg's autobiographical novel.
8. Note that the symbolic name "Clara Fried" translates as "clear, bright, famous peace." The character is modeled on Frieda Fromm-Reichmann, on whose treatment of Greenberg, see Hornstein (223–39).

9. The psychoanalytic dialogue here reproduces the Levinasian encounter with the Other: "The face before me summons me ... as if the invisible death that must be faced by the Other... were my business...as if, by my possible future indifference, I had become the accomplice of the death to which the other, who cannot see it, is exposed" ("The Face" 83).
10. My thanks to Elizabeth J. Donaldson for naming this a "queer" moment in the narrative.
11. Deborah's assertion occurs during Fried's vacation, a normal situation for Fried but one experienced by Deborah as equivalent to Fried's death. Dr. Royson, a British psychiatrist, fills in during her absence. While Fried differentiates between symptoms and sickness, insisting that she will not ask Deborah to give up her symptoms until she herself chooses to do so, Royson cannot make that differentiation, cannot accept Deborah's difference from himself, and thus cannot accept his own dependence and vulnerability.
12. Even more powerfully, Fried reflects on the impossibility of telling "a recovering patient that her own newborn health must grapple with symptoms of madness in the world" (218).
13. For discussion of the anti-Semitic association of Jews and illness, see, *inter alia*, Gilman, *The Jew's Body*, "The Jewish Disease: Plague in Germany 1939/1989" (211–33).
14. Readers today are likely to recognize the dybbuk from fiction by Isaac Bashevis Singer or countless adaptations of the 1964 Broadway show *Fiddler on the Roof*. On the associations of psychopathology and Jewishness, see Gilman and Thomas, *Are Racists Crazy?*, "The Holocaust and Post-War Theories of Antisemitism and Racism" (123–58).
15. In my forthcoming book-length study of this novel, I discuss examples, including Jay Neugeboren, *Imagining Robert*; Kim Chernin, *The Hungry Self* and *In My Mother's House*; and Susanna Kaysen, *Girl, Interrupted*. I argue the importance of *Rose Garden* to a tradition of innovative American Jewish life-writing identified by Aimee Pozorski as extending from Gertrude Stein and Henry Roth through Allen Ginsberg and Saul Bellow, and including writers such as Philip Roth, Tony Kushner, and Susan Sontag, whom Pozorski discusses.

Works Cited

Bérubé, Michael. "Disability and Narrative." PMLA, vol. 120, no. 2, March 2005, pp. 568–76.

Frank, Arthur W. *The Wounded Storyteller: Body, Illness, and Ethics*. University of Chicago Press, 1995.

Gilman, Sander. *The Jew's Body*. Routledge, 1991.

Gilman, Sander, and James M. Thomas. *Are Racists Crazy?* New York University Press, 2016.
Greenberg, Joanne. *I Never Promised You a Rose Garden.* 1964. Holt, 2004.
Hall, Alice. *Literature and Disability.* Routledge, 2016.
Halliwell, Martin. *Therapeutic Revolutions: Medicine, Psychiatry, and American Culture, 1945–1970.* Rutgers University Press, 2013.
Hornstein, Gail A. *To Redeem One Person Is to Redeem the World.* Free Press, 2000.
Kaiser, Wilson. "Disability and Native American Counterculture in *One Flew Over the Cuckoo's Nest* and *House Made of Dawn.*" *Journal of Literary and Cultural Disability Studies,* vol. 9, no. 2, 2015, pp. 189–205.
Levinas, Emmanuel. "The Face." *Ethics and Infinity: Conversations with Phillipe Nemo.* Translated by Richard A. Cohen. Duquesne University Press, 1985, pp. 85–92.
———. *Totality and Infinity.* Translated by Alphonso Lingis. Duquesne University Press, 1969.
Mitchell, David T., and Sharon L. Snyder. *Narrative Prosthesis: Disability and the Dependencies of Discourse.* University of Michigan Press, 2001.
Page, Anthony, dir. *I Never Promised You a Rose Garden* (film). New Concorde, 1977.
Pozorski, Aimee. "American Jewish Life Writing: Illness and the Ethics of Innovation." *The Edinburgh Companion to Modern Jewish Fiction,* edited by David Brauner and Axel Stahler. Edinburgh University Press, 2015, pp. 65–75.
Sherman, Gail Berkeley. "A Conversation with Joanne Greenberg." *Studies in American Jewish Literature,* vol. 28, 2009, pp. 86–101.
Snyder, Sharon L., Brenda Jo Brueggeman, and Rosemarie Garland-Thomson. "Introduction: Integrating Disability into Teaching and Scholarship." *Disability Studies: Enabling the Humanities,* MLA, 2002, pp. 1–12.

CHAPTER 11

Resistance, Suffering, and Psychiatric Disability in Jerry Pinto's *Em and the Big Hoom* and Amandeep Sandhu's *Sepia Leaves*

Srikanth Mallavarapu

In this chapter, I examine two novels that deal with the issue of mental illness and psychiatric disability in the Indian context, Amandeep Sandhu's *Sepia Leaves* and Jerry Pinto's *Em and the Big Hoom*. These novels, both of which are about a mother dealing with mental illness, allow for an examination of Arthur Kleinman's model of resistance and suffering in the context of the lived, embodied experiences of patients, families, and caregivers. Kleinman's body of work has explored the meanings of illness and pain and suffering in different cultural contexts. Kleinman's work explicitly challenges medical practitioners to engage in a substantive way with the human experiences of disability, suffering, and pain and the attempt to construct meaning in the context of chronic illness. Both *Em and the Big Hoom* and *Sepia Leaves* offer a nuanced representation of disability and mental illness, as well as the struggle to construct meaning.

Arthur Kleinman, a pioneer in medical anthropology and a strong advocate of cultural competency skills in medicine, urges medical

S. Mallavarapu (✉)
Roanoke College, Salem, VA, USA

© The Author(s) 2018
E. J. Donaldson (ed.), *Literatures of Madness*, Literary Disability Studies, https://doi.org/10.1007/978-3-319-92666-7_11

practitioners to listen and to work to relegitimize the experiences and narratives of those suffering from chronic conditions. In this context, it is interesting to see how Kleinman attempts to explore the question of resistance and suffering. When we hear the word "resistance" we immediately think of political struggles against oppressive power structures and hegemonic norms. Kleinman draws upon James Scott's work on weapons of the weak and everyday forms of resistance in his account of patients, some of whom are labeled as problem patients when they challenge or do not comply with the prescribed protocols of treatment (*Writing at the Margin* 126). Yet, for Kleinman, resistance is not just a political struggle against oppressive structures—it is linked up in a crucial way to suffering, which he defines as "the result of processes of resistance (routinized or catastrophic) to the flow of experience" (*Writing at the Margin* 126). A cursory reading of this definition might lead one to assume that Kleinman is advocating a reactionary political framework, arguing that "resistance... to the flow of experience" causes suffering, and therefore to reduce suffering, one must reduce resistance in the conventional sense.

However, when Kleinman is referring to resistance in the context of suffering, it is not in the standard political sense, but in the sense of the unfolding of life—bodies age and fall apart, there are earthquakes, accidents, things that we have to deal with in terms of our relationships with other people as well as injustice at different levels (*Writing at the Margin* 126). The standard use of the word resistance belongs to what Kleinman considers part of the domain of the many different responses to his definition of resistance—these include "grief, rage, fear, humiliation, but also...endurance, aspiration, humor, irony" (*Writing at the Margin* 119). Kleinman's redefinition of resistance is problematic in the way that it attempts to collapse these two different levels. Kleinman himself acknowledges that the way that he uses terms like resistance, delegitimation, and relegitimation is "admittedly inelegant" (*Writing at the Margin* 146). Nevertheless, the goal of Kleinman's critique is meaningful and worthwhile—to pay attention to the ways in which standard medical discourse, as well as anthropological discourse, can delegitimize the experiences and suffering of those dealing with chronic and serious illnesses. He asks practitioners working with people who are suffering "to witness, to affirm their humanity" (*Writing at the Margin* 146). Kleinman's work is replete with remarkable accounts of patients and examinations of resistance, especially when it comes to struggles around the delegitimation and the relegitimation of experience. Kleinman suggests that suffering and resistance are a fundamental part of human experience and that professionalized discourses that draw on preestablished explanatory frameworks fail to engage with the dynamic nature of experience and the process of suffering. The following sections of this paper explore questions of suffering and the delegitimation and relegitimation of experience in the context of two novels from India that deal with the impact of chronic mental illness.

On Mental Illness and a Love of Stories: Jerry Pinto's *Em and the Big Hoom*

Jerry Pinto's critically acclaimed novel *Em and the Big Hoom* (2012) is a fictionalized account of events in his life and his experiences growing up in a Goan Roman Catholic family in Mumbai. The title refers to the nicknames given by the narrator and his sister to their parents—their mother (Imelda) is Em, and their father (Augustine) is the Big Hoom. The central focus of the novel is the narrator's relationship with his mother, a woman who describes herself as being "mad" (*Em and the Big Hoom* 188). In the Library of Congress cataloguing system, the novel is described rather prosaically: (1) Women—Fiction, (2) Manic-depressive illness—Fiction, and (3) Domestic—Fiction. The novel itself is more subtle, even as it lists the various diagnoses applied to the narrator's mother, ranging from nervous breakdowns to bipolar disorder to paranoid schizophrenia as well as the range of pharmaceutical interventions and the fleeting relief brought by the initial use of Lithium Carbonate, which fades away. In Kleinman's accounts of patients, one of the themes that he returns to is the delegitimation of experience. Yet, in Pinto's novel, Em is never reduced to being just a manic depressive or a paranoid schizophrenic, even though her struggles lead to multiple suicide attempts and take a tremendous toll on the family. Pinto describes Em as trying to reclaim a degree of control over her narrative by being extremely direct while talking to her children. While the narrator is sometimes embarrassed by her frank conversations, especially those about sex, he is able to have honest conversations with her on a range of issues, including her illness.

The other way Em maintains control of her narrative and relegitimates her experience is by writing a diary, which she allows her children to read.

There is a directness in her writing and in her conversations with her family when she describes the voices in her head and the events in the past that mattered to her. She tells the narrator that "knowledge always helps" (*Em and the Big Hoom* 8). While he appreciates her strong sense of integrity, there are also things that she says that pain him deeply, especially when she tells him that "a tap [of sadness] opened when you were born" (*Em and the Big Hoom* 10). Pinto's emphasis on the family dynamics here is in keeping with Kleinman's framework, where illness and suffering have a social component and have to be understood as intersubjective experiences that include not just the patient but also the extended network of family and caregivers (*The Illness Narratives* 3). The narrator talks about his recognition as a child that there was something wrong, but instead of saying that there was something wrong with his mother he says "there was something wrong with all of us" (*Em and the Big Hoom* 9). His refusal here to isolate the mother is significant; in response to the delegitimating experience of individual madness, the narrator relegitimates the collective experience of the family.

The father, the Big Hoom, is also portrayed as a sympathetic character, someone who tries his best to take care of his family. He works as a sales manager, but before he got his degree he worked as a compounder for a doctor, filling prescriptions for him. The Big Hoom's degree is in engineering and the scientific worldview matters a lot to him, but he also values the fact that the doctor he worked for was kind and understanding to the patients, never mocking alternative forms of treatment—whether it was Ayurveda, Unani, or homeopathy—saying that "sometimes, they get in the way less than we do" (*Em and the Big Hoom* 82). The Big Hoom also models this kindness and understanding along with the scientific approach when he attempts to explain Em's condition to the narrator when he was a young boy, comparing nerves to power lines and saying that the nerves carry electricity through the body. The narrator knows that there is something wrong with his mother's nerves and visualizes "thoughts, like electric currents, and inside my mother's head they ran uncontrolled—flashing and sizzling" (*Em and the Big Hoom* 9).

Kleinman's work also acknowledges the importance of narratives of family members and caregivers in addition to the patient. While *Em and The Big Hoom* is a novel, it is based on the family history of the author and it is fascinating to see the layers of narratives in a text of this sort— the son, who is a writer, remembers his mother and his conversations with her, giving voice to her experiences, including excerpts from her diaries and letters and memories of conversations he had with her. But the novel is much more than that—it shows Em, the narrator, his sister, and his father also attempting to make sense, to construct meaning. One of the remarkable achievements of this novel is how Pinto captures the way in which this family develops a linguistic shorthand, playing with language in a way that draws on their shared history.

Another significant layer of Pinto's narrative is the medical discourse: the accounts of prescriptions, diagnoses, and interactions with doctors and nurses. The Big Hoom does try to get Em the best medical treatment possible, and there are a few instances when she is admitted to the psychiatric ward of the JJ Hospital when she is in danger of harming herself. Over the years, the nurses and doctors establish a rapport with Em, and there are times when Em chooses to admit herself, especially when things seem to be spiraling out of control. The Big Hoom is on deputation to Brazil on one of those occasions, but the psychiatric ward is full. The narrator and his sister make the unfortunate decision to admit her at the Staywell Clinic, run by Dr. Alberto D'Souza, a doctor who is described as looking like Alfred Hitchcock. She is administered electroconvulsive therapy (ECT) during her ten-days stay there, and when she returns she is a shell of the person she once was (*Em and the Big Hoom* 186).

The narrator and his sister struggle with guilt about the medical treatment that their mother received. The narrator is convinced that no matter what Em had done to them, what they did to her by admitting her to the clinic was worse (*Em and the Big Hoom* 191). The novel further engages with the ethics of ECT when the narrator describes a college class trip to the Thane Mental Hospital. The instructor asks the doctors whether the students can watch patients undergoing the procedure—the doctor permits it, but the narrator notices that the patients themselves are not asked for their permission. One of the students brings up the antipsychiatry work of R. D. Laing and challenges the instructor on ideas of "normality" and "success" in the context of this medical procedure (*Em and the Big Hoom* 179–80). The narrator keeps quiet, even though he is extremely critical of what this procedure has done to his mother.

In addition to the world of the family that forms the central focus of this novel, the novel also engages with the issues surrounding mental health in the Indian context. The narrator tries to set up a support group and places an advertisement in a newspaper—there are a few people who show up, some of whom are interested in a psychoanalytic approach, others who want to model it on Alcoholics Anonymous—but the majority seem to be looking for options and information about where they can admit a family member who is dealing with mental issues (*Em and the Big Hoom* 70). Pinto has been an advocate for reducing the stigma around mental issues in India. In an op-ed published in *The New York Times* in December 2014, he describes his memories of the police visiting his house after his mother attempted to kill herself. His father paid the police officers bribes in order to avoid a messy court case, something that is alluded to in the novel as well. The bribes were required because of "Section 309 of the Indian Penal Code of 1860, a piece of legislation designed by the very Victorian Lord Macaulay, which punished attempts to commit suicide with a fine or up to a year in jail or both" ("India and the Right to Suicide"). Pinto's op-ed was published a couple of months after India introduced a new national mental health policy in October 2014, which among other things finally set into motion the decriminalization of attempted suicide.

How mental illness affects identity is another element that concerns Pinto and is central to his novel. In "Identity, Disability and Schizophrenia: The Problem of Chronicity" Sue E. Estroff examines how certain chronic conditions end up defining the identity of a person—rather than being a person who has an illness, the illness takes over the identity of the patient. For example, a patient *has* diabetes, but he *is* schizophrenic (256). Estroff argues that in "I am" illnesses, "chronicity consists of a fusion of identity with diagnosis, a transformation of self to self and with others… a change of self from someone who has an illness to someone who is an illness or diagnosis" (251). Estroff goes on to define chronicity and disability in the following way:

> Chronicity and disability are thus constructed by: the temporal persistence of self and other-perceived dysfunction; continual contact with powerful others who diagnose and treat; gradual but forceful redefinition of identity by kin and close associates who observe, are affected by, or share debility; and accompanying loss of roles and identities that are other than illness related. (259)

Estroff's analysis of schizophrenia in the American context makes the argument that there are "various personal and political-economic reasons for espousing and maintaining diseased, disabled conceptions about the individual" (259). Estroff examines how the political economy of the professionalization of mental care in the United States impacts the ways in which a person is defined as being disabled as well as the debates about the allocation of resources.

The Indian context is substantially different, with a significant shortage of mental health professionals as well as a lack of legal and government support for people with chronic conditions and disabilities. *The New York Times* ran an editorial titled "India's Mental Health Crisis" a couple of days after Pinto's op-ed was published. This editorial, while appreciating the new mental health policy that aimed at destigmatizing mental health issues also pointed out that budgetary allocations for health issues were being cut even when "Indian youths between 15 and 29 years old kill themselves at a rate of 35.5 deaths per 100,000 — the highest in the world — and suicide has surpassed maternal mortality as the leading cause of death of young Indian women... [and] there is only one psychiatrist for every 343,000 Indians" ("India's Mental Health Crisis").

Even though the Indian context differs in significant ways from the American one, Estroff's broad definition of chronicity and disability can be applied to examine the ways in which Em's identity changes. Pinto does map out the trajectory that Em traverses as her illness worsens, as she goes from earning more than her husband to losing her job. When she was young, she worked as a schoolteacher. Given the financial barriers to pursuing a degree, she learns typing and shorthand at an institute and ends up getting a job at a company where the Big Hoom was a junior sales manager. When they decide to get married, she is working in a well-paying secretarial job at the American Consulate and actually earning more than the Big Hoom. She loses her job at the Consulate when "she started adding her own, and very alarming, comments to diplomatic reports. 'Personal interpolations,' they called them" (*Em and the Big Hoom* 169–70). The novel offers a moving portrayal of disability in the context of chronic mental illness, with Em's identity as a working woman being taken away from her. There are moments when her children have to take care of her and protect her, something that is a reversal of the conventional parent–child relationship. The episode of ECT therapy and the way that it is administered to her is also a powerful example of the delegitimation of her experience, where she does not have any say in what is being done to her. The suffering that she goes through is so profound that she tries repeatedly to kill herself and asks her children to kill her.

While the description of ECT and Em's stay at the Staywell Clinic offer an example of the delegitimation of the patient's experience and of the violence of some medical practices, the novel clearly does not offer a sweeping rejection or critique of modern medicine. Em's experience at the Staywell Clinic is significantly different from her experience at the JJ Hospital and the relationships she establishes with the nurses and doctors there. Em does not hesitate to strike up conversations with other patients in the waiting room, offering support and advice; it is clear that her voice is not silenced here. Pinto's implicit acceptance of medical concepts of mental illness is also evident in his edited anthology, *A Book of Light: When a Loved One Has a Different Mind*, which gathers narratives of family members writing about their experience of living with someone with a mental illness or infirmity. In the introduction to this anthology, Pinto acknowledges that he did try to be open about the diagnosis that his mother was bipolar, and that trying to understand what was wrong in terms of genes and a chemical imbalance did have its appeal (8). In *Em and the Big Hoom*, the narrator understands that the model of biological determinism means that he himself might have some risk of developing a mental condition himself. He sets up an appointment with a psychiatrist to discuss his risk, and his father also tell him to "fight his genes," exhorting him to exert whatever agency he could, while also realizing that the individual does not have complete agency when it comes to chronic mental conditions (*Em and the Big Hoom* 71).

Em also ends up with a psychiatrist that she trusts, Dr. Michael, and it helps that he is also a Roman Catholic. The narrator's sister and Em have discussions about patriarchy and guilt, but Dr. Michael's brief comment that some of her beliefs were old-fashioned actually helps Em to deal with her sense of guilt better than the conversations with her daughter about the insights drawn from critical theory and feminism. While the medication seemed to help with some of the symptoms, especially as Em grew older, the narrator also says that "underneath the mysteries continued, unchanged. Underneath, somewhere in the chemistry of her brain, there was something that could not be reached" (*Em and the Big Hoom* 195). As for trying to construct meaning in suffering, the narrator explores a range of options from religion to philosophy, finding no simple answers. The narrator says that he experienced a loss of faith, but developed a love of stories (*Em and the Big Hoom* 61). Rather than any simple explanatory framework, what we are offered is the act of witnessing and remembering, the act of acknowledging the shared humanity of a person and family members who suffered deeply.

In his introduction to *A Book of Light: When a Loved One Has a Different Mind,* Pinto makes it clear that the goal of the anthology was not to provide answers but to allow the stories of family members to be told, because "sometimes it would just help if someone could come and be there, sit quietly and offer companionship, let you talk when you wanted to but let you be silent if that was what might help you heal… This is how life is. Open-ended. Challenging. Terrifying…" (12–13). As the portrayal of Em makes clear, no label could capture the complexity of his mother and no explanation could account for the suffering that she and her family had to go through. And yet, she had her own voice with her frankness and sense of humor running through her own narratives in her letters and diaries. Framed through the narrator's memories, we get a sense of a complex human life, filled with deep suffering, but also moments of love, laughter, and joy. The novel ends with the death of the narrator's mother—she dies of a heart attack. The narrator tries to console the father as best as he can. At one stage, they order food from the local Chinese restaurant. The boy who brings the food refuses to accept payment. The narrator says, "This was the city, India's biggest, a huge city, but people heard and responded to what was happening in your life. Sometimes, this much was enough" (*Em and the Big Hoom* 212). To hear and respond is sometimes enough.

Memories and the Quest for Meaning in Amandeep Sandhu's *Sepia Leaves*

Amandeep Sandhu's *Sepia Leaves* (2008) is also a novel based on personal experience written from a son's perspective, focusing on his mother who was diagnosed with schizophrenia. The evening after the death of his father, the narrator pores over letters, diaries, and old photographs, trying to make sense of his memories of his parents and the impact his mother's illness had on their family. Estroff's definition of disability in the context of chronic mental illness includes a reference to "loss of roles and identities" and this is something that can be observed in both *Em and the Big Hoom* and *Sepia Leaves* (Estroff 259). The standard role of a parent is to be responsible for and to take care of one's children. With a mother struggling with a chronic mental illness, the relationship between the narrator and mother is redefined in both novels. In *Sepia Leaves*, the narrator strokes his mother's hair, thinking that "she has always been like my child, though I am her son" (5). This is after the death of his father, when the narrator is wondering whether his mother is fully aware of what is going on, and also reflecting on the reversal of roles, wondering who is there to console him.

Like Pinto does in his novel, Sandhu also does not restrict himself to the portrayal of a patient. The novel examines how the family (the father, mother, and son) had to contend with what the narrator refers to as a "disease of prejudice" in addition to the mental illness of the mother (*Sepia Leaves* 183). The narrator is a child when he begins to realize that there is something wrong with his mother, whom he refers to as Mamman. Her behavior is erratic, with moments where she threatens violence and attacks his father. She soils her clothes and seems oblivious to the smell of urine. When she wants to show affection to the narrator by cooking him something, she does not notice if she uses salt instead of sugar or if the food is burnt. The narrator hears other children in the neighborhood referring to her as "pagli," which translates as mad woman (*Sepia Leaves* 40). The narrator's father (referred to as Baba) is kind but helpless, and the fading photographs in the album typically have photos of the son either with the father or the mother—not the complete family (*Sepia Leaves* 55). The photos illustrate not just the fragmentation of the family, but also the struggle to construct a narrative from fading memories.

The narrator's quest to reconstruct his past is inextricably linked to his quest to understand his mother's illness. He discovers that his mother has preserved the piece of paper that diagnosed her with schizophrenia. He remembers the day that it arrived in the mail, a letter from his aunt (who was a doctor) with a diagnosis and prescription. His mother interprets the note as telling her that her brain is "precious" and is also happy that it does not include any reference to her married name—the prescription includes her maiden name and this is something that she finds satisfying, given the unhappiness she feels at being married (*Sepia Leaves* 23). The narrator tries to look up the meaning of schizophrenia but is unable to find the word in his dictionary. His father tells him that their dictionary is an old one, and that new words get added all the time, but this doesn't help him to understand. Even though the word "schizophrenia" is missing from their dictionary, the illness of his mother is an inexorable presence in their lives. Dr. Nanda, the doctor at the hospital in Rourkela where the family relocates for the father's job, concurs with the aunt's diagnosis of schizophrenia and the drug regimen that she has prescribed. However, some years later, the doctor departs from this treatment program and gives Mamman electric shock therapy at the hospital. When Baba wants to know why the treatment has changed, Dr. Nanda explains that some violent patients are given this therapy to calm them. Mamman becomes increasingly angry with Dr. Nanda and the nurses, who have also become frustrated with her. They have seemingly reached an impasse in treatment, and Dr. Nanda suggests that Mamman be admitted to the asylum in Ranchi, which is something the narrator's father is not willing to consider (*Sepia Leaves* 81). Both Estroff and Kleinman point to the ways in which the experiences, roles, and identities of patients with chronic conditions are delegitimized and their agency is reduced. Once Mamman is admitted to the hospital, she has no agency with regard to the treatment options, and these options are not discussed with Baba either. He is disturbed by the electric shock therapy, but is only able to put his foot down when it is suggested that Mamman be admitted to the asylum. Here Sandhu highlights the diminished agency of everyone in the family.

Estroff points out that patients diagnosed with schizophrenia have "deceptively simple questions or suspicions" addressed to them: "The questions are: *can't* or *won't, inability* or *refusal, dysfunction* or *defiance*?" (251, italics in original). Kleinman, meanwhile, suggests that people suffering from chronic conditions who are labeled problem patients are offering forms of resistance (*Writing at the Margin* 126). The choice between dysfunction and defiance is an artificial one. In Kleinman's framework, there is a certain amount of resistance in dysfunction, which is linked to suffering and the delegitimation of experience. This does not preclude the possibility of more conventional resistance or defiance. The rage and frustration shown by Mamman can be seen as both dysfunction and defiance. Mamman resents the fact that her marriage meant leaving her home in Punjab and moving to Rourkela. She has a formal degree and is qualified to teach and one of the long-standing grudges against her husband is that he does not have an engineering degree—he has a diploma. However, as her condition worsens, it is also clear that she is not in a condition to be employed. Her episodes of rage increase significantly when the narrator's father employs Mando, a young woman, as domestic help, and she accuses him of having an inappropriate relationship with her. While her outbursts of violent rage are linked to her illness, they could also be seen as a response to her unhappiness in being dislocated from her home environment. One might speculate that Mamman's outbursts of anger were maybe at least partly in reaction to the patriarchal framework where the status of the wife is linked up to that of the husband and where qualified women were relegated to the domestic sphere.

The violence of the patriarchal framework is made explicit by the relatives on the father's side when the narrator's uncle asks Baba to assert his masculinity and to "give her two slaps when she misbehaves, that is the only way women learn" (*Sepia Leaves* 107). When the narrator's father is away, the uncle hits Mamman and locks her up in a room. Baba is reduced to tears when he finds out what happened, and says that he will protect Mamman and make sure that this will never happen again. But he also finds it hard to confront his family members who have just assaulted his wife (*Sepia Leaves* 144). This is not the first time that she had been physically assaulted—her own father had hit her as a child and some of her family members speculate if that was when her problems had started (*Sepia Leaves* 155). The narrator's father struggles to maintain his composure. He is deeply influenced by Gandhi's *The Story of My Experiments with Truth* and Nehru's *Discovery of India*. He considers Gandhi a saint and finds his ideas about self-discipline, purity, and rejection of western medicine compelling, even though he finds it hard himself to implement these teachings. However, he also deliberately chooses to move to Rourkela and work in the steel plant because he is inspired by the Nehruvian dream of a modern progressive India built on science and technology. The narrator's father embodies the tension between the Gandhian framework and Nehru's ideas, a tension which is still unresolved in India even after more than fifty years of independence. While the Nehruvian framework was an idealistic one that hoped for inclusive development, the narrator is also able to see the dark side of modernity. One of the underlying themes in Sandhu's novel is the violence of the modern nation-state, and one aspect of that is the history of how the giant blast furnaces were built on land taken away from indigenous groups, who were then forced to either migrate to cities in search of livelihood, or to become underpaid and exploited laborers in these plants and the townships that came up around them (*Sepia Leaves* 86).

This section of the novel is also set during the turmoil of the 1970s when Prime Minister Indira Gandhi imposed a state of Emergency, threatening democracy in India. The narrator, a young boy at this juncture, is fascinated when he hears some people saying that Indira Gandhi is mad (pagli)—if a mad person could be the Prime Minister, then his mother could be the Prime Minister. When curfew is imposed, the police allow his mother to leave the house and walk on the streets, because to them she is a harmless pagli—but the narrator's mother thinks that the police are scared of her, because of her imagined connections with the President and Prime Minister of India (*Sepia Leaves* 96–97). Kleinman cautions about the tendency to impose structures of meaning onto experience, of giving "primacy to the search for meaning over the rest of experience" (*Writing at the Margin* 145). Sandhu constructs his narrative with his young narrator trying to make sense of a dysfunctional family and a dysfunctional nation, and even though the young narrator strives to link up the two worlds in his quest for meaning, he is also gently reminded by his father that "you know these are different things: Mamman and Indira Gandhi, and you and me. Don't make these connections" (*Sepia Leaves* 89).

The narrator remembers a conversation he had with his father about one of his acquaintances, Gurdev, who was obese. His father tells him that "It's an illness. Never laugh at him. It is like Mamman's illness. He is fat and Mamman is angry. They can't help their illnesses" (*Sepia Leaves* 69). In the epilogue to the novel, Sandhu speaks of schizophrenia in terms of chemical imbalances in the mind as well as genetics. The narrator struggles with the labels attached to his mother—whether it is the dismissive pagli or the piece of paper from the doctor that says schizophrenia. He says that "the doctors were right in prescribing medicines. It was just that the medicines were not right in curing her" (*Sepia Leaves* 183). The complex dynamics of pain, suffering, and resistance described in this novel cannot be captured by simple labeling or medicalization. Kleinman argues that established categories and discourses fail to account for the complexity of suffering and the flow of experience. The life of Mamman cannot be completely explained by recourse to genetics or chemical imbalances in the brain, just as it cannot be completely explained as a symbolic internalization of the dysfunction of the nation-state or as a performance of resistance against patriarchal violence.

While the novel deals with many difficult and painful experiences involving the mother, Sandhu also portrays her taking care of Baba after he has a stroke. His mother, who was the one typically being taken care of, was now helping to take care of his father (*Sepia Leaves* 183). The narrator is able to bring his parents to live with him in Bangalore after his father retires, and his mother seems to mellow a little with age. His father is also able to pursue some of his interests, and the narrator remembers him listening to ghazals and discussing poetry before dementia sets in and he passes away. Sandhu offers a moving account of the death of his mother after she is diagnosed with cancer in a short piece in the anthology edited by Pinto ("My Mother's Breast"). In the epilogue to *Sepia Leaves*, the narrator says that "my learning to speak up helped me" (182). The act of speaking, of telling one's story is crucial in the context of relegitimizing experience. Sandhu's novel offers a nuanced and complex portrayal of a family struggling with the impact of mental illness.

Conclusion

Novels like *Em and the Big Hoom* and *Sepia Leaves* offer us narratives that witness suffering and acknowledge the humanity of people dealing with disability and chronic mental illnesses, refusing to see them merely as patients or political actors with specific agendas. These two novels map out the struggle to construct meaning in a world that resists it. There is pain, there is suffering, and a struggle in order to legitimize the experience of both patients and caregivers. Kleinman says that his model of resistance "probably can never be entirely satisfying as an explanatory account of human suffering. And perhaps that is as it should be" (*Writing at the Margin* 146). It is human to want to construct meaning with regard to experiences, especially when these experiences have to do with the suffering of loved ones. Even when there are no easy answers and no overarching frameworks of meaning that explain suffering, the act of witnessing, of listening, of paying attention to the narratives of patients, family members, and caregivers offers some comfort and is a powerful reminder of the complexity of human experience.

Works Cited

Estroff, Sue. "Identity, Disability, and Schizophrenia: The Problem of Chronicity." *Knowledge, Power and Practice: The Anthropology of Medicine and Everyday Life*, edited by Shirley Lindenbaum and Margaret Lock, University of California Press, 1993, pp. 247–86.

Gandhi, Mohandas. *An Autobiography: The Story of My Experiments with Truth*. Translated by Mahadev Desai, Beacon, 1993.

"India's Mental Health Crisis." The Editorial Board, *New York Times*, 30 Dec 2014. www.nytimes.com/2014/12/31/opinion/indias-mental-health-crisis.html. Accessed 15 June 2017.

Kleinman, Arthur. *The Illness Narratives: Suffering, Healing and the Human Condition*. Basic Books, 1988.

———. *Writing at the Margin: Discourse between Anthropology and Medicine*. University of California Press, 1995.

Nehru, Jawaharlal. *The Discovery of India*. Penguin, 2004.

Pinto, Jerry. *Em and the Big Hoom*. Penguin, 2014.

———. "India and the Right to Suicide." *New York Times*, 28 Dec 2014. www.nytimes.com/2014/12/29/opinion/india-and-the-right-to-suicide.html. Accessed 15 June 2017.

———. "Introduction." *A Book of Light: When a Loved One Has a Different Mind*, edited by Jerry Pinto, Speaking Tiger, 2016, pp. 7–25.

Sandhu, Amandeep. "My Mother's Breast." *A Book of Light: When a Loved One Has a Different Mind*, edited by Jerry Pinto, Speaking Tiger, 2016, pp. 36–54.

———. *Sepia Leaves*. Rupa, 2008.

Scott, James. *The Weapons of the Weak*. Yale University Press, 1985.

CHAPTER 12

Mental Disability and Social Value in Michelle Cliff's *Abeng*

Drew Holladay

One of the fruitful characteristics of the word *madness* is the breadth and flexibility of its meaning, denoting insanity while also describing irrationality or a fit of emotion like anger or love. When literary criticism of Caribbean fiction investigates madness, the term is usually used metaphorically, either as a symbol for social dysfunction in the postcolonial era or as a detrimental effect of colonialism on an individual's psyche. Taking up the lens of critical disability studies, on the other hand, one would highlight instances of literal disability in literature and its function in narrative, including mental disability. From the disability studies perspective, the experiences and perspectives of characters with disabilities may drive the symbolic and political significance of a given text, carrying along with them the dubious history of disabled figures in literature, who largely appear as symbols of corruption, decay, dishonesty, failure, or simply evil.

D. Holladay (✉)
University of Maryland, Baltimore County, Baltimore, MD, USA

© The Author(s) 2018
E. J. Donaldson (ed.), *Literatures of Madness*, Literary Disability Studies,
https://doi.org/10.1007/978-3-319-92666-7_12

Some postcolonial Caribbean writers offer an alternative to these negative depictions when they propose a kind of collectivity that preserves difference, a configuration that I argue can include differences in dis/ability. Twentieth-century Caribbean fiction frequently portrays the detrimental effects of a colonial culture that disciplines subjects into normativity; some of these works, however, also embed spaces and roles for individuals that colonial culture would reject as mad, unintelligent, bizarre, or inefficient. Embodying these two types of representation, Michelle Cliff's 1984 novel *Abeng* critiques harmful reactions to mental disability in Jamaican society while also opening space for the inclusion and valuing of someone with a mental disability: to recognize not only impairment or difference but also strength and contribution.

In this chapter, I will describe pivotal characters in *Abeng* who have a mental disability and bear its stigma—but whose circumstances and relationships lead to varied consequences. Cliff's portrayal of these disabled characters reveals a new picture of difference and *créolité* in Caribbean literature, showing that disability can serve as a productive analytical lens interconnected with issues of race, gender, and class. While figures of madness certainly invite interpretation along the line of mental disability, Cliff's "mad" characters clearly show how racial identity, sexuality, and class position strongly delimit each person's path. *Abeng* demonstrates the power of race and class to determine one's experience of disability—but not vice versa. In this analysis, I focus on disability experience but ultimately situate it within the complex of relations that attach a particular social meaning to each individual's appearance and behavior; in the spirit of scholarship on intersectionality, I hope to illustrate how characters with mental disabilities represent "multiply marginalized subjects" whose perspectives should be considered "when crafting a normative vision of a just society" (Nash 3).

Madness, Fiction, and Narrative Prosthesis

Literary disability studies have a strong tradition of recognizing pervasive negative stereotypes of disability in narratives as well as building a connection between those narratives and the historical realities of people with disabilities. The majority of such studies take a stance of commentary or critique where the academic writer recognizes the use of disability stereotypes by an author or filmmaker. However, I aim to demonstrate how Cliff performs that same critical work within *Abeng*: Cliff's narrative both embodies and comments on disability stereotypes, in part by illustrating the diverging effects of madness or mental disability on a particular character according to their social position. Cliff's portrayals of characters with mental disabilities may be interpreted as remarkably consistent with a disability studies paradigm, and those portrayals parallel the related, and more explicit, commentaries on dominant constructions of race, gender, and sexuality.

In this way, characters with mental disabilities in *Abeng* call attention to disability's common function as a "narrative prosthesis," where disability is employed in a narrative so that the stigma of disability serves as a symbol but its material reality remains unaddressed. In their seminal book *Narrative Prosthesis: Disability and the Dependencies of Discourse*, David T. Mitchell and Sharon L. Snyder explain that the concept of narrative prosthesis serves as a "way of situating a discussion about disability within a literary domain while keeping watch on its social context" (9); Mitchell and Snyder use the term to capsulize a disability studies approach to literature, taking up the trenchant cultural commentaries of disability studies and directing them toward works of narrative fiction. In fiction, as well as culture, "disability has undergone a dual negation—it has been attributed to all 'deviant' biologies as a discrediting feature, while also serving as the material marker of inferiority itself" (Mitchell and Snyder 3). Recognizing the toxic representations of disability in past narratives, then, can allow us to create a "more variegated and politicized disabled subjectivity" in the present (Mitchell and Snyder 11).

In a related mode of literary criticism, Elizabeth J. Donaldson points out the problematic symbolic uptake of madness both in nineteenth-century literature and modern feminist writing. Donaldson argues that while the "madwoman…became a compelling metaphor for women's rebellion," this figurative use of madness "reinforces…an almost monolithic way of reading mental illness" and "indirectly diminishes the lived experience of many people disabled by mental illness just as the metaphoric use of terms like lame, blind, and deaf can misrepresent, in ways that have ultimately harmful political effects, the experience of living with those physical conditions" (100–102). If only understood as symbol, madness will remain a prosthesis, a supplement, and the progressive disabled subjectivity Mitchell and Snyder hope to build cannot become a social and political reality. As I will explore later, this inverse configuration of madness as a positive symbol appears also in the work of Caribbean writer Édouard Glissant.

My argument here is that Cliff's narrative foregrounds the issues that Mitchell and Snyder, Donaldson, and other disability studies scholars posit as critical for responding to ableist characters, metaphors, and narratives; she does so by representing the effects of mental disability alongside other concrete historical realities of racism, sexism, and other forms of social and economic inequality.

Caribbean Madness and Colonialism

While *Abeng* offers a counterpoint to the problematic constructions of disability that Mitchell and Snyder identify, many Caribbean writers fighting the brutal cultural legacy of colonialism reinforce rather than resist negative portrayals of disability. The influential writing of Aimé Césaire and Frantz Fanon, as I argue below, powerfully describes internalized racism and racial discrimination but continues the use of disability as a negative foil or a condition to be erased or overcome.[1]

Colonial exploitation in the Caribbean singled out genealogy and skin color as the most powerful of identity markers. Fundamental cultural beliefs about race governed not only the treatment of blacks by the government and European elite but also black individuals' negative self-conceptions, as Césaire and Fanon vividly describe. In addition, some racial categories in the Caribbean were historically figured as disabled. Stereotypes about individuals with African lineage included a deficit in intelligence, overabundance of emotion, pathological hatred of authority, as well as exceptional physical and sexual abilities. These stereotypes served to uphold the institution of slavery by constructing blacks as ideal for hard work but animalistic and distrustful, justifying both the endless labor of slaves and their repressive confinement and brutal treatment.

In *Abeng*, these divisions manifest in the protagonist, Clare Savage, who accrues privilege for her light skin but kindles her connection to an ancestral past represented by her mother, who is black. Clare, who exhibits a number of countercultural stances in the novel, gives a "first indication of...rebel consciousness" when she "verbalizes and explicitly acknowledges her mixed blood in the face of her father's contention that she is white because he is white, regardless of her mother's blackness" (Springer 56). Significantly, Clare seeks to transcend cultural dictates of race (and gender) through her friendship and pursuit of ritual with Zoe, whose skin is dark. Despite this "rebel consciousness," however, nearly every other person in Clare's life reinforces racial norms.

Authors in the *négritude* movement of the 1930s reasoned that the long oppression of blacks in European colonies had produced a host of social and psychological problems. Instead of internalizing negative white stereotypes about Africa and Africans, intellectuals like Césaire argued for a distinct and proud black culture to be celebrated in writing and politics. This celebration would allow the oppressed and self-repressed black individual to rise above the strong prejudices and structural obstacles placed in his or her life by colonial culture. Césaire's famous poetic volume *Notebook of a Return to the Native Land*, features examples of the verbal and physical abuse directed toward blacks in his home country of Martinique and the neuroses such treatment produced in those individuals and communities. As Césaire argues in the poem, the black subject should surmount neurotic reactions to colonial abuse via the celebration of *négritude*; and then she may "unexpectedly [stand]" in the face of racism (47).

The metaphors employed in this poem associate images of bodily and mental ability like posture, productivity, and intelligence with liberation, while images of disability represent repression, impotence, submission, and deterioration. Writing about the *négritude* movement, disability studies critic Christian Flaugh observes that "cultural movements...that seek the liberation of one population, do so, at times, through recourse to reductive, normative-based rhetorical constructions, of which bodily dis/ability is a regular component" (Flaugh 292). Césaire fights against the idea of black racial identity as disabled or inferior: his choice of imagery renders disability as a tragedy to be overcome in a movement toward agency and completeness. As we will see in *Abeng*, an alternative to this traditional binary exists in the affirmation and inclusion of people with disabilities as an essential part of societies committed to equity.

The psychiatrist and writer Frantz Fanon's writing, while incisive and inspiring, maintains the harmful binary that associates disability with regression or inadequacy. Fanon, a fellow Martinican and student of Césaire in France, elaborated on his theses of *négritude* and identified specific ways that an oppressive racist culture affected people of African descent in the colonial context. Like Césaire, Fanon saw the detrimental effects of colonialism manifested in the behavior and mental states of colonized people. Though his direct observation of patients at a hospital in Algeria shape his conception of the problems caused by colonialism, Fanon asserts in *Black Skin, White Masks* that the situation is similar in other colonies like Martinique, where he was raised. In the colonial education system, "the black schoolboy is repeatedly asked to recite 'our ancestors the Gauls'" and is "made to feel inferior" for his deviation from European ideals (*Black* 126–27). If he chooses to "climb up into white, civilized society" he "tends to reject his black, uncivilized family at the level of the imagination" as well as language (*Black* 128). Even before the destructive colonial war in Algeria, "colonization, in its very essence, already appeared to be a great purveyor of psychiatric hospitals" (*Wretched* 181). For Fanon, the etiology of the mental disorders he describes is clear, and it has nothing to do with racial identity or biological determinism, as the white European colonizers would assert: instead, it is "the direct result of the colonial situation" (*Wretched* 233). Again, like in Césaire's *Notebook*, madness and mental disorder are the cruel effects of colonialism; the liberated society will instead be cleared of these afflictions and have a populace exhibiting bodily and mental fitness. Mark Sherry connects the absence of other "power dynamics, such as sexism" in Fanon's analysis to his adoption of the medical model of disability, which "assumes that medical responses are unproblematically beneficial" (n.p.). Césaire and Fanon offer recognition of, and liberation from, racist discourses but do not alter the cultural associations of physical and mental disability with failure, impotence, violence, or evil.

Crucially, the reinscription of disability (stereo)types in the writing of Césaire and Fanon conceals another dimension of discrimination and inequity present in European and colonial contexts: the differential treatment of disability based on racial identity. The colonial system in the Caribbean, with its association of black and brown racial identities with inferiority and disability, predisposed a negative interpretation of non-white bodies. Further, the economic disparity connected to skin color affected the way individuals in the Caribbean were judged by one another, especially in speech and behavior—both used as everyday measures of mental health and cognitive ability. While some such judgments were direct and overt, other, more subtle, judgments involved overlap between the behavior of the colonizer and the colonized, privileged and marginalized. With relation to mental disability, behaviors considered pathological or delusional in colonized subjects would be interpreted as tolerable eccentricity in the elite. Thus, the experience and perception of mental disability were crucially dependent on one's racial identity and class position.

Mental Disability in *Abeng*

Michelle Cliff's novel *Abeng* illustrates this situation in great detail, with a range of characters who represent the possibilities and impossibilities laid before colonial subjects. Set in Jamaica in the 1950s, its central narrative focuses on a girl, Clare Savage, who is light-skinned and poised between racial identities: her white father's family with its history of slave-holding and her "red" mother's family steeped in the rural life of former plantations and descendants of maroons. *Abeng* centers on travel between the native rural town, associated with blackness and the body, and the colonial urban metropole, associated with whiteness, Western education, and separation from native ways of life. The novel weaves a family history of the Savages with Clare's reflections on spending time at her parents' home in the city and her grandmother's house in the country.

After Clare visits the old Savage plantation with her father early in the novel, Cliff shifts the focus to the land's past and the last slave owner in the family, Judge Savage. On the eve of Emancipation, Judge Savage tries unsuccessfully to secure an injunction and retain ownership over his slaves; drunk on rum and his own delusions about the "diluted white seed" that will result from the end of slavery, he gathers and burns one hundred of his slaves on the property. Judge Savage, "a justice...trained to assess the alternatives available to human beings," excuses himself from this act of murderous violence: "Later, he would look back on what he had done and assess that he was a man of passion who had been pushed to his limit. His passion had been misled into violence. He was not to blame" (Cliff 39). The narrator sarcastically confirms this reasoning and points to the nature of insanity as a cultural construction, saying that "lest anyone think the judge's behavior extreme or insane or frenzied, the act of a mad white man, it should be pointed out that this was not an isolated act on the eve of African freedom in Jamaica" (Cliff 40). In this cultural context, the murders Judge Savage commits cannot be treated as murder, a crime of anger, for many white men in power took similar action—and it is their behavior which serves as the benchmark for sanity in the colonies. Further, Judge Savage also uses his belief in black racial inferiority as justification for his action: "These people were not equipped to cope with the responsibilities of freedom...Their parameters of behavior were out of the range of civilized men" (Cliff 39). In the example of Judge Savage, one finds that the label of madness is dependent upon one's race and class, since as a "rational" white man acting like his brethren he cannot be insane. Additionally, the presumption of the slaves' fundamental disability becomes a pretext for the killing, and even though we may feel, as readers, that we see the true racist motivations for Judge Savage's actions, the dark logic of "mercy killings" of disabled individuals looms in his words.

Much later in the novel Clare encounters a white woman considered mad, Miss Winifred, who represents a different situation for disabled individuals with light skin. Miss Winifred was rejected by the family and developed a number of unusual behaviors and beliefs, most notably a debilitating fear of water touching her skin that keeps her from bathing. Beatrice, her sister, frames Winifred's madness as a defiance of cultural norms: she harbored ambitions, wanted to leave the island, and did not want to marry. After being dismissed from school "because they could not control her," Winifred was forced to marry but "made the poor man's life a living hell" and drove him away (Cliff 159). Winifred privately explains to Clare, however, that immediately after having a child with one of the black servants on her family's estate as a young woman, her father had sent her to a convent and her daughter went to an orphanage. Winifred's repetition of racial slurs for her child's father reveals the conflict inside her own mind—at once a shame related to her culture's view of race and a defiance to fondly remember her relationship with the man, a gardener, who "taught me how to grow things besides babies" (Cliff 163). Clare sees Winifred's vulnerability and tries to learn more about her, recognizing that she is not expressing hatred, unreason, or the effects of menopause (as Beatrice implies). Instead, Clare feels that Winifred is relating "something she had not made peace with—not something she had invented in what Miss Beatrice called her madness" (Cliff 163). Clare's insight into Winifred's mental state allows the reader to see beyond the constructions of madness dominant in the Jamaican culture of the time. Yet Winifred, for all her isolation and inner torment, has all her basic needs met: living with a servant far outside the city, she has ample space to move, food to eat, a shoreline to watch. The stability Winifred enjoys is a far cry from the homeless wandering of Mad Hannah, another disabled character in *Abeng*, though their mental disabilities manifested in similar ways, through unusual beliefs and behaviors. Winifred, as a white woman from a wealthy family, has access to a safety net—both economic and social—that allows her to live a stable life with no threat of institutionalization despite her "madness."

As part of an elite economic and political class, the lives of Judge Savage and Winifred stand in stark contrast to characters in different circumstances, like the character of Mad Hannah, who face a double challenge of unrelenting poverty and racial prejudice alongside mental disability. Judge Savage's future will be comfortable, despite the brutality of his actions; Winifred will remain ostracized but comfortable. As the narrator recalls Mad Hannah's story, her grief after her beloved son Clinton's death "turned her from being an *obeah*-woman into being a madwoman" (Cliff 62).[2] Specifically, she could not complete traditional burial rites for Clinton and thereafter sought out his spirit or "duppy" around the island, wandering from one town to the next and speaking to trees and lizards for word on the duppy's location. People in the area laugh at Mad Hannah and "thought her foolish and crazy" (Cliff 65). The narrator recalls the townspeople's "explanation" for her behavior, trying to avoid guilt by saying that "she had passed through change-of-life too quickly" and this had made her foolish instead of "stop[ping] to consider...her journeys as ceremonies of mourning, as expressions of her faith" (Cliff 65). All of her wealth gone with her son Clinton, saddled with the perception of madness, and with no support from her community, Hannah eventually steals a horse to ride out and "find some peace"; she is subsequently arrested and sent to an asylum (Cliff 66). We are left to speculate whether her life would have taken a different course if she was a woman of wealth or had white skin. The line that divides madness and eccentricity in colonial Jamaica insidiously coincides with the line dividing dark skin from light skin.

While the treatment of Judge Savage, Winifred, and Mad Hannah (and their state of in/sanity) depend upon interpretation and cultural belief, *Abeng* provides another intersection of disability and race by representing characters with undeniable mental disabilities and the effects of these on their quality of life. For the colonized and dark-skinned, the negative effects of disability are magnified by class and race inequalities, while the elite live with their disabilities in relative stability. A classmate of Clare's, Doreen Paxton, demonstrates this contrast. Doreen was a student at Clare's Catholic school in the city, St. Catherine's, which had a predominantly white population and where most of the dark-skinned students attended on scholarship. The nuns who run St. Catherine's show their prejudice when Doreen has an epileptic seizure during a hymn in chapel. Even though Doreen is in great physical danger, "cracking her nose and cheekbones on the flagstones with incredible force," none of the nuns move to protect her from the harm of the seizure (Cliff 96). Eventually one of the teachers, "tall and herself-dark," comes to Doreen and braces her against the seizure's movements. The next day, the children at St. Catherine's are told that Doreen "will not be returning to school because she was an epileptic and might be a 'danger' to herself" (Cliff 98). Doreen's story illustrates the tenuous position of those with dark skin in this society: access to what the elite class considers basic education is wholly dependent on the economic and personal "charity" of the white population. When Doreen's neurological disability appears, it no longer matters that she was "a genius at the western roll" and could high-jump better than girls at a rival school; her scholarship is revoked, her mother is left to care for Doreen on her own, and St. Catherine's only abiding interest is "[concern] that the school might be liable for any lasting injury" from the seizure incident (Cliff 96–97). Doreen's dark skin had already made a Western education nearly beyond reach, and the nuns cancel even this paltry hope because of her disability.

Disability, Collectivity, Inclusivity

Each of these characters from Cliff's novel makes clear that neither disability nor race are in themselves determinative but are instead interwoven in their effects on an individual. In the light of this social and literary complexity, the interpretation of madness in Caribbean literature as a simple metaphor seems less than feasible. If we accept the limits of madness as a metaphor for social issues in Caribbean society, questioning its ethicality in relation to the postcolonial subjects such a metaphor represents, madness itself need not disappear from the landscape of Caribbean fiction. As demonstrated by Cliff and other authors like Myriam Warner-Vieyra and Edwidge Danticat, rich accounts of disabled experience highlight the individual challenges that multiply marginalized populations face and open spaces for critique and intervention. In all of these situations, still, madness and mental disability figure as negative consequences and states to be avoided or cured. For many with mental disabilities, however, a "cure" is neither possible nor desirable, and everyday life must be ventured without a narrative prosthesis to clean up the messes.

Martinican writer and theorist Édouard Glissant champions radical inclusiveness—referred to as collectivity—as a specifically Caribbean quality. One of his core arguments about Caribbean society is the need for collectivity—not as a unity formed around common belief, but as a grouping steeped in difference. For Glissant, movements that claim a single history or boast a pure lineage crumble quickly in the Caribbean's diverse social environment. Consequently, a way forward can only be found by retracing the roots of division and acknowledging difference as a virtue and strength. Facing the myriad problems posed by difference allows collectivity to form, where Caribbean people can find "not a return to the longing for origins, to some immutable state of Being, but a return to the point of entanglement, from which we were forcefully turned away; that is where we must ultimately put to work the forces of creolization, or perish" (Glissant 26). Glissant's vision of a heterogenous collectivity directly incorporates issues of language, race, and culture. His formulation is also ideal for the inclusion of disabled individuals, who represent new perspectives and ontologies that contribute to the vibrant collection of subjectivities within the Caribbean. Unlike common representations where disability is expelled or erased, this vision of the Caribbean allows expressions of bodily and mental difference that do not disappear in the collective.

In relation to the concerns of this chapter, however, Glissant's frequent use of madness as a theme is problematic. Reflecting on Glissant's accounts of "cross-cultural contact," J. Michael Dash writes that Glissant does not describe "facile postmodern hybridity" but "reintroduces the ideal of radical difference" (42–43). Glissant uses the image of the madman to figure this radical difference, and like the association of madness with women's rebellion that Donaldson critiques, for Glissant "madness is an exemplary state of extreme consciousness...and not a form of pathological behavior" (Dash 41). Though this is an inverse configuration of the disability stereotypes Mitchell and Snyder decry—madness is framed positively rather than as a sign of inferiority—mental disability as a lived reality has been superseded by a symbolic gesture. Despite this issue, I believe that Glissant's idea of collectivity is amenable to the inclusion of mental disability as a category of difference and identity to be valued within a diverse and tolerant society.

Through the character of Clary, *Abeng* exemplifies alternative approaches to organizing social and personal identity—approaches that, in their inclusiveness, carve spaces for the social incorporation of individuals with mental disabilities. A brief but important section of *Abeng* illustrates how the swift judgment that many make against cognitive difference may be countered with direct experience with disabled individuals. As a child of seven, Kitty, the mother of the protagonist Clare, developed tonsillitis that required a surgeon's help. To make the long trip from their country home, Kitty's mother has a neighbor's daughter Clary take her to the hospital. The novel's description of Clary foregrounds her state of mental disability, as "not quite right in the head. A little slow. What they used to call dull" (Cliff 138). Clary's impairments do not prevent her meaningful action, though, and she "was the sweetest girl anywhere...faithful to any task assigned her, as long as it was carefully explained" (Cliff 138).

Once they arrive at the clinic, Clary comforts Kitty in the waiting room; after her operation, Clary sleeps on the floor beside Kitty's bed and helps the nurses with whatever they need (Cliff 140). Clary's devotion leaves a lasting impression on Kitty: though her husband believed she was choosing his grandfather's name, the protagonist Clare is in fact named after Clary, "the simple-minded dark girl who fought for her and refused to leave her side" (Cliff 141).

The story of Clary opens a small space for the inclusion and valuing of someone with a mental disability—to recognize not only impairment or difference but also strength and contribution. The stereotype of simple-mindedness moves to exclude and limit those with mental disabilities, but an inclusive vision of society recognizes the difference without effacing the individual's humanity. With this episode, *Abeng* offers us a picture of both the entrenched stereotypes that plague postcolonial societies and ways of viewing disability that disrupt those received norms. In doing so, the novel also casts disability, and mental disability in particular, as another window into inequality and exploitation, as well as radical inclusion.

Conclusion: Mental Disability and Postcolonial Fiction

In this chapter, I sought to reveal how Michelle Cliff's portrayal of a number of characters in the novel *Abeng* parallels a disability studies approach to literature and brings mental disability into focus in relation to lived experience rather than using madness as a metaphor for the effects of colonialism in Jamaica. Cliff, in turn, situates disability as a consequential aspect of social and political identity—illustrating how ableism is experienced alongside other forms of prejudice and oppression. The privileged characters Judge Savage and Winifred exhibit mental disability, as described by the narrator, but neither are deprived of wealth or the fulfillment of basic needs; in the case of Judge Savage, his murderous violence does not affect his social power in the community. By contrast, Mad Hannah's grief and fixation on her son's spirit make her a vagabond, derided in the villages she frequents and eventually institutionalized in a clear use of the asylum as an instrument of social control. Doreen, who has already battled poverty and racial prejudice to earn a place at a good school, has her support rescinded as soon as her disability appears—in that moment of her first epileptic seizure, the nuns close by do not even look after her immediate physical safety. Through the poignant stories of these characters with mental disabilities, Cliff demonstrates that postcolonial fiction is not simply amenable to disability studies literary criticism but may *already* be doing similar critical work.

The disability-focused analysis of *Abeng* illuminates a path for connecting disability studies and postcolonial fiction in a way that is faithful to lived experiences and recognizes the distinctiveness and interconnectedness between disabled and postcolonial identities. From two slightly different perspectives, Clare Barker and Stuart Murray and Mark Sherry caution against intersections of disability studies and postcolonial criticism in which either experience is metaphorized in service of the other: Sherry writes that "Postcolonialism should not be understood as simply a metaphor for the experience of disability; nor should the terms "colonialism" or "disability" be rhetorically employed as a symbol of the oppression involved in a completely different experience" (n.p.). Barker and Murray summarize the problematic simplifications in the past:

> While, in the broadest terms, postcolonial criticism tends to treat disability as prosthetic metaphor, Disability Studies problematically transports theories and methodologies developed within the Western academy to other global locations, paying only nominal attention to local formations and understandings of disability. (219)

In contrast to this formulation, Barker and Murray suggest a symbiotic relationship between disability and postcolonialism where "the details within representations and narratives of postcolonial disability reorient, in a fundamental fashion, our understanding of such disability" (220). In *Abeng*, a reader can find "case studies" of the relation of disability to society in postcolonial Jamaica with attendant details that show the effects and interactions of multiple marginalized identities in a specific cultural context. By working inductively from the narratives in postcolonial works like *Abeng*, scholars in disability studies can build a more nuanced, global/local conception of disability—"emerging from and informed by (rather than applied to) 'cultural locatedness'" (Barker and Murray 228).

As my analysis of *Abeng* indicates, I agree with Barker and Murray and Sherry in that postcolonialism and disability should not be reduced to metaphors and should instead be treated as distinct aspects of the characters' lives. A new, more progressive approach to this intersection does not conflate the two, privilege one above the other, or equate them with other concepts like racism; instead, the new approach traces each dimension of oppression as it is enacted in individual nations, cultures, and communities. Sherry "emphasize[s] the importance of examining the interconnections of sexism, racism and disablism in postcolonialism and in the study of disability" (n.p.), offering examples of how ignorance of the separate cultural issues leads to reductive criticism. For example, Fanon's stance of medical objectivity leads to a "masking" of sexism in his "study of one man's impotence following the rape of his wife" (Sherry n.p.). If we consider characters like Mad Hannah and Doreen through this lens, we find the different dimensions of oppression *interacting* according to their cultural context. Even in the stories of Judge Savage and Winifred, relatively privileged characters, we find obvious sexism interacting with racism. Judge Savage rapes his slaves with impunity, producing "illegitimate" progeny, and his actions are considered the norm for a white land-owning male; on the other hand, Winifred's brief relationship with a black gardener "contaminates" her and results in her exile from the community. Additionally, Winifred's behavior (as well as Mad Hannah's) is attributed to her experience of menopause. Explicating the interplay of dimensions of oppression in postcolonial fiction will allow disability studies scholars to assert the distinctive effects of disabled identity while expanding the field's understanding of disability in disparate cultural contexts. Further, this analysis demonstrates the value of adding both disabled and postcolonial identities to considerations of intersectionality, which Jennifer Nash defines as "the notion that subjectivity is constituted by mutually reinforcing vectors of race, gender, class, and sexuality" (2).

Nash argues that one goal of intersectionality is to address the absence of various minority voices in scholarship, including "feminist and anti-racist work." Returning to a quotation from earlier in this chapter, Nash sees the inclusion of "multiply marginalized subjects" as valuable as a matter of rights but also epistemology: "For intersectional theorists, marginalized subjects have an epistemic advantage, a particular perspective that scholars should consider, if not adopt, when crafting a normative vision of a just society" (3). One such vision is offered by Glissant, who describes an evolving Caribbean collectivity that values its heterogeneity. In the spirit of inclusion offered by Nash and Glissant, *Abeng* shows us that mental disability, and disability more generally, should be recognized as an essential part of the global project of social justice—to address ableism and associated systems of prejudice in Western, postcolonial, and other cultures; to cement disability's status as political identity; to include the perspectives and lived experiences of people with disabilities as a unique form of knowledge in academia, government policy, and public discourse; and to recognize the creativity and contributions of disabled people on their own terms, without making them objects of pity or fodder for non-disabled "inspiration." By viewing disability as part of social justice, scholars can move toward what Barker and Murray call "democratic criticism," which (building on the work of Edward Said) argues for "participation" in the "formation of a full and inclusive idea of citizenship, one radical and yet everyday in its appreciation of the real value of disabled lives" (234).

Notes

1. John Thieme explores the metaphor of madness in more recent Caribbean writing, as a number of novelists engage "in the search to move beyond the madness instilled by colonialism" (115).
2. The phrase, "*obeah*-woman," refers to a practitioner of Obeah, an Afro-Caribbean system of magical ritual and religious belief.

Works Cited

Barker, Clare, and Stuart Murray. "Disabling Postcolonialism: Global Disability Cultures and Democratic Criticism." *Journal of Literary & Cultural Disability Studies*, vol. 4, no. 3, 2010, pp. 219–36.
Césaire, Aimé. *Notebook of a Return to the Native Land*. Wesleyan University Press, 2001.
Cliff, Michelle. *Abeng*. Crossing Press, 1984.
Dash, J. Michael. "The Madman at the Crossroads: Delirium and Dislocation in Caribbean Literature." *Profession*, 2002, pp. 37–43.
Donaldson, Elizabeth J. "The Corpus of the Madwoman: Toward a Feminist Disability Studies Theory of Embodiment and Mental Illness." *NWSA Journal*, vol. 14, no. 3, 2002, pp. 99–119.

Fanon, Frantz. *Black Skin, White Masks*. Grove Press, 2008.
——. *The Wretched of the Earth*. Grove Press, 2004.
Flaugh, Christian. "Of Colonized Mind and Matter: The Dis/Abilities of Negritude in Aimé Césaire's *Cahier d'un retour au pays natal.*" *Journal of Literary & Cultural Disability Studies*, vol. 4, no. 3, 2010, pp. 291–308.
Glissant, Édouard. *Caribbean Discourse*. University Virginia Press, 1989.
Mitchell, David T., and Sharon L. Snyder. *Narrative Prosthesis: Disability and the Dependencies of Discourse*. University Michigan Press, 2000.
Nash, Jennifer C. "Re-thinking Intersectionality." *Feminist Review*, vol. 89, 2008, pp. 1–15.
Sherry, Mark. "(Post)colonising Disability." *Wagadu*, vol. 4, 2007, n.p.
Springer, Jennifer Thorington. "Reconfigurations of Caribbean History: Michelle Cliff's Rebel Women." *Meridians: Feminism, Race, Transnationalism*, vol. 7, no. 2, 2007, pp. 43–60.
Thieme, John. "Becoming a Madman, Becoming a Madwoman: Ex-centricity in Caribbean Writing." *Ex-centric Writing: Essays on Madness in Postcolonial Fiction*, edited by Susanna Zinato and Annalisa Pes, Cambridge Scholars Publishing, 2013, pp. 95–118.

CHAPTER 13

It Doesn't Add Up: Mental Illness in Paul Hornschemeier's *Mother, Come Home*

Jessica Gross

Comics are important for disability studies because, among other things that comics may accomplish, they can present the experiences of disability in images when words fail, or, at times, show complex realities by presenting words and images that conflict with one another. This capability is especially important when dealing with mental illnesses, which have symptoms that may be impossible to express in words and are also often not visible to others. *Trauma Is Really Strange*, a comic about traumatic symptoms and strategies for recovery, explains both the need for embodiment to recover from trauma (a concept that the comic I'll be analyzing here, *Mother, Come Home*, addresses) as well as the idea that sometimes trauma cannot be portrayed using language. In explaining how trauma works, *Trauma is Really Strange* quotes Dr. David Berceli who explains that sometimes "there are no words to describe the depth of human experience the trauma survivor has been plunged into" (Haines and Standing 8). When there are no words to accurately describe the traumatic experience, images can help portray the lived experience of trauma to readers; as such, comics can be an important mode of communicating disability experience.

J. Gross (✉)
St. Louis College of Pharmacy, St. Louis, MO, USA

In this chapter, I analyze Paul Hornschemeier's comic *Mother, Come Home* and its portrayal of trauma in its two protagonists. I first discuss David Tennant's trauma, and then end the essay with a look at why his son Thomas's trauma is so different from David's. Being able to *see* David's and Thomas's experiences allows us to understand in a more intimate way how trauma works in their lives; because trauma is an invisible illness, comics are an important way to understand this illness that might otherwise be incomprehensible to an outsider.

Mother, Come Home

Paul Hornschemeier's *Mother, Come Home* is a comic that focuses on father David Tennant and his young son, Thomas, in the wake of the death of Sarah, their wife and mother, respectively.[1] The book is divided into two distinct parts: an opening section, which is different in both content and visual style from the rest of the book, is from the perspective of David Tennant, a symbolic logic professor, and the main text of the book, which is narrated by an adult Thomas Tennant who is looking back on his childhood. The comic deals with the trauma of surviving a loved one's death, but with a significant twist. Toward the end of the book, after leaving a psychiatric hospital, David tells his son Thomas that he helped assist in Sarah's suicide because she was sick. This event makes David feel as if he had killed his wife, and shortly after admitting this to his son, he stands at the edge of a cliff, tells Thomas to put his hand on his back, and jumps to his death. David's body is not shown, but a partially eaten sandwich that he leaves behind becomes the symbolic substitute for his body.

Mother, Come Home is complex in its narrative structure. The title pages identify the authors as "Paul Hornschemeier, with an introduction by Thomas Tennant." Thomas Tennant, however, is a child character within the book and, as an adult, also its ostensible narrator, and not the book's flesh-and-blood author. The book, however, goes to great lengths to make it seem as if Thomas Tennant is a real person and the book's actual author. This artifice extends beyond the story the book tells, and even includes its paratextual elements. Thomas Tennant is even supplied with a fake author's e-mail address at the end of the book (Romero-Jódar 1198).

Perhaps most curious, however, are the elaborate section divisions at the end of the book. After the last page of the narrative proper, there is a full page with a picture of a lion mask (a recurring motif in the book), followed by a full page that bears only the words, "End of Introduction" (Hornschemeier 107–108). Turning the page again, there is another full page bearing the image of the lion mask, followed by a page that reads, "Chapter One" and "We Are All Released" (Hornschemeier 109–110). Thus, the entire text of *Mother, Come Home* claims to only be an introduction to a book whose first chapter is not included in the physical book we hold in our hands. This closing to the book is important not only for how it seeks to extend the artifice that Thomas Tennant is the book's author, but also for the argument it makes about trauma.

The Wound

In *Unclaimed Experience: Trauma, Narrative, and History*, Cathy Caruth discusses the origin of the word "trauma," and the way Freud's analysis of it has shaped our modern understanding of the word:

> …the Greek *trauma*, or 'wound,' originally refer[red] to an injury inflicted on a body. In its later usage, particularly in the medical and psychiatric literature, and most centrally in Freud's text, the term *trauma* is understood as a wound inflicted not upon the body but upon the mind. But what seems to be suggested by Freud in *Beyond the Pleasure Principle* is that the wound of the mind—the breach in the mind's experience of time, self, and the world—is not, like the wound of the body, a simple and healable event, but rather an event that…is experienced too soon, too unexpectedly, to be fully-known and is therefore not available to consciousness until it imposes itself again, repeatedly, in the nightmares and repetitive actions of the survivor. (3–4)

This sense of trauma as a wound inflicted upon the mind—a wound that is so unexpected that it is not fully available to the conscious mind—is illustrated by *Mother, Come Home*'s opening section, narrated by David Tennant, Thomas Tennant's father.

In this opening section, the father floats through a barren landscape, and the words "To drift merrily" appear near the top of the first page (Fig. 13.1; Hornschemeier 1). His head is unnaturally and cartoonishly large and distorted. In the pages that follow, he continues to float through this bizarre landscape, sometimes encountering obstacles and sometimes being grabbed at by alien-like creatures. Words accompany nearly every panel, and it soon becomes apparent that Mr. Tennant is speaking to his deceased wife, and that he is attempting to find her as he

Fig. 13.1 "To drift merrily," from Paul Hornschemeier's *Mother, Come Home*. Image copyright © 2017 Paul Hornschemeier, courtesy Fantagraphics Books

floats through this "traumascape"—a bizarre, surrealistic milieu that represents how the world seems to the traumatized David and which stands in stark contrast to the main narrative section of the book.

The full reason why David is traumatized is not revealed until much later, in the main narrative section, when David explains to his son, "Your mother killed herself…But I had to…I had to…help her…she couldn't do it by herself. She was too sick. She was too...scared. We were both scared of everything that was happening then" (Hornschemeier 88). The true emotional weight of David's part in his wife's death is emphasized a few pages later when David yells, shaking Thomas, "**Thomas! I killed** her! I helped her..." (Hornschemeier 98, emphasis in original). His hand in his wife's death is David's wound, and this event was too unexpected for his conscious mind to process. His role in his wife's death is clearly what traumatized David and eventually led him to suicide.

The main narrative of *Mother, Come Home* is, for the most part, a coherent chronological story. The opening traumascape section, however, shows a disorientation of time, space, and language. In her essay "PostSecret as Imagetext: The Reclamation of Traumatic Experiences and Identity," Tanya K. Rodrigue explains that individuals who have experienced trauma often have trouble remembering the traumatizing event, and usually cannot reflect upon it with discursive language. She explains that many experts say that trauma "dismantles language" and that trauma disconnects the experience from language; this disconnect often results in only fragments of the traumatic experience being remembered (Rodrigue 39). Rodrigue continues, "Much of the time, traumatic events are identified as an absence, or that which has not come to be understood," and goes on to ask, "How can one give presence to absence? ... How might a traumatized individual bear witness to the experience and testify about an event that has yet to be understood?" (39–40). The opening section of *Mother, Come Home* portrays the representation of a traumatic telling that never quite locates the absence at its center; although David repeatedly tells his wife he is looking for her, what is absent is the traumatic event itself; her illness, her suicide, and the role that David played in it are never directly represented in this section.

Throughout this section, David confusedly tells his wife that he is coming to find her, and sometimes replays memories of their lives together from long before her death. The first words that David speaks to his wife are, "Do you remember that summer—I think you were sixteen—when you went horseback riding? I am coming to find you, regardless, but do you remember? We had such wonderful weather that spring—it was late spring—and your hair had grown to just the right length for horseback-riding fantastic memories" (Hornschemeier 3). David then returns to this same memory shortly before he jumps from the cliff and is pulled under black waters to his death. The second time David repeats these words to his wife, the text is exactly the same, but this time instead of being spread out through four panels the entire monologue appears in one panel (Hornschemeier 7).

To use Rodrigue's language, David gives "presence to absence" by obsessively repeating a memory from his adolescent years with his wife and not giving representation to the true obsessive mantra of his trauma ("I killed my wife, I killed my wife"). In never giving voice to the actual traumatic event, David is lost in a traumascape that disallows his participation in his everyday life. By avoiding narrating the traumatic event, he instead obsessively repeats another, earlier memory of his wife.

Field

Art historian, novelist, and critic John Berger's 1971 short essay "Field" is not about trauma; rather, it focuses on the author's meditation on a field near where he lives, and the importance of his experiences in this field. Berger's meditation on the significance of this field is relevant to my discussion of the opening section of *Mother, Come Home* for its insight on how some experiences may take place outside normal narrative time.

In "Field," Berger explains his time in the field as being something that lies outside the narrative of his life; this concept is similar to Caruth's discussion of trauma as being something that is not fully known to consciousness. The traumatic event is something that is not fully knowable to one's everyday, lived experience of normal life; the experience of trauma can't be incorporated into what one knows about the world (hence why the traumatic event is traumatic; it shatters expectations for how the world operates).

The opening section of *Mother, Come Home* depicts David's inability to incorporate Sarah's death into the narrative of his life, and this failure is an increasing source of friction that culminates in his suicide. David's experience in the traumascape of the opening section shows that his everyday experiences now lie outside narrative time; although Berger is not discussing a traumatic event, Berger also experiences a landscape as outside the narrative experience of his life. Berger explains:

> By this time you are within the experience. Yet saying this implies narrative time and the essence of the experience is that it takes place outside such time. The experience does not enter into the narrative of your life—that

narrative which, at one level or another of your consciousness, you are continually retelling and developing to yourself. On the contrary, this narrative is interrupted. (204)

The narrative of his life that David—like all people—is continually constructing for himself is shattered when his wife dies, and he is never able to incorporate her death into his life's narrative. As a professor of symbolic logic, David sees all of life through this frame, and his wife's death—and the fact that he assisted her in her suicide—can never add up like one of David's equations. His wife's death does not enter the narrative of his life—a narrative that for David is not really a narrative, but rather an equation. David cannot accept a world that is absurd and arbitrary, and this leads to his suicide; David's equation for how reality works is too rigid to admit the variable of his wife's assisted suicide.

If Mary Loves Anyone, Then She Loves John

Mother, Come Home stresses the centrality of symbolic logic to David's life numerous times. The title and copyright pages of *Mother, Come Home* are bordered by symbolic logic notations, including the repeated sentence, "If Mary loves anyone, then she loves John" (title page). In *The Trauma Graphic Novel*, Andrés Romero-Jódar explains the significance of this phrase and the way it frames the presentation of trauma. Romero-Jódar notes that the formulae under this phrase are ways of representing it in symbolic logic. Symbolic logic formulae seek to reduce sentences to the logical relations between their parts, and thus suppress ambiguity of meaning. Surprisingly, however, there are *two* formulae given for this sentence. Romero-Jódar writes:

> Philosophical logic, in contrast to other disciplines, uses a special type of written language commonly known as "logical formalisms" and "well-formed formulas" (WFFs) .... the fact that two WFFs are given for one proposition ... implies duplicity of possibilities that seem to break the unity and simplicity of meaning postulated by David's philosophy. Centring the attention on his mental condition, it seems evident that Thomas' father is utterly unable to understand the death of his wife, and this leads to his own traumatization, internment, and suicide ... In his world of logic, there are no WFFs to express the loss of his wife. It is absurd, beyond symbolic logic. (1145–65)

Thus, even the paratextual elements of the book before the narrative begins show the centrality of symbolic logic to the way that David views the world and processes the trauma of losing his wife.

This emphasis on symbolic logic continues into the opening section of the book; the formula (T+a number) is found throughout many of its panels. As Romero-Jódar explains, in symbolic logic "T" can stand for Truth, and "The higher the quantifier, the more different the truth will be" (1329). At the end of the introductory section we see (T+20) when "...he [David] finally succumbs to his inability to understand reality as Truth in terms of logic, and he becomes trapped inside his own mind..." (Romero-Jódar 1329). David is trying desperately to apply the rules of logic to his experiences with his wife's death, but he can never make everything add up. The rules of logic simply can't apply in this traumascape where he finds himself.

As David floats along and continues to search for his wife, he comments on aspects of his current life as "distractions" that keep him from finding his wife. The gulf between David's trauma—his wife's death—and his everyday life has become so great that he is losing touch with reality. He is now fully engulfed by this traumascape that is without clear time, space, or even temperature: "...it's not hot, but it's not not hot. You see? There doesn't seem to be any temperature at all, is my general point. Specifically, I, for some reason, expect it to be hot, but instead feel only a dull neutrality, thermally speaking" (Hornschemeier 6, emphasis in original). This section makes it clear just how different David's traumascape is from his corporeal reality. As he speaks to his dead wife, he struggles to remember even the most important aspects of his everyday life:

> There are multiple distractions that somehow leak themselves in, even into these open spaces. Things about cleaning and creditors. ALL sorts of ephemera...
> Little ghosts to be brushed aside.
> There is one that keeps occurring to me though.
> Something that I think may be of some import.
> Something we created together.
> A doll? A talking something? Something that made us happy. (Hornschemeier 6)

Trauma takes place outside the narrative of one's life; in this traumascape where David searches for his wife, the realities of his life narrative are inaccessible to him. Even the existence of his son is just out of reach for David; he cannot reconcile the remnants of the life he built with his wife with a world in which his wife no longer exists.

On the following page, David admits that his attempts to figure everything out have been unsuccessful. An image of him floating above rocks from which a single flower grows reads, "I start to think I've got it figured out, but then realize I don't. Where are you?" (Hornschemeier 7). In the main narrative of the book, David also expresses his inability to make sense of his wife's death in his lived reality. After David enters the psychiatric hospital, a series of pages show his conversations with his psychiatrist. The psychiatrist exhorts David of the importance of keeping "an anchor in reality," for when that anchor is pulled up, one is in danger (Hornschemeier 55). This language is reminiscent of the traumascape section, which ends with David being pulled under black waters by alien-looking creatures.

Here, the psychiatrist's warning foreshadows David's eventual suicide and David's drift from reality into his traumascape. On the next page, David admits aloud to the doctor that his wife is dead. He then articulates his difficulty, and the crux of his trauma: "I **recognize** the **fact**… **not** the absurdity to which it leads" (Hornschemeier 56, emphasis in original). Trauma and death, this book argues, are absurd; they cannot be fit into logical formulae, nor quantified. David seems unable to cope with his trauma because of his insistence on viewing the world as rational and orderly; when that image of the world is shattered, David seems incapable of continuing to live in the world. Unlike in his symbolic logic equations, when David enters the correct variables into the equation of his life he still gets an absurd response.

David is unable to accept the absurd nature of life, as well as the absurdity that he played a part in his wife's death. When pressed by David to tell him if he is "crazy," his psychiatrist responds, "I think you know as well as I that these sorts of things are—for the most part—arbitrary. It's…nothing is as simplistic and clean as people would like" (Hornschemeier 62). And, this is what *Mother, Come Home* also portrays about trauma; it (and the event that caused it) may be absurd and arbitrary; responses to trauma are not clean, simple, or logical. The psychiatrist expresses that David is capable of recovery, but that his recovery will neither be quick nor simple. Although David cognitively understands that his wife has died, and is finally able to say this aloud, he cannot affectively process her loss.

Graphic Medicine

It is significant that the opening section depicts how different David's experience is from how it appears to the psychiatrist and to his son. This is important because it reveals why David behaves the way he does; the reader is forced to view the world as the same absurd traumascape in which David finds himself. Graphic medicine, which the 2015 *Graphic Medicine Manifesto* defines as "the intersection of the medium of comics and the discourse of healthcare" can help to theorize what contributions a book like *Mother, Come Home* might make to disability studies (Czerwiec et al. 1). Many in the graphic medicine movement have argued that one of the affordances of comics is that they can obligate the reader to contemplate illness from an individualized, often non-medical perspective, and therefore can counter the traditional depiction of disability from an able-bodied and medical viewpoint. David's actions at the end of the book—jumping off a cliff in front of his young son, and making his son complicit in his suicide—seem, in the main narrative, bizarre and incomprehensible. While *Mother, Come Home* does show the harm that this suicide caused, through the opening traumascape it also shows the reader what cannot be seen from an external view of David's life and actions: that David sees himself in a world where everything is bizarre, and where he sees no rational options.

The depiction of David's traumascape counters the representation of David in the psychiatric hospital, which is presented as antiseptic, orderly, even prison-like: David meets with his psychiatrist in a space that resembles a police interrogation room (Fig. 13.2; Hornschemeier 58). This opening section that offers an internal view of David's illness, differing from the way he is viewed by others, is an important aspect of what graphic medicine can accomplish. *Graphic Medicine Manifesto* explains:

> Graphic medicine...[offers] a more inclusive perspective of medicine, illness, disability, caregiving, and being cared for...Manifestos acknowledge that there is not one "universal subject"...So too graphic medicine resists the notion of the universal patient and vividly represents multiple subjects with valid and, at times, conflicting points of view and experiences. (Czerwiec et al. 2)

Comics, then, and this newly defined field of graphic medicine, are capable of showing a disrupting, individualized experience alongside

Fig. 13.2 David faces his doctor at the psychiatric hospital, from Paul Hornschemeier's *Mother, Come Home*. Image copyright © 2017 Paul Hornschemeier, courtesy Fantagraphics Books

a clinical, so-called "objective" representation of the same illness. The main text of *Mother, Come Home* shows David's symptoms of trauma and depression as they appear to others, whereas the opening section depicts the same period of time from David's perspective. The shocking difference in verbal and visual styles between these two parts of the narrative shows how different trauma appears from the outside than from the inside. Thomas responds to trauma in his own, very unique way, as will be discussed below. These differing representations of trauma within the same text demonstrate, as *Graphic Medicine Manifesto* argues, that the same illness may be met with "….conflicting points of view and experiences" (Czerwiec et al. 2).

I Was Much Older Then

For seven-year-old Thomas, a key symbol for the way he deals with trauma is his lion mask, which we see his mother giving him in the first scene of the main narrative of the book, immediately following the opening section (Hornschemeier 10–12). This scene establishes the connection between the mask and the way Thomas deals with trauma, and also shows the way that Thomas's trauma intrudes into his everyday life.

The last page in this scene is a mix of panels showing Thomas receiving and putting on the lion mask, and additional panels that interrupt this scene with traumatic flashbacks for the adult Thomas. That is, these intruding panels point to the traumatization of the adult Thomas, and show that he now associates these later traumatic events with the mask. Two panels interrupt the memory of Thomas receiving the mask from his mother; one is of his father's foot in the snow at his mother's funeral, and the other is of a half-eaten sandwich, the symbol of David's body after his suicide (Romero-Jódar 1353–71). Thus, this single page summarizes Thomas's trauma, and foreshadows the role that this lion mask will play in dealing with it. On the following two pages, David and Thomas are shown in front of the mother's gravestone at her funeral. Thomas is wearing the lion mask (Hornschemeier 13–14). In fact, Thomas wears the lion mask whenever he visits a site or does an activity that he associates with his mother. The mask is usually portrayed in ornate, realistic detail. However, there are several scenes in the book that are drawn in a childish style, and in these scenes we see a simplified version of the mask. These scenes represent Thomas's fantasy life and the way he is processing the events around him as a seven-year-old.

In one scene, the reader sees Thomas's dream in which he wears the lion mask. The dream scene is accompanied by the explanation that he would dream "…big, humid allegories," but Thomas as the adult narrator says that "…now I cannot exactly pull up [the dreams]…due in no small part…to hundreds of youthful daytime fantasies enacted to erase the nocturnal dramas" (Hornschemeier 52). This explanation is accompanied by a non-dream scene in which Thomas is wearing his lion mask and playing with a toy that had also just appeared in his dream. Thus, Thomas wears his lion mask as a way of overwriting the trauma of his mother's death with childhood fantasies.

While David deals with his trauma by attempting to use logic to reason through what has happened, Thomas takes an alternative approach by not only acknowledging that the world is absurd, but by intentionally escaping into absurd fantasies. Thomas transforms the difficult realities of his everyday life, such as having to live with his aunt and uncle after his father checks into a psychiatric hospital, into fantasy scenes wherein each character is an animal. Only through these fantasy scenes, and while wearing his lion mask, does Thomas seem capable of processing and understanding his new reality. If David would seem to argue that trauma can be processed through attempting to understand it through the laws of logic, then it seems that Thomas would argue that trauma can be processed only through fantasy and an abandonment of logic.

After staying with his aunt and uncle for a while, Thomas decides that he needs to save his father from the psychiatric hospital. Although his father is voluntarily in the hospital, Thomas does not understand this and devises a plan to liberate him. He sets out to walk to the hospital wearing his lion mask. The walk to the hospital is marked as a coming-of-age for Thomas, as he comes to the realization that he cannot save his mother (the never-uttered traumatic refrain at the center of the book, "Mother, come home") and that he can only save his father, if he can even do that. In the panel in which Thomas comes to this realization, his mask is shown in his hands and no longer on his head. When worn, the mask symbolizes Thomas's filtering of reality through layers of childish fantasy and denial; taking the mask off signifies that he is capable of understanding and facing his trauma head-on, and thus is ready to begin the journey of healing that can perhaps lessen the trauma that he will experience later in life.

Thomas makes it to the psychiatric hospital and helps his father "escape." They then run into the woods surrounding the hospital, and Thomas again wears his lion mask. David tells Thomas they need to stop for a minute, and Thomas tries to remove his mask. David says, "No… keep that on," and then proceeds to tell Thomas that his mother had killed herself, and that he had assisted because she was so sick (Hornschemeier 87–88). As David reveals this information, Thomas faces him, his face obscured by the mask (Fig. 13.3; Hornschemeier 88). David does not feel capable of telling Thomas this difficult news without the mediation of the lion mask, which, it seems, David sees as a way for Thomas to retain some childhood innocence while learning this traumatic information. The reader knows that Thomas has recently undergone a great maturation when he realized that he could not save his mother and he removed his mask; however, David does not know this. As this is the first time in the book that David has told anyone that his wife killed herself and that he assisted, he seems to need the mediation of the mask to speak this difficult truth.

The next morning, David stands at the edge of a cliff near where he and Thomas have camped overnight in the woods. David tells Thomas that he has to go because he killed his wife (Hornschemeier 97–98). Then, just before he jumps off the cliff, David instructs Thomas to put on his mask, which he does. David then looks at Thomas and says, "No…take your mask off. Just us, okay?" (Hornschemeier 100).

Fig. 13.3 Thomas, wearing his lion mask, faces his father, from Paul Hornschemeier's *Mother, Come Home*. Image copyright © 2017 Paul Hornschemeier, courtesy Fantagraphics Books

This is a turning point in how Thomas will present his trauma regarding his father's suicide in *Mother, Come Home*. Thomas had been dealing with his mother's death and his father's inattentiveness through fantasy, greatly aided by his use of the lion mask. This scene breaks the chain of Thomas using fantasy as a way to escape the harsh realities of his life; David requests that Thomas experience his suicide as a fact of reality, not something that is mediated through his fantasy life. The adult narrator Thomas comments that "It became clear he [David] would need assistance," and on the next page Thomas places his hand gently on his father's back as he jumps off the cliff (Hornschemeier 100–101).

This action, of course, perpetuates the trauma that David had suffered from. If David felt like he had killed his wife for having assisted in her suicide, then he has now put Thomas in the same position by involving him in his suicide. And yet, although Thomas does throughout his life repeat the mantra that he killed his father, he also says that he believes this to be wrong. Shortly after David has jumped from the cliff, the narrator states:

> I killed my father. I killed my father. In my guilty moments, when being reprimanded by a teacher or a sales clerk or a girlfriend, I would chastise myself with this simple mantra, though, even then, I knew it to be wrong. (Hornschemeier 104)

Thus, although Thomas is traumatized as an adult, as the flashbacks at the beginning of the book indicate, he is able to live with this trauma without blaming himself and without becoming suicidal. Thomas not putting on his mask as his father jumps from the cliff is a turning point for Thomas and for the form that his trauma will take. Although Thomas had worn the mask throughout much of the narrative, Thomas says that he never put the mask on again after his father's death: "I know that to wear it now would blur that final moment" (Hornschemeier 101). The lion mask has provided a kind of blurring for Thomas: blurring the distinctions between fantasy and reality, and of the differences between his life before and after his mother died. Wearing the mask was one way for him to preserve a sense of continuity with his life when his mother was still alive.[2]

To return to Caruth's definition of the trauma or wound, Caruth defined the traumatic wound as "…an event that…is experienced too soon, too unexpectedly, to be fully-known and is therefore not available to consciousness until it imposes itself again, repeatedly, in the nightmares and repetitive actions of the survivor" (3–4). Although Thomas does experience intruding thoughts from this experience, not wearing the mask during his father's suicide was an attempt to make this event more fully available to his consciousness; David had wanted just the two of them to experience this moment without the intrusion of Thomas's fantasy life or his connection with his dead mother. As such, the book suggests, Thomas has the possibility of incorporating this event, painful as it is, into the narrative of his life in a way that David could never incorporate Sarah's death into his life.

After his father's suicide, as Thomas walks away from the campsite where he and his father had camped the night before, Thomas-as-narrator states, "I was much older then" (Hornschemeier 105). Here Thomas walks with his lion mask in his hand, as he had on the highway on the way to the psychiatric hospital. Both moments of realization and maturation required that Thomas take off the mask. By taking off the mask, Thomas has taken off both his symbol of childhood and the symbol that represented his sublimation of trauma into fantasy. *Mother, Come Home* presents both David's attempts to logically analyze his wife's death, and Thomas's attempts to sublimate traumatic experiences into fantasy, as ineffective. Instead, as I'll discuss below, it is the power of storytelling that allows Thomas to break free from his trauma in a way that David never could.

WE ARE ALL RELEASED

Although the narrative action of *Mother, Come Home* ends with David killing himself in front of Thomas, I argue that the book ultimately has a hopeful message about the possibility of living through and with trauma. The adult Thomas, who is narrating the book, is not suicidal, and other than the page at the beginning of the book that features intrusive panels from later scenes, Thomas is able to narrate the story of his childhood lucidly and without traumatic flashbacks.

I have previously discussed how David and Thomas each had their own way of dealing with trauma; David tried to logically reason through it, and Thomas used his fantasy world to cope with the changes in his life. However, a more fundamental difference underlies David's and Thomas's way of coping with trauma. David did not tell anyone his story until right before he killed himself, and even then he told it in just a few words. Thomas, on the other hand, as the narrator and ostensible author of this book, has painstakingly told the details of his parents' deaths in this volume. This act of writing his story is central to Thomas's healing, and this fact is hinted at before David commits suicide. As Thomas walks to the psychiatric hospital to "free" his father, he has a fantasy scene in which he liberates his father. The drawing and words are childish, but this scene foreshadows the rest of the book and gives an abbreviated version of their escape from the hospital, run through the woods, and David's suicide (Hornschemeier 71–75).

In this scene, David says to Thomas, "I will go away now" (Hornschemeier 74). Thomas responds, "Will you write?" David answers, "A little bit. You will begin to understand later," and Thomas replies, "And then I'll write" (Hornschemeier 75). As these words are shown, David begins to float off the ground and he looks as he does in the opening section. As David completely flies away from Thomas he says, "Yes. And we all will be released" (Hornschemeier 75). This imagined conversation doesn't make sense until the end of the book, when the reader sees David's actual suicide scene. Shortly before he jumps, David writes a note for Thomas that he exhorts him not to read until the following day (Hornschemeier 99). Thus, the imagined conversation between David and Thomas points to David's short note (which Thomas refuses to call a "suicide note"), and to Thomas writing once he understands his father's note. Most significant of all, David's final words in the imagined conversation, "And we all will be released," foreshadows the title of chapter one of the book: "We Are All Released" (Hornschemeier 75, 110).

As discussed at the beginning of this essay, *Mother, Come Home* goes to great lengths to make it seem as if Thomas Tennant is its author and that it is only the introduction to the real book. After Thomas walks into the woods after his father's suicide, there is a whole page that reads, "End of Introduction" and turning the page reveals "Chapter One: 'We Are All Released'" (Hornschemeier 108, 110). This narrative structure indicates that what we have just read is only the beginning of Thomas's story; in fact, we have not even read chapter one yet. And what we *have* read is about a time when Thomas was not released. This "introduction," then, was Thomas's working out of his trauma, which was a necessary step for him before he could go on to narrate the rest of his life. His childhood imagined conversation with his father predicted that "we all will be released" after Thomas writes; now that Thomas has written the story of his trauma, he is released from its grip, and it seems as if somehow his father's memory is also released.

The reader, too, is included in this "all"; after this "introduction," the reader is released from this story of trauma into a chapter one wherein Thomas is released from his traumatic childhood.[3] The reader, too, is released from a story of trauma into a non-trauma story. It is the act of writing, then, that releases Thomas from the severity of the wound that afflicted David. David, unlike Thomas, writes only a little, and only after he has already decided to kill himself. This "introduction," which is in fact the entire volume of *Mother, Come Home*, is Thomas's releasing of himself from the double trauma of "Mother, Come Home" and "I killed my father. I killed my father." In the economy created in *Mother, Come Home*, neither logic nor fantasy is an adequate way to approach trauma; only through the power of storytelling are Thomas, his father's memory, and even we, the readers, all released.

Trauma is Really Strange explains that with trauma, "We lose connection with our body or parts of our body. It is hard to stay present and grounded" (Haines and Standing 5). Furthermore, the comic instructs, "Please don't try too hard to think or rationalize your way out of trauma…But we can use our body and senses to feel and orient our way out of danger" (Haines and Standing 17). *Trauma is Really Strange* suggests that embodiment—focusing on being in a body—is a key way to heal from trauma. As a visual medium, comics can illustrate embodiment, and *Mother, Come Home* visually illustrates how David literally becomes untethered from the world and his surroundings and floats through his traumascape, while Thomas literally changes the way his body interacts with the world by wearing a mask. Ultimately, it's Thomas's embodiment of trauma—remaining firmly on the earth, and accepting his body's ability to look at difficult things without the mask—that saves him, and it is the book's visual format that allows us as readers to see dissociation and embodiment in action. As the title of *Trauma is Really Strange* points out, trauma *is* really strange, and its strangeness can be difficult to portray in words to those who have not experienced it. One of the gifts of comics is the way they can allow us to see experiences that are externally invisible, and to understand characters whose worlds no longer make sense to them; they make visible an invisible wound.

Notes

1. I prefer calling this work a "comic" rather than a "graphic novel" for several reasons. "Graphic novel" was largely a marketing term that arose to separate "high culture" comics from "low culture" comics, and thus ignores the debt that "graphic novels" owe to the comics that came before them. A number of scholars have written on this problem of terminology, but in this context Scott T. Smith's chapter in the *Graphic Medicine Manifesto* ("Who Gets to Speak? The Making of Comics Scholarship") is especially apropos.
2. See 1080–1111 in *The Trauma Graphic Novel* for Romero-Jódar's analysis of Thomas's mask, which covers elements that I did not have time to discuss here, such as the significance of the doorknob in the shape of the lion's mask on the cover of the American edition of the book.
3. Romero-Jódar analyzes the significance of "We Are All Released" in *The Trauma Graphic Novel* on 1027–40; I owe my analysis of the importance of storytelling and writing for Thomas's release to Romero-Jódar. See also 1016–30 for Romero-Jódar's analysis of the fantasy scene in which David and Thomas discuss writing, which in its emphasis on narrative structure differs from my own reading above.

Works Cited

Berger, John. "Field." *About Looking*. Vintage International, 1991, pp. 199–205.
Caruth, Cathy. *Unclaimed Experience: Trauma, Narrative, and History*. 20th anniversary edition, Johns Hopkins University Press, 2016.

Czerwiec, M.K., et al. "Introduction." *Graphic Medicine Manifesto*, edited by Susan Merrill Squier and Ian Williams, Pennsylvania State University Press, 2015, pp. 1–20.

Haines, Steve, and Sophie Standing. *Trauma Is Really Strange*. Singing Dragon, 2016.

Hornschemeier, Paul. *Mother, Come Home*. Fantagraphics Books, 2009.

Rodrigue, Tanya K. "PostSecret as ImageText: The Reclamation of Traumatic Experiences and Identity." *The Future of Text and Image: Collected Essays on Literary and Visual Conjunctures*, edited by Ofra Amihay and Lauren Walsh, Cambridge Scholars Publishing, 2012, pp. 39–68.

Romero-Jódar, Andrés. *The Trauma Graphic Novel*. Kindle Edition, Routledge, 2017.

Index

A
Ableism, 17–19, 23, 28, 148, 159–161, 210, 213
Ableist, 23, 128, 134, 148–153, 156, 158, 160, 202
Abnormal psychology, 57
Africa, 203, 205
Agamben, Giorgio, 150
Agency, 63, 76, 78, 106, 123, 148, 190, 193, 203
Ahmed, Sara, 51
Alcoholism, 6, 128, 136–138, 140–142, 188
Alcott, Louisa May
  Little Women, 5, 91, 92
  Moods, 5, 91–93, 95, 96, 98–102, 105, 106
  "A Whisper in the Dark", 5, 92, 94–98, 102
  Work, 5, 92, 93, 98, 101–103, 105
Alvarez, Al
  The Savage God, 66
Americans with Disabilities Act (ADA), 15
Andersson, Bibi, 175
Anishinaabemowin, 83
Ansloos, Jeffrey, 77
Anthropology, 75, 183
Antipsychiatry, 6, 52, 187
Anti-Semitic stereotypes, 174
Anti-Semitism, 170, 173, 175, 177
Arranged marriage, 94, 98
Asylum, 4, 35, 52–54, 56, 58–60, 62–64, 67, 94, 95, 97, 105, 110, 115, 119, 122, 159, 193, 207, 211
Asylum novels, 4, 5, 52, 59
Aubrecht, Katie, 3, 13, 20, 22, 28
Autobiographical writing on mental illness, 26, 109–111, 165, 178–180, 186, 188, 191

B
Bannon, Ann, 5, 128, 131
  "The Beebo Brinker Chronicles", 6, 127, 128, 130, 131, 136, 140, 141; *Beebo Brinker*, 131, 132; *I Am a Woman*, 131; *Journey to a Woman*, 131, 133–137; *Odd Girl Out*, 131, 132; *Women in the Shadows*, 131, 133, 138, 139

Barker, Clare, 211
Basaglia, Franco, 147, 151, 158, 159
Beers, Clifford, 122, 123, 125
Beresford, Peter, 13
Berger, John, 220
Bernstein, Charles, 153, 154, 156, 161
Berryman, John, 167
Bérubé, Michael, 180
Bipolar disorder, 26, 33, 34, 80, 98, 112, 185, 190
Blackbridge, Persimmon
   Prozac Highway, 3, 4, 32, 34–36, 42, 45, 47
Braidotti, Rosi, 149, 151
Brontë, Charlotte, 94, 97, 106
   Bertha Mason, 94, 97, 98, 106
Brueggemann, Brenda Jo, 13, 170
Butch, 133, 138, 139

C

Caregivers, 7, 183, 186, 196
Caribbean, 8, 199–202, 204, 208, 209, 213
Caruth, Cathy, 217
Césaire, Aimé, 202–204
Chernin, Kim, 181
Chickasaw, 77
Chosen families, 35, 46
Civilian Public Service (CPS) program, 118
Clare, Eli, 12, 18, 154
Cliff, Michelle, 7, 200
   Abeng, 7, 199, 200, 202, 203, 205–207, 209–211, 213
Collective transformation, 81, 85
Colonial, 4, 7, 72–75, 79–81, 85, 200, 202–205, 207
Colonialism, 75, 78–80, 199, 202–204, 210, 211, 213
Comics, 8, 215, 216, 224, 232

Coming out, 3, 11, 13, 16–19, 21, 24, 26, 27, 42, 129
Communist Party, 115
Community, 2–5, 16, 19–23, 25–27, 31–34, 36–43, 46–48, 51–67, 76, 78, 80–85, 101, 103, 109, 116, 120, 123, 131, 146, 148, 153, 156, 158, 160, 161, 173, 207, 211, 212
Community Mental Health Act, 123
Conscientious objectors (COs), 118, 119
Consumer, survivor, ex-patient, and mad (c/s/x/m) communities, 3, 25, 32, 48
Consumer/survivor/ex-patient (c/s/x), 11, 14, 16, 18, 24, 25, 31, 32, 48
Couser, G.T., 26
Crazy, 20, 24, 32, 45, 48, 58, 75, 83, 111, 113, 114, 139, 167, 171, 172, 174, 181, 207, 223
Cree, 77
Créolité, 8, 200
Crip culture, 129
Cripping, 35
Crip theory, 35, 147
Crip time, 123
Critical disability studies, 6, 147, 199
Cure, 4, 38, 61, 63, 101, 103, 208
Custodial care, 118

D

Dachau, 176
Darkness Visible, 65
Davis, Lennard J., 134, 147, 149, 154
Death, 2, 12, 56, 57, 66, 71, 75, 81, 92–95, 100, 101, 106, 117, 119, 120, 124, 137, 161, 171, 181, 189, 191, 192, 196, 207, 216, 219–223, 226, 228, 229

de Havilland, Olivia, 117, 118
Deleuze, Gilles, 76
Delusion, 36, 80, 81, 168, 175, 205
Depression, 5, 8, 32, 42, 44, 46,
 65, 66, 74, 76, 80, 83, 95, 99,
 101–103, 105, 112, 166, 225
Desire, 4, 15, 25, 38, 43–46, 57,
 60, 73, 76, 99, 134, 136, 140,
 150–152, 157, 160, 161, 176
Despair, 92, 93, 98, 102, 105
Deutsch, Albert
 The Shame of the States, 119
Diagnosis, 6, 12, 14, 26, 34, 43, 83,
 84, 97, 102, 105, 111, 113, 127,
 140, 169, 188, 190, 192, 193
Difference, 4, 6, 7, 11, 12, 14–17,
 19, 21, 31, 33, 43, 52, 65, 92,
 140, 153, 154, 165–175, 177,
 179–181, 200, 209, 210, 225,
 230
Dis/humanism, 6, 145, 147, 150–
 152, 160, 161
Disability, 127, 165, 183, 191, 199,
 206
 identity, 13, 23, 25, 153
 studies, 2, 3, 5, 8, 11–24, 26, 27,
 54, 91, 110, 147–149, 153,
 166, 199–203, 210–212, 215,
 224
Disclosure, 17, 20, 22, 27
Disfigured body, 6, 134
Dismodernism, 147, 150, 154
Dissociative identity disorder, 34
Donaldson, Elizabeth J., 5, 55, 72, 97,
 106, 181, 201, 202, 209
Dybbuk, 177, 181

E

Electroconvulsive therapy (ECT) or
 electroshock therapy, 57–59, 114,
 118, 124, 187, 189, 190, 193
Elliott, Alicia, 4, 74–76, 83

Empathy, 168–172, 176, 180
Epileptic, 207, 208, 211
Eros, 3, 31, 42, 45
Estroff, Sue E., 188
Ethnic erasure, 165, 173–175
Ethos, 20, 21, 23
Eugenics, 119, 206
Eurocentrism, 75

F

Faludi, Susan, 2
Fanon, Frantz, 202–204
Female malady, 95
Femininity, 92, 98, 105, 134, 135,
 141, 142
Feminist disability studies, 105
Femme, 42, 133
Firestone, Shulamith, 1, 8
Flaugh, Christian, 203
Foucault, Michel, 31, 35, 36, 38, 45,
 47
Frank, Arthur, 166, 180
Freud, Sigmund, 80, 217
Freudian, 117, 122
Fromm-Reichmann, Frieda, 180

G

Gaertner, David, 81
García, Dora, 6, 146–148, 151,
 156–160
 Hearing Voices Café, 146, 147, 151,
 157–160
 Mad Marginal, 6, 146, 156–160
Garland-Thomson, Rosemarie, 106,
 135, 170
Gay, 35, 48, 127, 129, 130, 140, 141
gay and lesbian studies, 13
Gay bar culture, 137, 138
Gender, 35, 42, 48, 53, 94, 95, 104,
 106, 128, 132, 175, 200–202,
 212

Gender inequality, 92, 94, 95, 106
Genocide, 173–175
Gilman, Sander L., 54, 180, 181
Girl, Interrupted, 65
Glissant, Édouard, 201, 208
Goffman, Erving, 11, 59, 61, 180
Goodley, Daniel, 147, 150, 160
Gothic, 5, 94, 98, 104
Graphic medicine, 8, 224, 225, 232
Graphic Medicine Manifesto, 224
Graphic novel, 221, 232
Greenberg, Joanne, 6, 52, 165, 168–173, 177, 179
  I Never Promised You a Rose Garden, 7, 52, 165–168, 170, 172–174, 176–178, 180; film version, 7, 165, 174, 175, 177
Grief, 1, 84, 93–95, 97, 98, 102, 106, 184, 207, 211

H
Haida, 79
Haisla, 81
Hall, Alice, 180
Halliwell, Martin, 180
Hallucinations, 37, 38
Hampton, John G., 77, 79
Haraway, Donna, 73
Hearing voices, 6, 43, 56, 82, 84, 113, 114, 157, 158, 178, 186
Heiltsuk, 80
Hesitation, 4, 72, 73, 77
Heteronormativity, 6, 130, 133–135
Heterosexual, 43, 130, 131, 133, 135, 136, 140
Hitler, 173, 175
Homophobia, 128, 133, 137, 139
Hornschemeier, Paul, 8, 216
  Mother, Come Home, 8, 215–217, 223, 225, 228, 229, 231
Huffer, Lynn, 35, 47
Hydrotherapy, 118

Hypertext, 5, 78, 79
Hysterical, 139, 140

I
Identity, 3, 4, 6, 11, 13–18, 21–27, 34, 35, 39, 41–44, 47, 51, 53, 54, 63, 66, 94, 127–129, 131, 133, 141, 147, 148, 154, 172, 176, 179, 180, 188, 189, 200, 202–204, 209, 210, 212, 213, 219
Identity politics, 3, 13, 21, 31, 34, 43, 47, 51, 147
Illness, 4, 7, 14, 17, 21, 22, 26, 55, 56, 91, 98, 100, 101, 112, 113, 115, 117, 123, 127, 129, 140, 157, 159, 165–167, 170, 172, 175, 176, 180, 181, 183, 185, 186, 188, 189, 191, 192, 194, 195, 216, 219, 224, 225
Illness narrative, 166
India, 7, 185, 188, 189, 191, 194, 195
Indifference, 55, 93, 171–175, 181
Indigenous art, 77, 79
Indigenous Literature, 4, 5, 72, 75, 76, 86
Indigenous mental health, 77
Ingram, Richard, 12
Insane, 7, 12, 82, 92, 105, 116, 170, 171, 178, 205, 206
Insanity, 75, 102, 105, 116, 147, 173, 174, 176, 178, 199, 205
Institutionalization, 95, 96, 161, 206
Insulin therapy, 61
Intersectionality, 200, 212

J
Jamaica, 7, 205, 207, 210, 211
Jamison, Kay Redfield, 25
Jane Eyre, 94, 97, 106

Jewish identity, 165, 166, 174
Justice, 82, 83, 114, 115, 123, 205
Justice, Daniel Heath, 72

K
Kafer, Alison, 161
Kaiser, Wilson, 180
Kaysen, Susanna, 181
  Girl Interrupted, 66, 181
Kesey, Ken, 2, 52, 166, 180
  One Flew Over the Cuckoo's Nest, 2, 52, 59, 166
Kinship, 4, 35, 45, 47, 76
Kleinman, Arthur, 7, 183
Kuusisto, Stephen, 24

L
Laing, R.D., 180, 187
LeFrancois, Brenda A., 14
Lesbian, 6, 32, 43, 48, 127–133, 135, 136, 139–141
  as alcoholic, 127, 128, 141
  as mad, 128, 132, 141
Lesbian pulp fiction, 5, 128–131
Levinas, Emmanuel, 7, 168, 179, 180
Levinasian ethics, 173
Lewis, Bradley, 14, 18
Liberal humanism, 146–148, 150, 159, 160
Liminality, 84
Linton, Simi, 14, 18
Lobotomy, 59, 60
Lockridge, Ross, 112
Longhouse, 80, 82, 83
Love, Heather, 47, 51, 63

M
MadArtReview, 4, 31–34, 36, 38–41, 43, 47
Maddening, 35–37, 39, 44

Madness, 3–6, 8, 12, 13, 15–27, 31–40, 42–47, 53–55, 67, 72, 74, 75, 78, 79, 81, 92, 94–98, 102, 103, 105, 113, 115, 128, 136, 137, 140–142, 158, 168, 169, 173, 174, 177, 178, 181, 186, 199–202, 204, 206–210, 213
Mad studies, 3, 11–15, 18–22, 24, 26, 27, 31, 48
Madwoman, 6, 45, 94, 95, 98, 104, 129, 136, 138, 140, 141, 192, 195, 201, 207
  in attic, 94
Mania, 80
Manic depression, 26, 80, 98, 105, 185
Maracle, Lee, 4, 71, 73, 83, 84
  Celia's Song, 4, 71, 80, 81, 83, 85, 86
Marcus, Neil, 21, 23
McLean Hospital, 58
McRuer, Robert, 35, 43, 129
Medical discourse, 128, 161, 184, 187, 217
Medical model of disability, 6, 13–15, 21, 26, 33, 39, 46, 54, 83, 85, 95, 103, 118, 128, 129, 152, 153, 166, 180, 187, 190, 195, 204, 212, 224
Melancholy, 92, 95, 98, 99, 103, 104, 106
Menninger, Karl, 123
Menninger Clinic, 121
Mental disability, 3, 7, 8, 15, 16, 20, 67, 101, 113, 124, 128, 136, 137, 141, 147, 149, 159, 160, 199–202, 204, 205, 207–210, 213
Mental Health America, 122
Mental Health Care Act, 120
Mental hospital, 5, 52, 58, 59, 109–111, 118, 120, 168, 174, 178, 187

Mental Hygiene Program, 118, 119
Mental illness, 1, 3–5, 7, 8, 14, 16, 17, 21, 22, 24, 31, 36, 37, 43, 44, 52–58, 60, 64–67, 83, 94, 95, 97, 105, 111–113, 118, 120, 127, 130, 166–168, 172, 175, 177, 178, 183, 185, 188–192, 196, 201, 215
Menzies, Robert J., 14
Meyer, Adolf, 125
Michi Saagiig Nishnaabe, 81
Mise en abyme, 171
Mitchell, David T., 167, 180, 201, 202, 209
Moddelmog, Debra, 13
Mohawk, 74, 76, 83
Moods, 91–93, 95, 96, 98, 100, 101, 105, 106
Morrison, Linda, 14
Motherhood, 133
Mourning, 80, 207
Murray, Stuart, 211

N
Narrative, 5, 8, 15, 20, 21, 23, 24, 32, 42, 63, 83, 94, 95, 97, 101, 102, 106, 113, 122, 133, 165–172, 174–181, 185, 187, 192, 195, 199–202, 205, 216–225, 229–232
Narrative prosthesis, 167, 200, 201, 208
Nash, Jennifer, 212
National Committee for Mental Hygiene, 122
National Institute of Mental Health, 120
National Mental Health Foundation (NMHF), 109, 119, 122
Nazi Germany, 173, 174

Nazi(s), 119, 175, 176
Négritude, 203
Neugeboren, Jay, 181
Neurodiversity, 16, 21
Neurological disability, 208
Neuroses, 203
Nishnaabeg, 81
The Noonday Demon, 65

O
Oral history, 72, 73
O'Toole, Corbett Joan, 17
Out of Sight, Out of Mind, 119

P
Page, Anthony, 174
Paranoia, 2, 33, 36, 116, 138, 139, 185
Physical disability, 25, 28, 98, 106, 141, 166, 180
Physical impairments, 127
Pinto, Jerry, 7, 183, 185
  Em and the Big Hoom, 7, 183, 185–187, 189–191, 196
Plath, Sylvia, 4, 52, 63, 66, 67, 166
  The Bell Jar, 4, 52–55, 59, 61, 65, 66, 166
Pornography, 130, 131
Postcolonial, 7, 199, 200, 208, 210–213
Posthumanism, 6, 147, 149
Potlatch, 75, 85
Pozorski, Aimee, 181
Prendergast, Catherine, 113, 124, 149
Price, Margaret, 3, 13, 18, 20, 67, 149
Prozac Nation, 66
Psychiatric aides, 118, 122
Psychiatric disability, 2, 5, 7, 11, 12, 16–18, 21, 23, 28, 91, 92, 97, 98, 105, 123, 166, 183

Psychiatric hospital, 8, 37, 114, 115, 120, 158, 187, 204, 216, 223–227, 229, 230. *See also* Mental hospital
Psychiatric survivors. *See* Consumer/survivor/ex-patient (c/s/x)
Psychiatrist, 2, 26, 113, 120, 125, 147, 151, 158, 169, 172, 181, 189, 190, 203, 223, 224
Psychiatry, 11, 12, 14, 18, 22, 24, 31, 39, 45, 47, 48, 54, 105, 117, 127, 151, 158, 159
Psychoanalysis, 75, 81, 122, 124, 169, 174, 175, 187
Psychosis, 36
Public Access Poetry, 145, 146, 151–155, 157, 160
Pyle, Kai Minosh, 83

Q
Queer, 3, 31, 32, 34, 35, 42, 43, 46–48, 51, 63, 127–131, 135, 141, 142, 171, 181
Quest plot, 167
The Quiet Room, 65
Quinlan, Kathleen, 175

R
Rape, 82, 86, 139, 140, 212
Raven, 84
Reaume, Geoffrey, 14, 47, 48
Recovery, 5, 54, 56, 101–103, 215, 223
Residential school, 71, 72, 76, 82
Responsibility, 82, 84, 109, 120, 170, 172, 179
Revitalization, 81
Robinson, Eden
Monkey Beach, 81
Romero-Jódar, Andrés, 216, 221
Roosevelt, Eleanor, 119, 120

Runswick-Cole, Katherine, 147, 150–151, 160

S
Samuels, Ellen, 123, 128
Sandahl, Carrie, 128
Sandhu, Amandeep
Sepia Leaves, 7, 183, 191–196
Schizophrenia, 2, 7, 12, 112, 113, 152, 153, 161, 169, 178, 185, 188, 191–193, 195
Self-harming, 54
Settler, 72, 75, 77–81, 83, 85
Sexual orientation, 128, 137
Sexual violence, 81–82, 86
Shame, 51, 100, 206
Sherry, Mark, 204, 211
Shoah, 165, 173, 176, 177
Showalter, Elaine, 94, 95
Shutter Island, 36, 37
Siebers, Tobin, 21, 148
Simpson, Leanne, 81
Slaves, 202, 205, 206, 212
Smith, Jeffery, 66, 67
Snyder, Sharon L., 124, 167, 170, 180, 201, 202, 209
Socialist Party, 114
Social justice, 8, 112, 117, 118, 148, 213
Social models of disability, 180
Stereotypes, 7, 54, 165, 166, 173, 174, 200–204, 209, 210
Stigma, 7, 11, 21, 23, 98, 111, 120, 166, 188, 200, 201
Stó:lō, 73, 80, 81, 83, 84
Styron, William, 167
Suicide, 1, 8, 12, 41, 46, 53, 56–58, 60, 61, 63, 65–67, 75, 78, 80, 92, 93, 98, 101, 102, 105, 112, 137, 167, 185, 188, 189, 216, 219–221, 223, 224, 226, 228–231
Symbolic logic, 216, 221–223

T
Take Shelter, 36–38
Terminology, 13, 16, 17, 21, 32–34, 39, 43, 232
Thieme, John, 213
Thomas, James M., 181
Titchkosky, Tanya, 23
Tradition, 3, 35, 67, 72, 81, 94, 130, 148, 181, 200
Traditional knowledge, 80
Translation, 76, 79, 157
Trans person, 24, 25, 48
Trauma, 8, 34, 38, 76, 82, 215, 219, 228–231
  intergenerational, 76, 177, 228
Traumascape, 8, 218–220, 222–224, 232
Tuberculosis, 134, 137
Tuscarora, 74, 77
Two-headed serpent, 80, 81, 83

V
Visions, 6, 73, 75, 80–82, 85, 145, 152, 153
Vizzini, Ned
  It's Kind of A Funny Story, 52, 65
Voice-hearers. See Hearing voices
Vulnerability, 6, 130, 166–170, 173, 174, 176, 177, 179–181, 206

W
Ward, Mary Jane, 5, 52, 109–123
  Counterclockwise, 109, 110, 119–124
  The Other Caroline, 109, 120, 124
  The Snake Pit, 5, 52, 59, 109–113, 116–118, 120, 123, 124; film version, 5, 109, 117, 118, 122
Weiner, Hannah
  Clairvoyant Journal, 6, 145–147, 151–156, 158, 160, 161
Weldy, Ann. See Bannon, Ann
Where the Roots Reach for Water, 66
Wilkerson, Abby L., 129
Willow Weep for Me, 66
Withers, A.J., 3, 13, 20, 22–28
Wollstonecraft, Mary
  Maria–or, The Wrongs of Woman, 94
Woman on the Edge of Time, 59
Wounded storytellers, 166
Wrongful confinement, 94, 95, 98
Wurtzel, Elizabeth, 66–67

X
Xenophobia, 165, 173

Y
Yiddish, 175, 177
Young, Suzanne
  The Program, 52
Youth suicidality, 77

The manufacturer's authorised representative in the EU is Springer Nature Customer Service Centre GmbH, Europaplatz 3, 69115 Heidelberg, Germany. If you have any concerns regarding our products, please contact ProductSafety@springernature.com

Printed and bound by CPI Group (UK) Ltd, Croydon, CR0 4YY

23/03/2026

02076682-0005